HENRY
BLOFELD
My A-Z of Cricket

Also by Henry Blofeld:

Over and Out
Cricket's Great Entertainers
Cricket and All That
A Thirst for Life

HENRY
BLOFELD

My A-Z of Cricket

A Personal Celebration
of our Glorious Game

HODDER

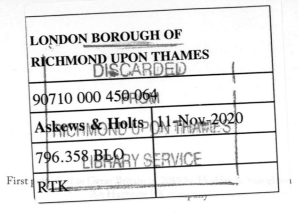
First p

This paperback edition published in 2020

1

Paperback ISBN 9781529378511
eBook ISBN 9781529378504

Typeset in Adobe Caslon by Hewer Text UK Ltd, Edinburgh
Printed and bound in Great Britain by Clays Ltd, Elocraf S.p.A.

Hodder & Stoughton policy is to use papers that are natural, renewable
and recyclable products and made from wood grown in sustainable
forests. The logging and manufacturing processes are expected to
conform to the environmental regulations of the country of origin.

Hodder & Stoughton Ltd
Carmelite House
50 Victoria Embankment
London EC4Y 0DZ

www.hodder.co.uk

To Valeria, with huge thanks for her love, patience and enthusiasm – and to my daughter, Suki, for hers too.

CONTENTS

PREFACE

The idea of this book came to me two years ago when I was writing *Over and Out*, a collection of stories from my long life in the *TMS* box. While I was putting them together, so many other things came to mind about the various facets of cricket and all those curious names connected with it. At the same time, a number of the players I had watched since 1947, when cricket and I took a firm hold of each other, also flashed in front of me. That was the year of the monumental run-scoring feats of **Denis Compton** and **Bill Edrich** for Middlesex and England, who both figure in this book, and there is **Godfrey Evans** of the same vintage, although he had to wait another three years until I had taken up wicketkeeping before he gained my lasting affection. In later years, of course, a grinning Godfrey, mutton-chop whiskers and all, was a frequent visitor to the BBC commentary box as the representative of a firm of bookmakers. By then, thanks to Brian Johnston, he had become 'Godders' to one and all. The result of all this was that I felt I had to write another book, and mercifully Hodder and Stoughton were of a like mind.

I have gone much further back than 1947 too. No less a figure than **W.G. Grace** loomed large in my early life, partly, I think, because of the Grace Gates at Lord's, but mainly because of his beard, which I found thrilling, and I remember my mother continually mentioning him by name. As you will see, W.G.'s record must win him a permanent place in the Best XI of All Time and so I had to have him. My mother had an eclectic bunch of elderly cricketers she loved to talk to me about. Learie Constantine, who narrowly failed to win a place here, was one. His fielding deeply impressed her and, as a result, when a new labrador puppy who was a spectacular fielder of a rubber ball arrived at Hoveton, he was immediately renamed Learie. Another old-timer who was on her list was **K.S. Ranjitsinhji**, the one batsman of all those long gone who I would still give my right arm to see play. He had a bit of luck in becoming the Jam Sahib of Nawanagar, but he lived up to it well and there is an irresistible Oriental magic and majesty about him. I could never have left out Ranji. For a time, I owned the formal cane he used in the years he spent at Cambridge when he first came to England in the 1880s. With amazing stupidity, I let it go at an auction.

After England's incredible victory in the 2019 World Cup, the slightly enigmatic **Ben Stokes** has pride of place among the moderns, with **Joe Root** and **Jimmy Anderson** tugging at his coat-tails. I could not have everyone, but **Graham Gooch** and **David Gower** have earned their places, although they are the very antithesis of one another, and **Sir Alastair Cook**, a knight in every sense of the word, could not be left out. Two of my special favourites are **Alan Knott**, surely the best wicketkeeper ever, and **Colin Bland**, who was, with a apologies to my mother and Learie Constantine, undoubtedly the greatest fielder the game has ever seen. I am pleased, too, to have been able to find a place for **Cyril Coote**, a pillar of Cambridge University cricket and probably a unique groundsman/coach figure in the history of the game. **Miss Paterson**, a redoubtably determined lady and a no-prisoners-taken cricket coach at my preparatory school at Sunningdale, fully deserves her entry. She set me on course and there has never been anyone quite like her.

While writing this book, I understood all too well the agony selectors must go through when they have to make the decision of who to leave out. I have no doubt I shall be pilloried from all sides about the household names I have not selected. I could say that lack of space was one reason and pass the blame on to my amazing publisher, Roddy Bloomfield, but I will not. Roddy, a great friend, still eagerly fastens on his publishing pads four or five days a week, and over the past fifty years or so has published more than 100 books on our great game of cricket.

The danger in calling this book *My A–Z of Cricket* is that some people may grasp it expecting to find in these pages a glossary of the game. It was never intended to be anything more than a personal look at some of the players and events I have enjoyed the most, whether reading about them or watching them from either the press or the commentary boxes. Some others are key figures in the development of the game and its art. W.G. and Ranji are important here. Then there are more recent players whom I have not known and cannot therefore telling amusing personal anecdotes about, but who have made a great impact on the modern game. **Chris Gayle** and **Virat Kohli** both fit in here. It has amused me to dip into a few of the idiosyncratic and incomprehensible terms that the game enjoys. I have also tried to explain the part that many unsung and unnamed individuals play in making the game what it is, such as **The Groundsman** and **The Scorer**. There are others I have chosen for reasons that will, I hope, become clear as you read about them. I have always loved players who have brought humour and style to the game and there are some of those. And some who were jolly good chaps and could also play cricket pretty well. There are a few other things that simply need explaining, as well as skulduggery that must be dealt with. **Obstructing the Field** is a case in point, and while it is perhaps appropriate that the illustration I use here saw the departure of Stokes, England's newest and somewhat controversial hero, it is a term that might have the uninitiated scratching their heads. **The Doosra** is a little bit of inexplicable Indian magic, and at first glance **A Pair** may not be exactly what it sounds like.

This gives you, dear reader, a little bit of the menu, but now it is time for me to cross my fingers and leave it to you. Before I go, I would like to take this opportunity to thank my brisk and vibrant agent, Ralph Brünjes, for the part he has played. He is always such a huge help and, although I need quite a bit of steering, he usually manages to get me down the right path, and mostly with a smile on his face too.

Henry Blofeld
Norwich, August 2019

A

JIMMY ANDERSON

Watching Jimmy Anderson bowl was one of the highlights of my last decade as a commentator. He is one of the great swing bowlers of all time, a fiercely individual and controlled human being, a man of immense determination who has learned his trade the hard way and, above all, someone who knows his own mind and will not easily be deflected.

Anderson summed up his approach to cricket to perfection in the Test match against the West Indies at Lord's in 2017, after he had taken his 500th Test wicket by knocking out Kraigg Brathwaite's middle stump: 'Normally it's anger, but today it was a bit more, not quite teary but emotional in that way. I don't get like that when trying to focus on my job and it took me a bit by surprise.'

Anderson is a most interesting character. In private life, he has a reputation for being shy and something of a loner if he does not have close friends around him. Until he has confidence in other people, he is wary, not to say suspicious, of them – never more so than when some ageing fast bowler tries to tell him how to bowl. It took Anderson a while to learn the consistency that, in the second half of his international career, became his hallmark.

It is extraordinary to think that he had played only three limited-over matches for Lancashire when he was sent out to join England's one-day squad in Australia in 2002–03. He did not have a name, let alone a number on the back of his shirt, but he was quick to show what he was made of. Playing in Adelaide in great heat, he produced an astonishing spell of ten overs which cost only 12 runs.

That remarkable start won him a place in the England side for the following World Cup, but his form in those early days was very much in-and-out, and he also had problems with his back. He spent two years trying to change his action so that it was kinder to his back, and this destroyed his rhythm. He suffered a stress fracture which kept him out of things for much of 2006, but was back in the side for the 2007–08 tour of New Zealand, where he teamed up with Stuart Broad in the Test side for the first time.

He had a successful season in 2008 and became one of *Wisden*'s Five Cricketers of the Year, yet you were never quite certain what you were going to get from Anderson in those days. In spite of his considerable success, he was worried by his lack of consistency and in 2010, with a remarkable display of character and admirable singleness of purpose, he decided to reinvent himself. He made up his mind that accuracy and therefore control was all-important and he worked hard to make sure he gave the batsman nothing. Length and line were paramount and maiden overs were the order of the day.

This new approach meant that even if Anderson was not taking wickets, he did not let the batting side take control, which was of enormous value to his captain. It also meant he would have to work that much harder because his captain would now give him more to do, which was probably part of his plan. All through this, Anderson never stinted himself and his dedication to his cause shone through, just as his tally of almost 600 Test wickets is testimony to its effect.

The story I love about Anderson came to me from Graeme Swann – they are great friends. England were playing Pakistan at Lord's in 2010 and Anderson bowled a succession of beautiful outswingers which kept going past the outside edge of the bat. When this had happened for the umpteenth time to the same batsman, Andrew Strauss, the captain fielding at first slip, said to no one in particular, 'I think it's time for the inner [inswinger]. Matt, go and tell him.' Matt Prior, keeping wicket, declined the invitation, as did Swann, at second slip, a few moments later. 'I suppose I had better go and do it myself, then,' the captain said, and in that characteristic way of his which made him look like a horse in a dressage contest, he ran, knees up, to the other end. Anderson was walking back to his mark and watching events behind him on the big screen. When Strauss was three or four yards away, Anderson looked over his shoulder and said in a loud voice, 'F*** off, Strauss.' Whereupon his captain, as instructed, turned round and strutted back to first slip. The inner came along eventually – when Anderson was ready for it – and the batsman was lbw.

In spite of having a prickly nature, for the most part Anderson kept his feelings under control out in the middle. The new Anderson had a wonderful season in 2014, when he took 37 wickets in seven Tests against Sri Lanka and India, although he boiled over briefly in the game against India at Trent Bridge. He got involved in a slanging match with India's Ravi Jadeja and lots of pushing and shoving went on as they walked into the pavilion. There is no fixed rule, but fast bowlers, by their very nature, tend to have a fiery side to them. While it would be better if these incidents did not happen, it is all part of the game and I certainly do not hold it against Anderson. When bowling, he was always wrapped up in intense concentration, which made him unforgiving towards batsmen, and if on the occasions they took him on he sometimes spilled over, so what? He was also, of course, England's leading sledger. He claimed this chatter was essential to help him rise above his natural shyness.

I met Anderson no more than a couple of times, and very briefly at that. Once was in the bar in the players' hotel not long after his regular partner-in-arms, Chris Broad, had destroyed South Africa in the second innings of the Test in Johannesburg in 2015–16. He was with Alastair Cook and, while enjoying the victory as much as anyone, he was charming in a fairly distant way. There was a wary look in his eye, and even then it was abundantly clear that he was very much his own man, with his own agenda, yet he was a very agreeable companion over a celebratory drink or two and revealed a good, if slightly reluctant, sense of humour.

His determination was also evident in his batting. For a long time, he was England's regular nightwatchman, and he even batted for a record 54 innings before he was out without scoring. In his left-handed way, he will have irritated many bowlers with his homespun defensive technique, and none more so than Australia's at Cardiff in 2009. He and Monty Panesar, the last-wicket pair, survived for the last 69 balls of the match, thereby enabling England to escape from the first Test with a draw. At the end of it, I well remember Anderson leaving the field just as he would at the end of any day's cricket – without any sign of emotion. It was job done and that was that. His other great moment with the bat came at Trent Bridge in 2014 in the first Test against India. Batting at number eleven, Anderson made 81 as he and Joe Root put on 198 together, which is a world record for the last wicket. Anderson was certainly no mug with the bat and had a left-handed off drive Graeme Pollock or Frank Woolley would have envied.

A

APPEALING

'Howzat' is cricket's wake-up call. At any level of the game, a screeched appeal is always electrifying. It produces a moment of glorious suspense when all eyes swivel to the umpire and anything is possible. It is one of the most entertaining aspects of cricket, especially as interpretation of the Laws can be alarmingly imprecise, and an appeal can unleash the most amusing and surprising chain of events.

For example, Law 36 states that a batsman is out lbw if his pads prevent the ball from hitting the stumps. But – and this is where the fun starts – a number of other provisos have to be met before the decision can be made. Is the ball, beyond reasonable doubt, hitting the stumps? Did it pitch outside the leg stump? Did it hit the edge of the bat? And so on. The suspense then continues for a while before the ultimate decision is flashed up on the screen.

In recent years, umpires have been put under increasing pressure by players who do their utmost to try and push the Laws to the limit in the hope of getting a decision in their favour. In the old days, the appealing was mostly done by the bowler and the wicketkeeper, but these days just about the whole fielding side joins in. The close fielders often turn round and point expectantly at the umpire. Some even run towards the umpire when an appeal is made, an example of the intimidation that has been allowed to creep into the game, although this is now illegal. The players will claim innocence, but they know exactly what they are doing as they submerge the umpire under a cacophony of organised screams. Then there is absurd appealing, when it is palpably obvious a batsman is not out. This happens too often and especially when a fielding side has taken a number of wickets and is expecting one to fall just about every ball. Or it can be the vocal product of frustration for the fielding side when things are going badly. Whatever the excuse, it can become extremely irritating. But imagine cricket if there was no appealing. It would not be half such fun, and what a boring life the umpires would lead.

Down the years, there have been all manner of idiosyncratic appealers and, for me, this has been one of the delights of the game. The loudest appealer I can remember was Robin Jackman, a wonderfully ebullient cricketer who bowled at fast-medium for Surrey and England. The umpires did not take offence because he was generally such a chirpy and friendly chap and his appealing was more of a gimmick than anything else. The umpires were not being threatened. The game had not yet reached that stage. Jackman's lung power was awesome, nevertheless. It earned him the nickname of the Shoreditch Sparrow in Alan Gibson's wonderful daily match reports on county cricket in *The Times*.

Perhaps the loudest, and most cheerful, appealer of all time was the old Lancashire and England wicketkeeper in the 1920s, George Duckworth. He was a short man, but a bundle of noisy joy and happiness. When I began my commentary life in the 1960s doing a number of county matches for ITV, George was our splendid scorer, and what fun he was, with his rumbustious sense of humour. In his playing days, Duckworth's appealing was legendary, especially when Lancashire played Cambridge University at Fenner's. The ground is not much more than just across the road from Parker's Piece, a vast area of grass where it always seemed that no fewer than twelve games of cricket were going on at any one time. It was said that whenever Duckworth unleashed an appeal on Fenner's, at least five batsmen were given out on Parker's Piece.

Bill 'Tiger' O'Reilly, the pre-war Australian leg-spinner, is reputed to have had a ferocious and frightening Irish/Australian appeal which was intended to leave an umpire with no option. An appealer I greatly enjoyed was Godfrey Evans, whom I have written about elsewhere in this book. He was splendidly noisy and those red wicketkeeping gloves helped the whole exciting effect, as did the ball which with both hands he threw high above his head. If it was not out, it had to be an injustice, or so it seemed. I found the spectacle of an Evans appeal more irresistible than any firework I have ever seen. Alan Knott also made his feelings known with an appeal which was both shrill and piercing. Even so, this was one aspect of the game in which he had to bow his head to Evans. In the modern game, the decibel content of appeals is higher than it used to be, not least because everyone now joins in. I suppose this is only natural in a game which has acquired a much more openly aggressive attitude, especially in the shorter game, when it is distilled into the highly exciting, showbiz-inspired, anything-goes T20 jamboree, where colossal sums seem to be at stake and players are bought for millions.

As a player I was right in the middle of the appealing industry, for I was a wicketkeeper and it is our business to appeal. My hero in those days, as you will have gathered, was Godfrey Evans and, to the mild dismay of my parents and maybe the masters at Sunningdale school, I managed to acquire a pair of those gloves with the irresistible Evans lookalike scarlet rubber palms – and I remember practising my appealing. I cannot remember who the donor was – I probably shamed my parents into it – but I don't think I have ever owned any more precious and closely guarded possessions.

Cricket without any appealing would really be like Samson after Delilah had been at work on his hair with the scissors. Whenever I see pictures of cricketers in the late 1700s or 1800s I wonder just how their appeals would have sounded. If a bowler wearing a top hat had shouted his head off, his hat would have fallen off and he would have looked ridiculous. Did they simply turn round and politely ask the umpire if that might just possibly have been out? I doubt they went down on their knees – not that I can think of any bowler who has actually done that unless in a state of exasperated amusement. When did appealing become raucous? I cannot imagine Australians at any time in their history forgetting to give it everything when they asked the question. Towards the end of the nineteenth century, an Australian Aboriginal side toured England, and I wonder how and in what language they appealed. Cricket without appealing would be as unappetising as a regimental sergeant-major with laryngitis.

A

ARGENTINA

In parts of South America, cricket has been surprisingly vibrant over the years, but Argentina have always led the way. The game there has been well organised and the standard good enough for a number of English touring sides, including MCC, to have gone there. At their peak, before and after the last war, an Argentine side would probably have held its own in the Minor County Championship.

I was lucky to be selected to go to Argentina in 1980 as part manager and mostly social secretary of a side taken round South America by Derrick Robins. He was a businessman who was a notable cricketing benefactor and for a long time the owner of Coventry City FC. We had an amazing four weeks, starting in Caracas and going down to Buenos Aires by way of Bogotá, Lima and Santiago. We ended our tour in Rio and São Paulo, where the night life was hot and some of us had greater difficulty in distinguishing between transvestites and the real thing than we did in winning cricket matches.

In Argentina, we stayed just outside the main city of Buenos Aires at the Hurlingham Club, a close relation of the club of the same name down by the river in south-west London. The sporting facilities were extraordinary and centred around polo and golf. Hurlingham has a splendid cricket ground too, near the impressive clubhouse in which we stayed. Robins's team was made up of young county cricketers, many of whom it was hoped were destined for higher things. Chris Cowdrey was the captain and the manager was my old Norfolk friend and England batsman Peter Parfitt, while Robins had also brought along Les Ames, who had been such a wonderful wicketkeeper-batsman for Kent and England before the war.

The hospitality for that week in Buenos Aires was formidable, bordering on the outrageous. We played games at Hurlingham and at the other two main clubs, Lomas and Belgrano. The Belgrano ground was in the middle of the business district, with high-rise blocks all around. In many ways it was not unlike the Honourable Artillery Club ground in the City of London. These sides all played to a good standard and the cricket was always competitive, although Robins's side was never in any danger of losing. The locals were kept up to the mark by the national coach, Brian Ward, who had opened the batting for Essex a few years earlier. Ward was continuing a tradition, because in the 1960s another Essex opener, Mickey Bear, would go out in the winters as the Argentine coach.

Like many sporting benefactors, Derrick Robins always liked to be on the winning side. With the cricket in South America this was never a problem, but Robins was a fierce competitor at all levels. While we were staying at Hurlingham, we had the party's official golf day. Derrick himself arranged the pairings and had decided to play with Bill Athey, another Yorkshireman, who opened the batting for his county and England. During a practice round, Robins noticed that Graham Stevenson, the Yorkshire all-rounder, could hit the ball a huge distance off the tee. When the pairings were posted the evening before the competition, they had changed. Derrick was now playing with

Graham Stevenson, which caused a certain predictable amusement. The following day, Robins was full of it, but his frown soon reappeared when Stevenson hit his first drive an immensely long way, but over cover point's head. To everyone's great delight, he continued to do this for the next seventeen holes and Derrick was not within sight of figuring in the final round.

I have always had a soft spot for cricket in Argentina. In 1955, my first captain in the XI at Eton was Clem Gibson, whose family had settled in the Argentine. His father, also Clem, had played for Eton and Cambridge as a medium-fast outswing bowler who had good variety and remarkable control. He was one of eleven amateurs who had played for Archie MacLaren's XI at Eastbourne in 1921 against Warwick Armstrong's unbeaten Australian side. MacLaren had promised to pick a side to beat the Australians at the very end of their tour – and they won an extraordinary game by 28 runs. In 1955, several of our games at Eton were watched by young Clem's mother and father, who were a delight. I can still remember old Clem, modesty personified, talking about that game at the Saffrons at Eastbourne and also about cricket in the Argentine, where his family owned a considerable amount of land. He would complain that the only problem he had with cricket in that country was that he never got enough practice.

A

ARTIFICIAL PITCHES

Some people throw their hands in the air at the mention of artificial pitches, rather as if they have caught someone passing the port the wrong way at the dinner table. Artificial pitches are not to be sniffed at, especially when it comes to teaching the young how to play the game.

When I was still very young, my father put down a concrete pitch for a net at Hoveton, which the village used for practice when it was too wet to play on the grass. In the spring holidays from prep school, Alan Brazier, who batted intermittently for Kent and Surrey, came down for a week to coach us. I remember the coconut matting that was stretched tightly over the concrete being watered, although I am not sure why. Maybe it was done in order to keep the bounce of the ball a little lower. I was spellbound by actually being able to talk to and be coached by a real-life county cricketer. It was an enormous thrill. Alan instilled in me the rudiments of the game and my infantile strokes became a little more polished. My father had settled for an artificial surface because of the advice of a friend and near neighbour, Mike Falcon, himself a considerable cricketer, who had captained Norfolk from 1911 to 1946 and was a member of Archie MacLaren's side which beat the Australians at Eastbourne in 1921. Falcon's family had installed a concrete pitch at their house near Hoveton (a house now lived in by Matthew Fleming, who captained Kent with great skill and determination and was a more than useful all-rounder and brilliant fielder who played in eleven ODIs for England). Falcon told my father how important it was to learn the game on a surface with an even bounce, and I am delighted to say my father saw the point.

An excellent by-product of having an artificial pitch out in the middle is that it means a new ground does not have to be anything like so big. If a ground has a turf pitch and the club has a good-sized fixture list, the square from which the pitches are cut has to be much larger. The ground therefore needs to be bigger to accommodate a big square and prevent some of the boundaries from being ridiculously short. An excellent example of the benefits of an artificial pitch is the charming but small new ground at Biniparrell, the home of the Menorca Cricket Club. They have a big fixture list, with many club sides coming over each year from England, as well as a climate which allows a long season. Their artificial pitch is essential for what has become an amazing cricket ground.

So artificial pitches have their place, but I hope the day never comes when they are again used for first-class cricket, or indeed county limited-over matches, for natural pitches are always more interesting. They bring extra possibilities into the game that, by their very nature, bland artificial pitches are unable to do.

A

THE ASHES

The Ashes is the Holy Grail of cricket. The first ever Test match was played between Australia and England at the Melbourne Cricket Ground in March 1877, even though it had to wait a while before that match was granted Test status. As far as England are concerned, Australia are the old enemy and vice versa. We should not forget that England's first overseas tour, in 1859, was to Philadelphia, yet it was England versus Australia that was to become the centre of cricket's universe.

The Ashes themselves, which came along five years after this first Test, are really a practical joke made good. In late August 1882, Australia beat England at The Oval by seven runs in a game which was over in two days. The next day, the *Sporting Times* published an obituary notice, saying that the body of English cricket would be cremated and the ashes taken to Australia. The following winter, an England side captained by the Honourable Ivo Bligh, later Lord Darnley, went to Australia. They lost the first Test in Melbourne and played the second on the same ground two and a half weeks later. This time they won by the convincing margin of an innings and 27 runs.

Soon after this second game, the England side went to Sunbury, which is near Tullamarine, Melbourne's airport, where they were guests of Sir William Clarke and his family. Two of the Clarke daughters were spirited young ladies and, knowing all about that obituary notice, they got to work and burned two bails and maybe one or two other things. Nobly assisted by a friend called Florence Morphy, who within a year had married the England captain, they all then scooped up the resulting ashes into a small urn, which they presented to Ivo Bligh in recognition of his team's victory in Melbourne.

Bligh brought the urn back to the considerable family pad at Cobham in north Kent, where it took up its position on the mantelpiece in a biggish room at one end of the house. There it remained until one day an over-zealous parlourmaid got to work with the duster and knocked the urn off its perch. When it hit the floor, it broke open and some white dust-like stuff poured out. The parlourmaid ran from the room and summoned a no doubt irritated butler. He saw at once what had happened and tried to scoop the contents back into the urn, but it was little more than dust and he was not able to get much of it back. So, brimming with imagination, he scooped up a good bit of ash from the fire-place, put that inside the urn as well and then stuck it back together again, before putting it back on the mantelpiece.

That was the last time the sacred urn was opened. It was given as a present to the MCC at Lord's by Ivo Bligh's descendants after his death in 1927. It therefore belongs to the MCC, being a private gift, which is why the urn remains permanently at Lord's in spite of the fact that it is occasionally won by Australia. It has, in fact, made two state visits to Australia, both at a time when they held the Ashes. But Australia had to hold its breath on each occasion when it was put back on the aeroplane and flown back to the museum at Lord's. Those two Clarke girls will have had no idea of what their charming practical joke began, but thank goodness they burned those two bails when they did.

The Ashes have remained as cricket's defining trophy ever since. There have been times when they have caused bitter conflict, as with the Bodyline series, and there was even one series when the two countries played each other without the Ashes being at stake. For two years, the cricket world had been split down the middle by Kerry Packer, who wanted exclusive rights to televise international cricket in Australia. When the Australian board refused to sell him the rights, Packer had set up his own international cricket there, buying up most of the world's best players. When an armed neutrality rather than a peace was declared in 1979, England responded by sending a side to Australia in 1979–80 to play three matches and test the waters, but on the understanding that the Ashes, held by England then anyway, would not be at stake. Australia won 3–0.

For all the magnificent cricket we have seen over the years from the other Test-playing countries, and the West Indies in particular, the Ashes has always held pride of place. Now the major force behind the game is India, thanks to the huge popularity the game has in that country and the extraordinary success of the Indian Premier League, the world's major T20 competition. Where this will leave the Ashes is anyone's guess. It is hard to imagine that the Ashes could ever become a devalued trophy, but these days just about anything is possible. Personally, I cannot believe we will ever see England and Australia not playing each other for the Ashes, but maybe this is yet another case of the wish being father to the thought.

B

JONNY BAIRSTOW

Jonny Bairstow is a fine example of a thoroughly modern international cricketer, an all-rounder worth his place in all three forms of the game. He is a batsman who can also keep wicket pretty well and, when not wearing the pads, he is an extremely able fielder. His father, David, had kept wicket in four Test matches for England and the Bairstows became the thirteenth father-and-son combination to play for England, and the first to have both kept wicket.

Jonny Bairstow is not only a formidable cricketer, he is also a most impressive figure. His zest for life and cricket shine through in everything he does and although he is still not quite the first name the selectors write down when choosing an England Test side, there is something wonderfully reassuring about his presence. He clearly relishes every moment and has become an important figure in the dressing room, especially when things are not going according to plan. There is a spirit and energetic determination about everything he does. When he comes in to bat, England's opponents know they have a fight on their hands. His life is all the more remarkable because he has had to get over the shock of his father taking his own life when he was only eight years old. No one could have lived better in his father's memory.

Quite possibly, it has all made Jonny even more determined to get where he has. His progress as a player, both at school at

St Peter's, York, where he won the Young Wisden Schools Cricketer of the Year award in 2007, and in his early days with Yorkshire always showed a great single-mindedness. He began playing for Yorkshire Second XI in 2007 and, after making 202 for them in June 2009, he was promoted to the First XI. In his first game, he made 82 not out in the second innings and also had to take over behind the stumps when the official wicket-keeper was injured, and he held four catches. The following year, he played regularly as a batsman, finishing with just under a thousand runs. In 2011, he took over as the number-one wicketkeeper and that year was also the only Yorkshire batsman to score a thousand runs. By the end of the season, he was chosen for the England ODI squad and played as a batsman in the last game against India. He made 41 in 21 balls, taking England to victory and impressing no one more than Alastair Cook, his captain.

In 2012, he was in the side for the first three Tests of the summer, against the West Indies, making his debut at Lord's. He did not play in the first two Tests against South Africa later that summer, but was brought back for the third at Lord's. He came in after England had lost four wickets for 54 and he had made 95 before he was bowled by a beauty from Morne Morkel. I was commentating on that match and when Bairstow was out I remember saying, 'I wonder how important those missing five runs will be for him.' A century would have done wonders for Bairstow's confidence, while an innings of 95 might have left him with a mite of uncertainty, even though it was then his highest Test score.

It was at this point that Jos Buttler became a threat to Bairstow's place as wicketkeeper in the ODIs and T20s, and for the next few years Bairstow was in and out of the side. Bairstow always wanted to keep wicket and I am sure he felt that this gave him an important second string to his bow. Buttler did not keep wicket for his county, Somerset, but in New Zealand in 2012–13 he got the job in front of Bairstow and is currently England's one-day keeper. It was Buttler who broke the stumps at the end of the final at Lord's in 2019 when he ran out Martin Guptill, enabling England to win their first World Cup. In this same tournament, Bairstow fulfilled a most important role as Jason Roy's opening partner. Together, in England's last two qualifying games and in the semi-final, they gave England the perfect start after which they went on to beat India, New Zealand and then Australia. While Bairstow allowed Roy to get on with it at the other end, he also played the new ball with great skill, but without suggesting he should be considered as an opener in Test cricket. The game is different, with the red ball tending to swing more and a predatory field of four slips and a gully waiting for those edges. With the advantage of hindsight, I wonder if Bairstow may at times have felt it would have been better for him if he had given up wicketkeeping altogether and had been able to concentrate everything on making sure of his England place as a specialist batsman. He has spent a lot of effort trying to prove that he is a better wicketkeeper than Buttler and this may have been at the cost of his batting. For such a fine batsman, he made too many low scores, which might not have happened had so much of his time not been consumed by worrying about his other job.

When Bairstow first played for England, the wicketkeeping position was filled by Matt Prior and while he was around, Bairstow was only ever likely to play as a batsman. In

2013–14, England went to Australia, where they lost the series 5–0. Prior's form suffered badly and so Bairstow took the gloves for the last two Tests, doing the job competently enough. Prior then returned for the first two Tests against India in 2014, before injury made him withdraw from the side. It was then that the selectors plumped for Buttler, who kept the job for the Ashes series in 2015. Bairstow played in the last three Tests of that series as a batsman, but he got another chance behind the stumps after Buttler had had a poor series in the UAE late in 2015 against Pakistan. Bairstow was now proclaimed as England's first-choice wicketkeeper. He kept in the four Tests in South Africa in 2015–16 and in the series against Pakistan the following summer. During the fourth Test against South Africa in 2017, he became the seventh English wicketkeeper to claim a hundred victims in Test cricket, and this included two matches in 2016 in which he held nine catches, against South Africa in January and Sri Lanka in May. In that same year he scored 1,470 Test runs, the record for an England wicketkeeper in a calendar year. These figures reflect the confidence Bairstow clearly gains from being able to do both jobs.

It is one of those odd coincidences that Buttler and Bairstow should be around at the same time. In their different ways, both are such splendid cricketers, and while it would be wonderful to have the two of them in the England side at the same time, their rival products are too similar. Two wicketkeeperbatsmen are often one too many, but Bairstow's form with the bat in the 2019 World Cup showed that this may not necessarily be true. I personally would always want him in my side in whatever capacity. His is a reassuring presence.

For me, Jonny Bairstow has been a delight as a player, if at times a little frustratingly so. His spirit has always been unquenchable, and increasingly I feel that all is not lost when he comes to the crease. He is of the stuff of roast beef and Yorkshire pudding and he is a great team man. In paying credit to Jonny, we must never forget the part that his mother, Janet, has played in making all this possible. In the face of dreadfully difficult circumstances, she provided the family background that enabled his talents and personality to come through and flourish as they have.

B

PETER BAXTER

Backers, as I like to call him, became the producer of *Test Match Special* in 1974 and it was not until 2007 that he passed the reins on to Adam Mountford. He was in the hot seat for thirty-four years and I wonder if he will ever be given full credit for the way in which he allowed *TMS* to develop. No one could have shown greater loyalty to the programme than Backers. He was enormously proud of it, and not the least of his achievements was to protect *TMS* and fight its corner when it came under surprising attack from within the BBC itself. He won a fair number of battles which I dare say no one ever knew that he had to fight, let alone win. There was a period in the 1980s when *TMS* was never sure which network, if any, was going to be its home. There were many agonising discussions within both the BBC and the *TMS* team as to what our fate would be. Questions were even asked on the floor of the House of Commons. *TMS* was a much-cherished institution, yet there were times when it appeared that our ultimate bosses did not appreciate this.

Backers, with rare determination, never took his eye off this particular ball, and in this he had no greater supporter than Brian Johnston. There was an occasion during a Test at Old Trafford in the 1980s when the then head of sport, 'Slim' Wilkinson, came up to our hotel in Bucklow Hill to try and assure us that a future broadcasting home would be found for us, that we would be safe and that stories of our imminent extinction were nonsense, but he was far from convincing. We were then the property of Radio 3 and went to air on their medium-wave network, but there was talk of closing this down, which would have meant that we no longer had a home. Mrs Thatcher had set up the Peacock Committee to look into the BBC and the suggestion was there were too many radio networks. We naturally felt his was an extraordinarily cavalier attitude for the BBC to take with one of their flagship programmes and no one was more upset than Brian Johnston at the way he felt we were being treated. He was far from overjoyed by Wilkinson's lack of conviction on the subject. The meeting that evening was the only time I saw him lose his temper, and the following day a much-chastened Slim Wilkinson caught the train back to London, having been left in no doubt about the feelings of those of us at the pit face. It was difficult for Backers to shout the odds at his immediate boss, but he did not mess about either and made sure Wilkinson got the message.

Backers became a good commentator himself, although he was unfairly criticised from within when he first clasped the microphone – something he did for the excellent reason that it saved the BBC money because he was there anyway. In his role as producer, he understood how the programme should sound and was always quick to prevent bad habits taking hold. He was never afraid to take a commentator aside and tell him where he was going wrong and we had great respect for him. The one exception to this was Don Mosey, a resolute Yorkshireman (even though he had decamped across the Pennines to Morecambe). The Alderman, as he was nicknamed by Brian Johnston, took an extreme northerly approach to all things to do with *TMS* and was reluctant to appreciate Backers's views. He undoubtedly felt that he should have had Backers's job himself. The two of them had their moments, but blood was never spilt.

Peter Baxter became a great friend of mine and, in a moment he may privately regret, he later agreed to tiptoe onto the boards with me and take part in a two-man show about all the fun we had had and the pranks we had got up to on *TMS*. On a very cold evening, in a chapel near his own home in north Buckinghamshire, we amused the locals just about enough to be persuaded to give it a go in theatres around the country. Five and a half years and nearly 400 shows later, having shared many remarkable adventures, overnight stays in unusual lodging houses, some hectic drives and much losing of the way from one venue to another, we decided to call it a day. It was an awful lot of fun and Backers was wonderful, always ready with a smile as well as a stern producerly wag of the finger, although I fear he now found me a little harder to control.

We did three years at the Edinburgh Festival without getting anywhere near showing a profit, but we had colossal fun. We made some terrific friends and rubbed shoulders (occasionally) with famous theatrical and broadcasting names and thought we were hugely important. We once helped stage a cricket match on the Meadows in Edinburgh between Festival performers and the managers of the venues, and once or twice drove to Leith to sample Tom Kitchin's unrivalled culinary skills. Putting up with me as he did through all these adventures, you can see why Backers is a great deal more than just a saint. I have never had a much better friend – in the commentary box, on the stage or surrounded by Arlottian-sized glasses of red wine. Oh yes, I was one of two people whom, as the *TMS* producer, he had to take off the air because we had had at least a couple of glasses too many. But that's another story.

B

COLIN BLAND

In the evening after my final day's commentary for *TMS*, at Lord's in early September 2017, I was walking back across the ground to the Media Centre after being given a glass of champagne in the England dressing room. The ground was empty and I stood in the crease at the Nursery End having a last nostalgic look round. Suddenly two incredible moments of cricket at Lord's which I had watched as a spectator but had not thought about for a long time came racing back to me.

In my mind, I was watching the first Test against South Africa in 1965. Ken Barrington and Jim Parks were batting for England and Colin Bland was fielding for South Africa. Bland, a Rhodesian, was the greatest fielder of all time and a magnetic entertainer. A tall man, long in the leg, lean and lithe, he moved like a two-legged panther. His long-striding run leading into his swoop at full stretch was irresistible. The authority and control of his hands made even the hardest-hit cricket ball blink. Then, in an extraordinary movement which combined balance, athleticism, elasticity and supple agility, his low, flat throw homed in on the stumps with an accuracy no other fielder in the game's history has been able to match. This was the product of a highly unusual natural aptitude, rigorous and consistent practice and a mind which must have been as tough as granite. Bland had a fierce self-control and a personality which was not given to frivolity; he was modest and under-stated, a charming yet reticent man.

That day at Lord's, Bland ran out Parks (32) and Barrington (91), both with direct hits on the stumps, which together summed up the extent of his genius. Parks was the first out and unluckily so, in that he was batting with Barrington, who seldom called his partner for a run, but just ran, which could be disoncerting. When he played a shot and sensed a run, he just set off, presumably confident his partner would respond. On this occasion, Barrington was facing at the Nursery End and he pushed the ball to the right of extra cover. Parks, at the non-striker's end, saw Barrington start to run and was late in starting himself because there had been no call and he had been following the ball. He quickly realised he was in trouble as Bland swooped at extra cover. Parks did his best to run down the line between Bland and the stumps to try and block the throw. This did not deter Bland and his throw zipped between Parks's legs and hit the stumps when he was still two yards short of his crease. (Parks later told me, with a twinkle, that he was run out four times in Test cricket: once by a mute, Barrington, and on one occasion by a batsman who was deaf, the ever-cheerful Fred Titmus.)

Later, Barrington played a ball to Bland's right at midwicket and set off for what looked like a straightforward single. Bland pounced on the ball. He was completely off balance, with his weight falling away from the wicket at the bowler's end, but he somehow managed to turn while in the air and hit the one stump he could see – for he was effectively square on with the wicket. Bland did not drop catches either.

He was a more than useful middle-order batsman too, scoring 1,669 runs in his 21 Test matches at 49.08, but it was as a fielder he will be longest remembered. He was an important member of Ali Bacher's South African side, which swept all before it in the 1960s until South Africa were ostracised by the world's sporting bodies in protest at the hideous system of apartheid which operated in South Africa at that time. But even that cannot take away from Bland's genius as a fielder.

B
BODYLINE

Until Kerry Packer's televisual invasion of international cricket in the second half of the 1970s, Bodyline was the greatest controversy the game had known. It was the brainchild of a hard man with a Machiavellian mind who also happened to be captain of England. When Douglas Jardine was given the captaincy of the 1932–33 England tour of Australia, Rockley Wilson – a master at Winchester, Jardine's old school, who had bowled for England in one Test match, in Sydney in 1920–21, and was a man known for his pithy humour – poignantly said, while clutching his Adam's apple, 'We may win the Ashes, but we'll probably lose a Dominion.'

Jardine knew that if he was to win the Ashes, he had to stop Don Bradman, who had made a record 974 runs in the series in England in 1930. He devised a plan for which he needed the collaboration of his two main fast bowlers, Harold Larwood and Bill Voce, both stalwart Nottinghamshire miners. Jardine wanted them to pitch the ball short and aim at the batsmen's bodies. He would give them a field with as many as five or six short legs up for the catch when the batsmen fended the ball away from their bodies. He would also place two men back behind square on the leg side waiting for the catch if the batsman tried to hook.

It was a form of attack that had never been used before and it had a remarkable shock effect. The Australians generally had no answer to it. Bradman, in particular, found only a partial answer. In the four Test matches he was able to play, he averaged 56. By his extraordinary standards, this was failure. Sticking to his plan enabled Jardine to win the Ashes by four matches to one.

Australia managed to hang on to their Dominion status, but these barbarous tactics had serious repercussions at the highest levels among the politicians of both countries. Jardine and England were effectively condemned as cheats, even though Bodyline was within the Laws of the game as they then stood, if not the spirit. They were thought most emphatically 'not to be playing the game' and the Australian nation shrieked in protest – and some of it is still shrieking.

While Bodyline became an international incident, it also caused problems within Jardine's side. One of his fast bowlers, Gubby Allen, who captained England on the next tour of Australia, in 1936–37, refused to bowl short at the batsman's body and was utterly opposed to this form of attack. It is interesting that he still took 21 wickets in the series. It may have been that the Australian batsmen were so relieved to be up against normal bowling that they let their concentration wander. Another opponent of Bodyline was the Nawab of Pataudi, who made a hundred in the first Test in Sydney, his first Test match. When Australia batted, Jardine did not use his new tactics at the start of the innings, but after a few overs he clapped his hands and called up the Bodyline field. Pataudi had been fielding on the off side and stood his ground when Jardine indicated that he wanted him to join the short legs. Seeing this, Jardine said, 'I see His Highness has conscientious objections.' Pataudi played only one more Test in that series. It was an irony that Pataudi later decided to send his own son, who became an autocratic captain of India in the 1960s, to Winchester, Jardine's old school.

Another important figure in the whole business was the manager of the England side, the pusillanimous Pelham Warner. One can only wonder if Warner ever tried to change Jardine's mind about Bodyline. I rather suspect Jardine's character was too strong for his more timid manager. He will almost certainly have regarded Warner as his servant rather than his landlord, which he effectively was as the principal representative of the MCC. In those days, the MCC controlled English cricket and organised and ran the overseas tours.

When Bodyline was used on that tour of Australia in 1932–33, it was the first time short-pitched fast bowling had become more than an occasional weapon. Batsmen had never seen a barrage like that before and they had no idea how to cope. Nowadays short-pitched fast bowling has become a way of life at the top level. It played a big part in the success of that great West Indies side in the 1980s. Batsmen have learned to deal better with this form of attack, although fast bowlers can no longer create quite the same problems as Larwood and Voce because the Laws have been changed. Nowadays, only two fielders are allowed behind square on the leg side, whereas Jardine could have as many as he wanted. Also, fast bowlers are now permitted to bowl only two short balls an over, while the Bodyline lot were able to bowl as many as they wanted.

B

IAN BOTHAM

Ian Botham's cricket has always been as damaging as a hurricane. Magnificent, destructive, magnetic, irresistible, heroic, courageous, impossible, generous, maddening, pugnacious, pigheaded – just some of his many sides. Without them, Ian Botham would not have been the same man or the same cricketer. You could not have one without the other. He has been an extraordinary phenomenon who has touched us all and brought joy and amazement to many lives. His genius has left cricket, and not just English cricket, in a stronger place.

There is much more to Botham than cricket. He was quick to realise he had been extremely lucky in life and his heart went out to those who were less fortunate. He took on the battle against leukaemia after he had seen young children who were dying from the disease in the Musgrove Park Hospital in Taunton. This inspired him in 1985 to set out on his first fundraising sponsored walk, from John o'Groats to Land's End, which took thirty-five days and raised a million pounds. Since then he has organised many more, including one across the Alps in April 1988 following in the footsteps of Hannibal. These much-publicised and highly successful walks raised many millions for leukaemia research. When he was given a richly deserved knighthood, this charity work will have been at least as big a reason for it as his incredible performances on the cricket field. He may have got into trouble with his antics during his playing days, but so what? He has a huge heart and what he has managed to do is extraordinary. No praise is too high, even if from time to time he shows that he has still not lost the ability to score an own goal.

I was lucky to witness much of his career, starting with a fine performance in a one-day game against Hampshire in 1974, when he steered Somerset to victory over Hampshire with Andy Roberts bowling at his fastest. I was in the commentary box at Trent Bridge for his first Test, against Australia in 1977, when he had his first haul of five wickets in an innings. I was also at Headingley in 1981, for the Test match against Australia just over a week after he had resigned from the England captaincy. He was able to shrug off the ignominy of that and play one of the great innings in the history of Test cricket. After England had followed on 227 runs behind and had slumped to 135–7 in the second innings, he played the most destructive innings I have ever seen, making 149 not out after taking six wickets in Australia's first innings. England went on to win one of the greatest ever Test matches by 18 runs. I also watched Botham take 5–1 in 28 balls to win the next Test, at Edgbaston, and then saw his 118 at Old Trafford in the match after that, which effectively made sure of the Ashes and was technically the best innings he played for England. I was at The Oval in 1991 when, in one of his many comebacks after injury, he trod on his stumps trying to hook Curtly Ambrose and triggered the famous 'leg-over' moment in the *Test Match Special* commentary box. And there were so many wonderful and inspiring moments in between.

I must come clean. Ian and I locked horns when he was captain of England and took the side to the West Indies in 1980–81. His captaincy was not especially helpful to England's cause in the first two Test matches, in Trinidad and Barbados. I was a new recruit for the *Sunday Express* and wrote about his captaincy in disparaging and rather unkind terms. He was sent a cutting of my piece, which only came to light when the side flew home from Jamaica at the end of the tour. It was found in the top pocket of his blazer. We had a slight altercation in the transit lounge at Bermuda airport. It reached the Sunday papers the next weekend and he and I then had a much-photographed public forget-and-forgive soon afterwards at the old Newlands Road ground in Southampton, where Hampshire were playing Somerset. I have to hang my head in shame.

I do not think there can be much doubt that the best all-rounder the game has ever seen was Garry Sobers, but Botham was not far behind. He played at a time when there were several outstanding all-round cricketers. India had Kapil Dev, while Imran Khan was playing for Pakistan. New Zealand had Richard Hadlee, although he was perhaps not quite a genuine all-rounder, being more of a bowler than a batsman, and the West Indies side featured Malcolm Marshall, like Hadlee, a bowler who could bat extremely well rather than the real thing. Another bowler who could bat pretty well was Pakistan's Wasim Akram. They were all wonderfully exciting cricketers. What a time it was to watch international cricket.

The most remarkable aspect of Botham was his zest for play-ing the game and for living life to the full. His spirit could never be dampened and he would take on any challenge, however much the odds were against him. Every captain would want to have a player like Botham in their team. Shrinking violets in the dressing room must have found it almost impossible to resist his buoyant enthusiasm. His confidence was hugely infectious. When Botham was at his best as a player, nothing was impossible. With the new ball in his hand, wickets seemed bound to fall. He had a great knack of taking a wicket early in a new spell, and even at the end of his career, when he was in and out of the side because of injury, he almost always took a wicket in his first over. It can be tempting to paint him as a lucky bowler, but great cricketers make their own luck and Botham certainly did that.

There were also the off-duty moments when he kicked over the traces in a spectacular way, which guaranteed the involvement of the red-tops and brought a beaming smile to the face of Kelvin MacKenzie, the editor of *The Sun*. I have always likened Botham to a young golden Labrador who kept wagging its tail and knocking valuable objects off the table. There was never any malice in what he did; he was a vibrant young man living life to the full and he found it hard to resist temptation.

Although he has kept his hand in as a commentator on Sky Television, his life away from cricket is in some ways strongly reminiscent of those hirsute amateurs of more than a century ago. Shooting and fishing form a big part of his life and he has become highly skilled at both. He also loves his wine, mostly at the receiving end, but, initially with the help of a friend who owns vineyards in South Australia, he now has his own range of wines which can be bought in top-of-the-range supermarkets. When he was a player, Botham became a good friend of John Arlott and for a time he also had a house in Alderney. This meant that he learned this particular trade from a reliable tutor, even if, from time to time, quality became confused with quantity. Botham will have found nothing wrong with that either. The bottom line is that this planet would have been a much duller place without Ian Botham – and John Arlott too.

B
THE BOX

This is arguably a batsman's most important piece of equipment. Even with a box in place, a delivery from a fast bowler that makes a direct hit causes acute discomfort. Play will be held up as people rush out with glasses of water and anything else they feel may solve an insoluble problem, and it will be a while before play restarts. Misadventures of this sort inevitably reduce many people to laughter, but never the poor chap who is on the receiving end.

When I first contemplated using a box, I felt it was another step completed in the complicated process of growing up. It was some while before I discovered that a jockstrap was an essential accompaniment. I remember only too well inserting the box for the first time and then feeling badly let down when, after a couple of strides, it came to rest somewhere near my right knee-cap. I sought further advice and was severely disappointed when told that at my age it was an irrelevant piece of equipment anyway. I need not have worried, because by the time it became relevant I had graduated to a jockstrap and all was well.

Nowadays batsmen bind up the rest of their bodies so that they look like men-of-war. It would not surprise me if modern boxes have been developed and streamlined in perhaps some rather surprising ways, but even if that is so, it does not appear to lessen the pain that a direct hit can cause.

Most cricketers have a good box story. Mine happened in 1959 when I played for Cambridge against Sussex at that charming ground in Eastbourne, the Saffrons. We had a lot of fielding to do, not least because it was a game when the Reverend David Sheppard momentarily deserted his flock and took up his bat again for Sussex, this time against his old university. Inevitably, he made a hundred and it was a joy to watch him. In the middle of the order Sussex had a short, rather stocky left-hander who always seemed to be smiling called Ken Suttle, who had gone on a tour with England to the West Indies in 1953–54 without playing in a Test match. He was now facing another left-hander, Simon Douglas-Pennant, who bowled left arm over the wicket at fast-medium.

Suttle, who had a crouching stance, decided to hook a short delivery which may not have been quite short enough for the purpose. He swivelled and got an edge on the ball, which hit him amidships with a horrifying clang. He doubled up in considerable pain and had to suffer the usual laughter. When he had recovered, and before facing another ball, he fished out his box and found there was a huge dent in it which made it difficult to wear. This did not faze the fearless Suttle in the least. He put down the box and, using his bat handle as if he was tapping a stump into the ground, casually knocked out the dent. After holding the box up for inspection, he seemed satisfied with what he saw, so slipped it back into position and prepared to face Douglas-Pennant's next ball. *Wisden* tells me he went on to make 34 and took his place in the Sussex side for their next game. Happily, no lasting damage was done, although it is to be hoped that this particular box was promptly sent into honourable retirement.

B
STUART BROAD

Thirteen fathers and sons have played cricket for England, although none have been at opposite ends of the pole more than father Chris Broad, an impressive opening batsman, and son Stuart, an extraordinary fast bowler. Chris made three hundreds in the 1986–87 Ashes series in Australia, while Stuart (at the time of writing) has taken 450 Test wickets and is still running in as fast as his increasingly apprehensive limbs will allow. In spite of his occasional glaring looks and brusque manner, when watching Stuart, whatever he was doing, I always felt that deep down he was hugely enjoying himself, even if he was not prepared to let on.

Too often, talented sons are overawed by highly successful fathers. Interestingly, Stuart Broad began life as an opening batsman like his father, but as he shot up in height he decided he wanted to be a fast bowler. He was approaching things, therefore, from the opposite end of the scale to his father, who knew all about facing fast bowling but not as much about the art of delivery. They explored different territories.

Stuart has become one of England's greatest fast bowlers and his tally of Test wickets is ample evidence of this. No two fast bowlers have ever been the same. They shape their job the way it suits them best. Broad makes full use of every inch of his height – he is six feet five inches tall. His deliberate, menacing walk back to his mark, the long-striding, fierce run-up and the high, furious action all help him to find pace, bounce and unrelenting hostility. A slight paradox in Broad is that it is surprising that someone with such boyish and innocent looks should be so hostile as a bowler and so forthright in his views in general. Visually, his bowling seemed out of character.

The only problem Stuart has had is that for all these component parts to work at their best, they have to be harmonised by rhythm. Sometimes, even soon after one of his great spells, this rhythm mysteriously seems to disappear. I have seen Broad run in on mornings when the pitch and the elements are entirely in his favour. All he needed to do was pitch the ball up and bowl at the off stump, making sure the batsman was kept on the front foot. Yet, instead, he bowled repeatedly short and wasted the ball still further by bowling wide of the stumps, allowing the batsman to play no stroke. It seems strange that such a marvellous bowler should not be able to fall back more on automatic pilot to produce the required length and line, even at the cost of some pace. No one can have been more frustrated than Broad himself about this. After each wayward ball, he must have been angry with himself, and yet the next ball would also be short and wide. It was his rhythm that was missing. Broad is not alone here, for every fast bowler goes through periods like this, and even Jimmy Anderson at the other end cannot always get it right.

Broad has tended to be a little wary of the press and media, and he may have inherited from his father the cussed side to his nature that is revealed from time to time. When things have gone against him on the field or he has received what he thought was unfair criticism, Stuart has not held back. I was lucky enough to be in the commentary box for three of Stuart's most destructive and heroic spells of bowling. I completed his hat-trick against India at Trent Bridge in 2011; I conveyed the news of the two wickets he took in his first over against Australia at Trent Bridge in 2015 when he took 8–15 as Australia were bowled out before lunch on the first day for 60; barely six months later, I was on the air at Wanderers in Johannesburg when he destroyed South Africa in their second innings, taking 6–17, including a spell of 5–1 in 36 balls. The main threat to England then was likely to be A.B. de Villiers. He came in at 28–2, after Broad had removed both openers, and I was on the air with former South African captain Graeme Smith alongside me in the commentary box. With his mechanism working to perfection, Broad raced in to bowl to de Villiers, who had not yet scored a run. De Villiers was in two minds and pushed belatedly at a ball which came back a fraction into the left-hander on pitching, flicked the inside edge of the bat and Jonny Bairstow held on to the catch. It was the moment South Africa knew they were beaten and it is one of the imperishable memories of my commentating career. I cannot remember seeing a better ball, unless it was the one from Freddie Flintoff that accounted for Ricky Ponting in the second Test against Australia at Edgbaston in 2005. That was a perfectly placed lifter from only just short of a length which no one would have been able to avoid and Ponting was also caught behind.

When I shut my eyes now, I can see this fair-haired giant striding in to bowl like a human Ferrari that has just slipped comfortably into overdrive. On all three of the above occasions Stuart Broad was an irresistible force of nature and it was as magnificent as anything I have seen from a fast bowler. After that Test in Johannesburg, we moved four days later across to Centurion, little more than an hour away from Wanderers, and in that match at least one cog was missing as he ran in to bowl. This will always be the way with Broad. He can now see fast-bowling old age on the horizon, but he still has it in him to give us one or two more of those great spells to relish, and will surely end up with more than 500 Test wickets. He will go down not only as one of our greatest fast bowlers, but as half of one of the best fast-bowling partnerships, Anderson and Broad, who have propped up the England side for a long time.

Just occasionally, Stuart Broad batted well enough, in his flashing left-handed way, to suggest he should bat higher than number nine. It is still something of an affront to human nature that he should once have made 169, against Pakistan at Lord's in 2010, batting at number nine. He came in when England were 102–7 and, standing upright, slashed, drove and pulled his way to more runs than any England number nine had made before. He rode his luck and it was wonderful to watch. What a shame it is that this match will be remembered longest for the organised cheating by some of the Pakistanis. They deliberately bowled some prearranged no-balls, for which three of the side went on to serve prison sentences.

Stuart Broad's batting was almost always a little bit more miss than hit, but in that one innings he showed that if he had put his mind to it he would have scored more runs. But I am sure he was right to put most of his energies into making himself the wonderful bowler he became. His batting undoubtedly suffered when, in 2014, he had his nose broken by a bouncer from Varun Aaron in the Test at Old Trafford against India. After that he was more concerned about getting out of the way of anything short, not that it has deterred him in the least from serving up plenty of short stuff himself.

B

BUMP BALL

The bump ball is one of the mysteries of cricket. Sometimes, when the batsman plays a full-length ball, he will hit it straight into the ground and the ball then flies into the air. When it is caught by a fielder, it looks to the uninitiated like a genuine catch. John Arlott, the greatest commentator of them all, would invariably describe a ball so caught as a 'spectator catch' in those wonderful Hampshire tones of his.

How can you tell? I think anyone who has ever played cricket will know that a bump ball has a different look to it. It is not a catch as the ball has been hit into the ground and is therefore not out. Every time this happens, part of the crowd go up as if it is a genuine catch. Having said that, I have no doubt that over time many bump balls have been given out, especially when it comes to the grassroots game at village or club level. Even as a batsman, I don't think you are always absolutely certain you have hit the ball into the ground and it is therefore a bump ball. If you hit your boot with your bat at the same time as the ball, or if you thump the bottom of your bat into the ground as you make contact with the ball, it is not always easy to be certain what has happened. I am equally sure that many batsmen, on returning to the pavilion, have claimed that a genuine catch was a bump ball. It can be a useful excuse.

I can just remember the most famous bump or non-bump ball ever. When England went to Australia immediately after the war, in 1946–47, cricket had already penetrated my consciousness even though I was only just seven years old. Don Bradman had not been well for some time, but he was keen to play in the series, although Australia were taking a bit of a chance in playing him. In the first Test, at Brisbane, he won the toss and was soon batting himself, for Australia's first wicket fell when the score was only nine. Bradman struggled for more than an hour while making 28. He then faced Bill Voce and tried with a diagonal bat to chop a ball of yorker length away behind square on the off side. The ball flew at chest height into Jack Ikin's hands at second slip.

The fielders were amazed when Bradman, who believed his bat had struck the ball into the ground, stayed where he was. The England fielders then appealed vigorously for a catch. All eyes turned to Umpire Borwick, standing in his seventeenth Test match. He found in favour of the batsman and Bradman went on to make 187. The innings did wonders for him when it came to helping him back to full health and rekindling his full enthusiasm for the game. If he had been out for 28, there was a feeling that he might have decided that at his time of life a return to Test cricket was a step too far. As it was, he stayed to lead Australia to a 3–0 victory in that series and, of course, took his Invincibles, as they came to be named, to England in 1948.

I well remember this incident being talked about at the time by Freddy Hunn, who was in charge of the grain store in the farmyard at Hoveton and in his spare time looked after the village pitch. A few years later, when I was playing Minor County cricket for Norfolk, we played a game against Staffordshire at

Lakenham, Norfolk's lovely old ground in Norwich which some years ago sadly fell into the hands of property developers. Bill Edrich, who had begun his career with Norfolk before the war, had come back in 1959 to captain the county while Jack Ikin had finished his cricket with Lancashire and now captained Staffordshire. After the first day of this game, several of us fore-gathered in a pub in the middle of Norwich and listened while Bill and Jack, both in the slips that day in Brisbane, talked through the incident. Neither was in the least doubt that the ball had flown straight from the edge of Bradman's bat into Ikin's hands and that it was a fair catch. As their memories took hold, they became increasingly adamant.

C

CHEATING

Cricket, like every sport, moves and changes in step with society. We, alas, live in a more unprincipled age than we once did and all sorts of unholy practices have crept into the game, just as they have into life in general. Some may always have been there, but a host of new horrors have been spawned thanks largely to the thriving and alarmingly imaginative illegal betting industry in India. We live in an age, too, in which the constant and intense scrutiny of the media means that it is much harder to keep anything secret.

The most unexpected culprit I ever came across was Arthur Mailey, the Australian leg-spinner. I was lucky to meet him three or four times when playing boys' cricket in Norfolk, where Mailey often stayed. I have a collection of his delightfully humorous drawings. He was a man of enormous good cheer, was loved by the establishment and was the sort of character you would never in a million years have suspected of breaking the Laws. Yet, in his splendid autobiography, *10 for 66 and All That*, published in 1958, he happily owns up to keeping resin in his pockets when bowling and to lifting the seam quietly and carefully for Jack Gregory and Ted McDonald, Australia's opening bowlers. When I first read that, I found myself wondering what Moses might have got up to on that walk down from the top of Mount Sinai.

Match-fixing and ball-tampering may have been going on for a long time, but not perhaps to the extent that almost certainly happens today, and in a more discreet way. In the days of Mailey, it is extremely unlikely there were the financial inducements that are flying around today. Spot-fixing is a newer sin and is a by-product of spread-betting, itself a relatively recent invention. These days vast sums are bet on the outcome of every ball. When Mohammad Amir deliberately bowled his first ball in the Lord's Test match in 2010 to the fine-leg boundary for five wides, there were a number of people in the know who were able to take huge advantage of the extremely good odds the bookmakers were offering against the first ball of the match going for five runs. The deliberate cheating in this match was orchestrated by the Pakistani captain, Salman Butt, who was the bookies' man on the ground.

Cheating will always be around, for human nature has made sure there will always be punters who are ready and willing to exploit these illegal methods of grabbing some money. Every cricket team has its new, young players who may be susceptible to pocketing a bit of cash in this way. Then there are the members of any side who are unlikely to remain there for long. They will often be tempted to cash in while still in a position to do so, and in an increasingly greedy world, most if not all men have their price. We live in a murky age.

The game desperately needs a damage-limitation exercise, but the people who run cricket, the International Cricket Council (ICC), sometimes seem hopelessly confused. It is their job to control the game and, above all, to keep it as clean and respectable as they can, but an awful lot is going on under the watch of the present people in charge. Cheating is never going to be obliterated, but it must be possible to restrict it more successfully than is happening at the moment. The ICC makes disapproving noises, says 'Tut tut', but does nothing, even though there seems to me to be a straightforward course of action: every cricketer caught with his hand in the till while playing in international competition should never again be allowed to play for his country.

Of course, one or two young players, coerced by their seniors as Cameron Bancroft was in the ball-tampering incident involving the Australians in South Africa in 2017–18, are going to be unlucky. Infinitely the more important issue is the greater good of the game, and, therefore, so what? Top sportsmen earn enormous sums these days and even though cricketers may consider themselves the poor relations of international sport, they are still doing a great deal better than they once were. If young players like sandpaperer Bancroft are put under pressure to cheat, many of them will not want to go down that road when they know that they risk facing a lifetime rather than a one-year ban. As for older players like David Warner, apparently the orchestrator of what happened in Cape Town, and his captain, Steve Smith, who must surely have known what was going on even if he did not have the guts to stop it, it was good riddance, but only for a year and that is not nearly long enough. Maybe their arrogance led them to think they were untouchable. The sheer stupidity of what they did is underlined by the fact that the sandpapering was carried out in front of thirty-odd television cameras positioned around the ground. It was bound to be spotted. Mailey had not had to face that problem when he got to work with his resin.

Because the Australian psyche needs winners and recently they have been losing, they were bound to bring back Smith, such a wonderful player, but not as captain, for that would have been one step too far. As I write, he has just scored two magnificent hundreds in the first Ashes Test at Edgbaston in August 2019. I was surprised Warner was also recalled to arms, for it had seemed clear that he was the instigator of this whole business, but if he had not been brought back, perhaps Australian cricket would have been dragged lengthily and expensively through the courts. If Warner ever writes a 'tell-all' autobiography, we may find that there is much more to come from this story, although for the present it is on hold. In his second incarnation, Warner has found runs harder to come by than Smith. There may be a moral here.

Sadly, it is the authorities themselves who consistently refuse to stand up and be counted on this issue. Much wringing of hands goes on, but the moral high ground remains unoccupied and there is no one prepared to thump the table and say that enough is enough. Of course, we live in an age which is ridiculously litigious, and solicitors and legal advisers will be busy wringing their hands as well, for the seemingly ungodly keep discovering legal ways of turning the tables on their bosses. The result may be that the ungodly will continue to flourish and the ICC will go on shaking its collective head, not daring to do anything but speak pious words which will never solve anything, and the game will be made to look even more foolish.

C

DENIS COMPTON

Denis Compton was a present from Paradise and my supreme hero. Just occasionally a cricketer appears who does not have to obey the laws which control other mortals. He makes his own, and because they are sublime they cannot be copied or written down. Compton's bat was truly a magic wand balanced on two mercurial feet guided by a unique instinct.

In 1947, under the hot sun which shone for most of the summer, Compton treated the large post-war crowds to a prolonged exhibition of batting, the like of which had never been seen before. That summer, he made 3,816 first-class runs and hit 18 centuries, records which may never be broken. His innovative approach to batting took the art to new levels. Established technique was not ignored, but adapted and reorganised to suit the needs of genius.

Compton was never one for the record books; he was not tangible or precise as a man or as a batsman. He was as unconcerned by batting averages as he was by the vicissitudes of life. He shrugged off injuries and bowlers alike. At his pure, unimpeded best, as he was in 1947, nothing was beyond him. Having given him the ultimate key to the art of batting, fate then crept up behind him with a solid chunk of lead piping in her hand.

Football was his second love and he lent his talents to the right wing of Arsenal at Highbury. When his right knee was damaged, it probably stopped him from playing full international football for his country, but it undoubtedly prevented him from reaching his proper place in cricket's record books, not that it will have worried him in the least. At the top level of cricket's Valhalla, his only companion would surely have been Kumar Shri Ranjitsinhji, the game's other remarkable, innovative and unconcerned genius.

Denis Compton first turned out for Middlesex in 1936 at the age of 18. He played for England against New Zealand the following year and in 1938 made a hundred in his first Test match against Australia. The requirements of Highbury prevented him from touring South Africa with England the following winter. Then, like all the players of his generation, he was robbed of what would surely have been six of his most productive years by the Second World War.

During the war, Compton did play some cricket in India, which included an extraordinary innings of 249 not out for Holkar against Bombay in the Ranji Trophy final. The runs were made during the fourth innings of the match when Holkar had been left to score 867 to win. He shared a long partnership with Indian Test batsman Mushtaq Ali, who later commented on the excellence of Compton's running between the wickets. (He was the only man to do so throughout Compton's entire career. That was one part of the game he never quite got the hang of.)

Before the match, an Indian tycoon keen to see Holkar win had offered Compton fifty rupees for every run he made over a hundred. After reaching three figures, each time he hit a four it was worth £30 to him. When the match was over, Compton reckoned he was owed the not inconsiderable sum of £1,300.

C.K. Nayudu, the Bombay captain, took Compton to the tent where the wool tycoon had been watching. When he arrived, a large silver salver bearing an envelope was set in front of him. He tore it open, only to find a hastily scribbled note saying, 'Sorry, have been called to Calcutta on very urgent business' – and that was the nearest he got to his money. For all that, it had been a typically thrilling innings and was very much a forerunner of all that was to come from his bat and his footwork three years later in England.

The 1947 season was the first in which I took a serious interest in the daily county cricket scoreboards and, of course, Denis Compton became my hero. I kept my own tally of his runs and every morning I could not get down the stairs quick enough to read the Middlesex or England score. I wallowed in Compton's success. The greatest moment of my early life was when I first went to Lord's with my parents to watch the third day's play in the second Ashes Test in 1948. Alas, Australia were batting in their second innings, but I saw Don Bradman, swamped in the baggy green cap, make 89. I was disappointed when he was caught at first slip by Bill Edrich off Alec Bedser just before the close of play – I wanted to see him make a hundred – but not half as disappointed as I was not to see Compton bat. I was left to wonder at him as he wandered about in the field, Brylcreem glistening in the sun.

Back at school, at Sunningdale, I wrote a letter to him including a stamped addressed envelope, asking for his autograph. About ten days later, a letter addressed to me in my own handwriting was sitting one morning on the table outside the library with all the other boys' letters. Feverishly, I tore it open and there in my hand was a slip of paper which had 'With

Compliments' printed at the top and a delightful and highly legible 'Denis Compton' written underneath. I don't think I have ever felt quite so excited as when I first held that slip of paper. I still have it. It was my own personal Magna Carta. It got even better. Two years later, the Sunningdale First XI, into which I had just slipped as a keen but decidedly variable leg-spinner, were taken by bus to a lovely ground in Taplow to watch a benefit match for Compton. I wanted to get another autograph from him that day. Sadly, the queue was too long, but my puny box camera managed to get him in the frame. I went through agony – suppose it had not come out – until the photograph came back, safely developed.

Now in his thirties, Denis the batsman was becoming increasingly handicapped by that wretched knee. I also had to suffer his dreadful tour of Australia in 1950–51 when he averaged under ten. During that series, I was ridiculed at school for my hero-worship of the great man. My support never wavered, although it was a long time before I completely forgave him for what he had put me through. He managed to make up some of the lost ground when he scored the winning runs at The Oval in 1953 when England won the Ashes for the first time for twenty years.

By then I had moved on to Eton where, if you can believe it, I found myself keeping wicket to Denis Compton three years later. During the previous winter he had had his right kneecap removed. In May 1956, his old county captain Walter Robins brought the Forty Club, a club for the over-forties, down to play against Eton, and Compton, in his first outing since the operation, was in his side. We batted first and the Great Man bowled a couple of overs without being able to take any run-up.

He just stood at the crease and brought his arm over. Then, shortly before tea, he hobbled in to bat. His movements were badly restricted, but his instinct and inclination were not. With his right foot painfully anchored, his left came enthusiastically forward, almost on the prance, looking for the chance to despatch the ball as it had always done. And I was just a few feet away. He was so charming to us all and full of laughter. It was an amazing day. There was one remarkable coincidence to it too. The Forty Club side also included Arthur Morris, the former left-handed Australian opening batsman who had just retired and who was to become a lifelong friend of mine. When England were in Australia in 1946–47, the fourth Test was played in Adelaide and in that match Compton made a hundred in each innings for England and Morris did the same for Australia. That day I caught Morris behind the wicket and never let him forget it.

The Australians were touring England in 1956 and, having seen Compton play for the first time since his operation, it was unthinkable that he would be fit enough to play in a Test match that summer or, indeed, ever again. As it was, his recovery was astonishing. He was back in the Middlesex side in July and chosen to play in the fifth Test at The Oval after England had already won the Ashes. In England's first innings he made 94, an innings which Don Bradman described from the press box as the best piece of batting in the series.

I also had the luck to play against Compton in one of his last first-class matches. In 1959 he turned out for the MCC against Cambridge University at Lord's. All the old flair and instinct were there, as vibrant as ever, and he made 71 magical runs in their first innings. His footwork, his improvisation and his versatility were extraordinary. Even with the handicap of his right knee, he left me with impression that he could have hit every ball he received to any and all points of the compass. The hair, no Brylcreem now, was as dishevelled as ever, the calling for runs was characteristically imprecise and his spirit was, as always, unquenchable. His bat, too, which I was lucky enough to see from the gully, was every bit as much a magic wand as it had ever been.

C

ALASTAIR COOK

I cannot think of any batsman I have wanted to see make runs more than Alastair Cook. It was not his strokeplay or his style as a batsman that I was anxious to watch, and I would not have driven miles to see him bat either, but I did desperately want him to be successful. He was not a lithe and graceful thoroughbred at the crease, but although I was usually a dispassionate viewer in the commentary box, I always felt perhaps unreasonably sad if he should get out. I had a huge loyalty, admiration and affection for Cook – and that is the only way I can put it.

The reaction of those at The Oval who gave him an ovation which lasted for many minutes when he made 147 in his last Test innings, and also of the country as a whole, was evidence that this was the public perception of Cook, too. Few cricketers can ever have laid claim to such respect and affection.

He was the most charmingly understated of men and I cannot believe he has an enemy in the world, give or take Kevin Pietersen. Everyone must hope their daughter marries an Alastair Cook. He was as modest as a cricketer as he was as a man, and yet there was an impenetrable core of steel in him as he faced the world's opening bowlers for 161 Test matches. His figures bore an overwhelming testimony to this. He made more runs in Test cricket than any other Englishman and his 33 Test hundreds is also top of the list. He held more catches, too, than anyone else except a wicketkeeper and, perhaps the most remarkable of all, he played 159 successive Test matches, which is a world record.

Cook shuffled almost unnoticed into the side in India in March 2006. He had been playing with the England A side in the Caribbean when he received an urgent call to fly to Nagpur for the first Test. In spite of jet lag, he made 60 in England's first innings and 104 in the second. He may go down as the last England batsman capable of playing the long innings which is so important in the context of Test cricket. This attribute was never more evident than it was right at the start in Nagpur. He was never going to be an Ian Botham, a David Gower or an Allan Lamb; he was simply going to be an unpretentious, hardworking, old-fashioned Alastair Cook who fought his way to 12,472 Test runs.

His England career was not one long fairy story, for he survived a number of anxious periods. He was not the only England captain to be messed about by Pietersen's extraordinary ego, although he arguably suffered the most. Their 'battle' undoubtedly had a profound effect on Cook. The irony was that he was happy to take Pietersen with him to India in 2012–13 and did all he could to reintroduce him into the England fold after he had been dropped for sending messages to the South African dressing room at Headingley in August 2012 that undermined Andrew Strauss both as a captain and as a batsman, an incident I have gone into more fully in the entries I have written about Pietersen himself and Strauss. England won the series in India, and that was maybe Cook's greatest achievement as captain. A year later, in 2013–14, he took a side which must have left England with high hopes to Australia, where they lost all five Tests. It was a series that was bedevilled by a power struggle orchestrated behind the scenes by Pietersen. The fall-out was considerable. Andy Flower, the coach, resigned, Pietersen himself was banished by England and although Cook stayed on, he lost the series to Sri Lanka in England the following summer. He did not make runs himself and must have been close to throwing in his hand. His career was probably saved by a stubborn innings of 95 against India at the end of that summer. It is fair to say that if there had been an obvious replacement, Cook might well have been persuaded to give the job up at that point.

As captain, Cook stood solidly at first slip until the spinners came on and then he would venture to short midwicket or short extra cover. There was nothing very imaginative about his captaincy and if he had a motto it would have been 'steady as she goes'. Cook comes from farming stock and, as a breed, farmers are not great risk-takers. He was happy to let the game plod along in the hope that something would turn up rather than take a considered risk to try and unsettle the batsman's concentration and make something happen. He was not one of England's greatest captains, but he did not do a bad job, either.

He had no more important supporter than his wife, Alice, who was a tremendous help at times of crisis. When he had those problems with Pietersen, and when he lost form himself, her support was invaluable to him and almost certainly made the difference. If it had not been for her, I think he would surely have resigned the captaincy a year or two before he did. It was a measure of the man that however badly things were going, on the field and in the dressing room, he managed in public to be the same charming, unassuming individual, no matter what was churning around inside him.

I remember meeting him on the 2015–16 tour of South Africa coming off the field at Wanderers in Johannesburg three-quarters of an hour before the start of the third Test. He made a point of coming up and having a friendly, unhurried conversation even though at that moment there must have been many more important things going on in his mind. Yet he put all that to one side and made me feel I was the only person he wanted to talk to. He even suggested that he and I should one day have a long chat in front of television cameras, which sadly has never happened.

I think the essence of Cook was a complete lack of self-importance, which made me feel that although he was captain of England, a job which has turned some people into remote and isolated figures, he remained a genuine friend. This is the reason I could not bear to see him out, even if I did not always particularly enjoy the product when he was battling away in the middle.

Few captains can have inspired such feelings of loyalty in his team. He had no greater supporter than Graeme Swann, who tells one amusing story against Cook, who has a good sense of humour. When England won the Ashes in 2009, the Australian batsman Mike Hussey, who had been a colleague of Swann's with Northamptonshire, was facing him when England needed one more wicket to win the match and the Ashes in the final Test at The Oval. Hussey, who had made 121, pushed forward and the ball flew off the edge onto his pad and into the hands of Cook at forward short leg. As the celebrations began, Swann noticed Cook slip the ball into his pocket and thought, 'How lovely, he's keeping it for me.' Later, in the dressing room, he asked Cook for the ball. Cook laughed and said, 'Give it to you? Why, this will be worth a lot of money in a few years.' Cook eventually let Swann have the ball and it is now in the museum at Lord's.

The full story of Alastair Cook's contribution to cricket will never be told by his figures alone, impressive as they are. It was the manner of the man: his modesty, his strength of character; a resolute ability to stand firm and an innate knowledge of what was right and what was wrong and the determination to act accordingly. All of this, allied to an extraordinary ability as a cricketer, made the knighthood he received after his retirement his just reward. Cricket would have been a poorer game without Sir Alastair Cook.

C

CYRIL COOTE

It is impossible to define Cyril Coote. He is best known for being the head groundsman at Fenner's at Cambridge for forty-five years, but he was so much more than that. A successful opening batsman for Cambridgeshire in the Minor County Championship, he had a great knowledge of the game and became a formidable coach. It was almost as if Fenner's was his private domain. He was in control of every aspect of the ground and its activities, including the finances, even to the extent of owning the concession for catering and bar services. In my two years at Cambridge, I found him a wonderful coach, adviser and friend, although he was a man who let few people get close to him.

He was in all senses a benevolent despot. Cyril had a marked limp, which came from an accident while playing hockey in his teens, a limp which in time became synonymous with Fenner's. When he was appointed custodian there he was only 25 and had been on the point of succeeding his father as groundsman for Trinity Hall. As it was, at Fenner's he succeeded Dan Hayward, the brother of the great Tom Hayward who batted for Surrey.

When I first met Cyril as an 18-year-old, I was initially alarmed by this commanding figure with a huge head, a strong body and a no-nonsense limp. Ted Dexter was captain of Cambridge that year and when he and Cyril were locked together in conversation, they seemed an unapproachable combination. I soon discovered this was not so. Cyril was always ready to talk and to help. He invariably made me feel he was on my side, in his slightly distant way. He had been a good player himself and was also the most objective watcher of others. He made a study of the techniques of the best players who came to Fenner's with the county sides. He was always happy to offer his advice and fifteen minutes in the nets with Cyril watching was time well spent. He had a ready smile and a determined voice, but was never domineering or hectoring and he always respected other people's opinions. Away from Fenner's, he was a brilliant game shot and an able fisherman and in his youth I am sure he must have given the pretty girls a run for their money.

Not the least of his attributes was his ability to teach the art of groundsmanship, and as a result Fenner's became an excellent training ground for young groundsmen. Bernard Flack, who went on to become the groundsman at Edgbaston and, eventually, the official inspector of pitches, was his most successful pupil. Cyril was greatly helped in the pavilion on the catering side of things by his wife, small, petite and blonde, who in her day must have been outstandingly pretty. I remember having the odd glass with Cyril in the pavilion after the close of play, but I do not ever recall him coming over to the Prince Regent on Parker's Piece for a drink. He was a prodigiously hard worker and at the end of the day, the job done, he and his wife would just go home. They were often the last to leave Fenner's.

Cyril was a perfectionist in everything he did. I can well remember him in the old Fenner's pavilion expounding his beliefs at the end of the day. Wearing a brown jersey with sleeves rolled up to the elbow, he would be bustling up and down helping Mrs Coote collect the last remaining cups and glasses. He was eternally restless – at least in public – and while clearing up he would sometimes talk about the way he worked. Maybe his rare moments of contemplation occurred at home in the evenings. He worked by controlled instinct and when it came to preparing pitches he was innovative and certain he was right – which he almost always was. For example, worms had traditionally been a problem for groundsmen, but Cyril liked to keep them because they aerated his soil. He always hoped, too, for sharp frosts in the winter, for they lifted the soil evenly, enabling the roller to bind the surface together better in the spring. He would say that the secret to groundsmanship, like so much else in life, was timing.

In the post-war years he prepared a series of wonderful batting pitches at Fenner's. There was an extraordinary game there in 1950 against the West Indies. By the end, Cambridge had made 594–4 declared and in reply the West Indies reached 730–3, which meant that 1,324 runs had been scored for the loss of seven wickets. The university batting was always much stronger than the bowling and the authorities at Cambridge tried to persuade Cyril to alter the balance of his pitches. His response to this was interesting and sensible. He refused to comply with their wishes and his argument was that although the university might take more wickets, the county batsmen would cope much better with the more testing conditions. It was better, he felt, to have pitches on which the university would score around 300 runs, which would then give the bowlers something to work with. Now that Cambridge no longer play first-class cricket, the importance of the game at Fenner's has probably diminished. The pitch is still reasonably good for batting, although you are unlikely to find one of the exceptional surfaces Cyril used to produce.

In later years, when I went back to Fenner's to write about university games, it was fun to sit in the new pavilion with Cyril and listen to him reminiscing about the players who had passed through his hands. He was always adamant that David Sheppard was the most complete batsman to come up to Cambridge as an undergraduate, with Peter May in second place. Ted Dexter was another who really caught his eye. He reckoned Majid Khan, already a Test cricketer when he arrived at Cambridge, played the best innings he ever saw from a university player. He made 70 not out against Worcestershire in 1972 on a hard pitch which became almost unplayable for a short time after a heavy shower of rain. He also considered Majid to be the best captain in all the years he was at Fenner's. Cyril had been a great supporter too, of Jahangir Khan, Majid's father, who was in the Cambridge side when Cyril first took over in 1935. His outstanding Cambridge bowler was Ossie Wheatley who, in 1958, took 80 wickets for Cambridge, moving the ball about at fast-medium – one or two even caught behind the stumps by one H.C. Blofeld. Wheatley went on to play for Warwickshire and then captained Glamorgan. His record at Cambridge is unlikely ever to be broken.

Cyril's resonant chuckling laugh and strong handshake still seem to greet me every time I go to Fenner's. No one would have deplored more the removal of first-class status from Oxford and Cambridge. If he had been ageless, perhaps it would never have happened.

C

CORFU

The two principal remaining legacies of the fifty years of British rule in Corfu between 1815 and 1864 are cricket and ginger beer. In many of the more unlikely parts of the world where cricket has been left behind by the British colonists and now has little more than a toehold, it has mainly been the expatriate community who have kept the game going. While this must initially have been so in Corfu too, over the years the Greeks themselves have not only taken an interest in cricket, but have also learned to play the game competitively, if occasionally in a spirit that is not entirely orthodox.

My only experience of cricket there came around 1980 when I was asked to go out with a team put together by Ben Brocklehurst, a former captain of Somerset. At this time, Ben owned and ran *The Cricketer* magazine, which was also the marketing tool used by Ben and his wife, Belinda, to promote their travel business, to a large extent centred around cricket.

We were a splendid mixture of the past and the present and of hope over experience. Our captain was none other than Bill Edrich, who features elsewhere in this book. He was well into his sixties but still a most capable player, and I don't think I have ever met anyone who enjoyed the game more than Bill. He played it with a wonderful spirited intensity and enjoyment. In Corfu, I remember him enjoying the retsina almost as much.

But when we took the field no one was more determined than Bill that we should conquer. Another Test cricketer in our party was Bruce French, who kept wicket for Nottinghamshire and England in a charmingly efficient and impish way.

The ground was in the square in the centre of Corfu Town. It had an artificial pitch covered with coconut matting and along one side of the ground there was an impressive line of shops and bars, with much outside seating under the olive, eucalyptus and plane trees where defeated batsmen could drink their sorrows away. On the other side, the grass at deep-ish extra cover gave way to the tarmac surface for the local bus car park. At the start of the match it was empty, with the buses out on their business, but in the evening they were back, tightly parked. This meant that the side batting first had to hit the ball much further to reach the boundary than the side batting second, when the parked buses became the boundary line.

Our first game was against Gymnastikos, the local champions. They were captained by a Corfiot called Contos, whose attitude would have given W.G. Grace and Douglas Jardine plenty of food for thought. In spite of the bus situation, Bill decided to bat first and I remember our innings well because Bill and I put on over a hundred for the second wicket. Contos, at a mean medium pace, was the best of their bowlers and the most outrageous appealer. He was not naturally attracted to umpires either. We scored somewhere just over 200, but we then ran into problems we had not anticipated. Gymnastikos made a reasonable start, but then lost a couple of wickets and the redoubtable Contos, on the short side and stocky with wide shoulders and not much of a smile, walked to the middle looking more than ever like a local Napoleon.

He took a most deliberate guard and began to bat as if he was brave Horatius defending the bridge. He had scored a few runs before he could not make up his mind whether to play back or forward and the ball removed his off bail. This did not deter him in the least. He bent down, picked up the bail, put it back on the stumps and took up his stance, ready to face the next ball. It was now that Bill, fielding as usual at first slip, gently reminded Contos that he was out. Contos affected not to understand and to be unable to speak English – which was far from the truth. A lively discussion ensued, with Bill's English making little headway against Contos's Greek, which resembled machine-gun fire. Talk about Greek meeting Greek. The long and short of it was that Contos won that particular battle and duly faced the next ball. He was out soon afterwards and Bill wished him a happy journey back to the pavilion. In the end, we won and Bill and Contos finished the day slapping each other's back over their retsina and telling each other what good chaps they were.

Cricket still goes on in Corfu and I am sure that bar under the awning just over square leg does more business than ever. A cricket tour to Corfu is, I can assure you, one of the best cricketing adventures. Ginger beer never gets a look-in these days.

D

BASIL D'OLIVEIRA

I can still see Basil D'Oliveira's lovely amused smile, with more than just a touch of mischievousness creeping in at the corners. No sportsman did more than D'Oliveira to help break down the barriers of apartheid. His was an extraordinary story. Born a Cape Coloured, he was, because of his colour, denied the chance to play cricket for his country of birth or, indeed, first-class cricket within the country.

His story can never be told too often. He came to England in 1960, the money for the journey having been raised by his friends in the Cape. He began in the Central Lancashire League, was selected for Commonwealth XI tours in the winter and by 1965 had been taken on by Worcestershire and, scoring six hundreds that year, did much to help them retain the County Championship. The following year he was picked for England against the West Indies. In 1967–68, he had a disappointing tour for England in the West Indies and when it came to the Australian tour of England in 1968, his place was in doubt. Nevertheless he played in the first Test at Old Trafford, making 87 not out in England's second innings, but was surprisingly dropped for the next three matches.

The following winter, England were touring South Africa, whose segregational policies turned D'Oliveira's possible selection into a political problem. He was not originally in the team for the fifth Test against Australia at The Oval, the final Test of the summer, but a few days before the match began, Roger Prideaux pulled out with an injury. D'Oliveira was chosen to replace him. Batting at number six, he played a magnificent innings of 158 and took a crucial wicket on the last day, and his passionate hopes of touring his home country with England seemed certain to be realised. To make even more sure of this, he made a hundred for Worcestershire the day after the Test match ended, but that same day the side to tour South Africa was announced and he had been left out. There was an immediate furore and loud accusations were made that the MCC – it was they who still chose England touring sides – had bowed to political pressure from the apartheid regime in South Africa. They were accused of racial discrimination.

Almost three weeks later, one of England's bowlers, Tom Cartwright, had to pull out of the tour because of injury and the same selection committee that had originally refused to pick D'Oliveira now brought him in as a substitute for Cartwright. A bowler had dropped out and a batsman had replaced him – as the South African prime minister, B.J. Vorster, was quick to spot. He had already told Sir Alec Douglas-Home, the former prime minister and president of MCC in 1966–67, that D'Oliveira would not be acceptable as a member of the England touring party. That message must have been relayed to Lord's. Vorster announced on 17 September in Bloemfontein that he was not prepared to accept 'a team thrust upon us'. A week later, after meeting officials from the South African Cricket Association at Lord's, the MCC, their arm twisted by Harold Wilson, the prime minister, called off the tour, even though they had done everything in their power to make sure it went ahead. In the end, Harold Wilson had summoned the president and secretary of the MCC to Downing Street and instructed them to cancel it.

The MCC president, Ronnie Aird, at once paid tribute to 'the great dignity D'Oliveira has maintained throughout the whole business'. D'Oliveira was rewarded with the OBE in the Queen's Birthday Honours the following year. South Africa's intransigence over D'Oliveira's selection had a major part to play in their complete isolation from international sport and to the eventual disappearance of apartheid. It had been his greatest desire to return to South Africa as a member of the England cricket team and it was, of course, of even greater importance to him to see equal opportunity given to all the coloured people in South Africa. He was denied the first, but played a bigger part than maybe he knew in fulfilling the second.

D'Oliveira, who was 34 when he first played for England, went on to play in 44 Test matches. I was lucky to know him reasonably well. He never lost that smile or his sense of humour and it would have been impossible to invent a better role model for all that he did. His delightful strokeplay and easy bowling action were very much the product of the man you saw in front of you.

No one had more to do with D'Oliveira's original journey to England than John Arlott, who had seen apartheid at work when he had commentated on England's tour to South Africa under George Mann in 1948–49, and abhorred it. It was Arlott who steered D'Oliveira towards Middleton, a club in the Central Lancashire League, and kept an avuncular eye on him thereafter.

It is interesting to reflect on that 1967–68 tour of the West Indies under Colin Cowdrey, himself a somewhat enigmatic figure in the above drama (The England side did not tour in the

winter of 1966–67, and this alone shows what a different cricketing age we were living in back then. In Test and/or one-day
mode, England these days can have as many as three short tours
in one winter and never go without.) It was D'Oliveira's first
overseas tour and when he arrived in Barbados, he could hardly
believe his luck – and given the events of his life so far, who
could blame him? He did not have a good tour on the pitch and
perhaps allowed the joys of what he was finally embracing to go
to his head. It was perhaps the only time in his life when he
took his eye off the ball. The irony was that because of this, he
was not an automatic choice for the England side when the
players returned home for the series against Australia in 1968.
He was chosen for the first Test, however, but strangely, after
making that 87 not out, he was dropped. If he had had a good
tour of the West Indies, it would have made subsequent events
even harder to understand.

I sometimes wonder who had a word with whom behind the
scenes after that first Test. Was their conversation something
like 'If we don't drop him now, we may be forced to keep him
throughout the series and have no choice but to pick him for
South Africa'? If that was so, and it is only my conjecture, it is
an even bigger mystery why D'Oliveira was brought back when
Prideaux decided he was unfit to play in the fifth Test. Doug
Insole was chairman of the selectors then and the other three
were Alec Bedser, Don Kenyon and Peter May.

If D'Oliveira's exclusion for those three Tests had been polit-
ically motivated, as I have suggested, how did he get picked
right at the end of the series? Those selectors were a pretty
conservative bunch and seem likely to have toed the party line.
Or did they suddenly have pangs of conscience about

D'Oliveira? I am not certain that Doug Insole was known for having pangs of conscience or for changing his mind. Cowdrey, the captain, would certainly have gone along with the thinking that came out of the committee room at Lord's.

Maybe the selectors felt that it was a risk worth taking because they thought D'Oliveira was unlikely to make much impact and if he did not it would be helpful when they left him out of the side for South Africa. Maybe the fact that Prideaux pulled out at the last moment and D'Oliveira was close at hand had something to do with it. Even with all the advantages of hindsight, it is a story which still does not quite add up, and with so few of the personnel involved still around, we will probably never get to the full truth, be it straight or, as I suspect, more than a trifle twisted.

D
THE DOOSRA

In recent times, spinners, who were fast becoming an endangered species, have had to reinvent themselves. In the process they have got up to all sorts of unholy tricks. Orthodox finger-spinners – off-spinners and the orthodox left-arm spinners – no longer give captains their traditional attacking options. They have become principally containing bowlers, ending the innings with figures of, say, 3–94 off 37 overs without ever having the old-fashioned luxury of, say, 8–26 in 15 overs. The chance of a finger-spinner returning the latter figures decreased hugely when it was decided that pitches should at all times be covered against the elements. They now never have the chance to grab the rich rewards which once came from drying pitches.

To make themselves more competitive, finger-spinners have realised the importance of being able to bowl the ball that turns the other way. It was this which inspired the imaginative Saqlain Mushtaq from Pakistan to develop the 'doosra', which enables an off-spinner to turn the ball from leg to off. In Hindi and Urdu, *doosra* means 'second' or 'other', hence its use here. The doosra is the off-spinner's equivalent of the leg-spinner's googly, the 'wrong 'un', which turns the ball from off to leg.

It is important to remember that a leg-spinner is a wrist-spinner. This makes it possible for the leg-spinner to bowl the the googly without any suggestion that the ball is being thrown.

On the other hand, when the mechanism behind the finger-spinner's doosra is dissected, it is not easy to be convinced that such a ball can be bowled without a kink in the elbow at the point of delivery. I once sat near Saqlain Mushtaq as he explained in great detail how he had invented the delivery. Saqlain, the nicest, most genuine of men, was in no doubt that his doosra was a legitimate ball. I am not sure his audience was.

While I did not doubt Saqlain's sincerity, it all sounded more than a trifle strange. Throwing is the reddest of cricket's red lines. A chucker is the game's chief pariah. I think there are quite a number of off-spinners who have that tell-tale kink. There have been many likely candidates and the most glaring is, of course, the Sri Lankan off-spinner Muttiah Muralitharan. He was the main suspect for many years before he retired. There is no doubt that Murali was a genius and the game would have been much the poorer without him. What a wonderful 'bowler' he was – and also the most delightful and cheerful of men.

My own rather extravagant view of this is that I do not think it matters if spin bowlers throw – they are not going to injure batsmen in the way that fast bowlers who chuck almost certainly will. This is something for the legislators to work out and it should not be too difficult to determine a speed of delivery above which bowlers must have a straight arm at the point of delivery. I can hear the shrieks of horror when people read this, but would this be a more severe interruption to the world of cricket than the introduction of the T20 game, to say nothing of England's forthcoming 100-ball curiosity?

Under current legislation, I do not believe the doosra is a legal delivery, but I think this ball makes cricket a better game and helps preserve off-spinners. The administrators have already gone part of the way by enlarging the legitimate angle a bowler is allowed to have in his elbow at the point of delivery to 15 degrees. If that is not legalising throwing, I don't know what is. Whatever they may say, this was done to make sure Muralitharan was accommodated within the laws of the game, to prevent the whole of Sri Lanka going walkabout. The cynics may suggest that political pressure was brought to bear on the legislators over the issue of the Sri Lankan. I am sure it was, although we could debate for ever the point at which stage whispered words in dark corridors become political pressure.

Long live the doosra.

D

THE DRAW

I now propose to blow out of the water for ever the ridiculous belief that a drawn cricket match is a waste of time. It is a myth that has been propagated for far too long by our American friends when they deign to consider the workings of cricket. It is none of their business anyway. There can be no doubt that some of the best games of cricket ever played have ended as draws. Yes, after five hard-fought days – as far as Test cricket is concerned – a game may end without either side winning, and hallelujah to that. I am now going to ram a couple of supreme examples of positively electric draws down the collective throat of any disbelievers.

I watched almost every ball of the second Test between England and the West Indies at Lord's in 1963 from the top deck of the Warner Stand. The West Indies were the most thrilling side and they had won the first Test match by ten wickets. For three days this Lord's Test ebbed and flowed as one exciting subplot followed another. The West Indies were four runs ahead on the first innings and in the England innings we saw a magnificently heroic 70 in 75 balls by Ted Dexter, England's aristocratic-looking captain. 'Swashbuckling' is the right word to describe Dexter that day.

The weather was cloudy and dull and the light was barely adequate at any stage of the match. West Indies had the two most formidable fast bowlers in the world at that time, Wes Hall and Charlie Griffith. Hall, now a benign Protestant minister in Barbados, was tall, vibrant and the embodiment of hostility. He ran in to bowl with arms and legs going like a collection of demented windmills. You could feel the power he generated. Even watching him was like touching a live electric wire. For any batsman, that flailing run-up was nothing more than an elongated definition of terror. At the other end, Griffith, also tall but a less cheerful man than Hall, came in to bowl as if he wanted to knock the batsman's head off. Added to that, there was a suspicious kink in his elbow at the point of delivery when bowling his faster ball. At times, he undoubtedly threw the ball, thereby posing a serious physical danger for the batsman.

England had almost two days to make 234 runs to win, but rain saw to it that much of this time was lost, which heightened the drama still further. There was a basic, primeval, almost caveman atmosphere as this last innings spun out its course in between the showers. England 31–3: both openers were blasted out by Hall and then Ted Dexter was undone by the guile of off-spinner Lance Gibbs. Ken Barrington, a cheerful character and so much more than the ultimate professional, in spite of his general solidity at the crease, was now joined by Colin Cowdrey, who also had what it takes. When he had made 19, Cowdrey faced Hall in the gloaming. Hall tore in from the Pavilion End, where there was no sightscreen and the ball came out of the dark background of the windows of the Long Room. A furious short ball cracked into Cowdrey's right arm and broke it. Brian Close took his place and gallantly played the merciless fast bowling as much with his body as with his bat. The latter was dented and cracked, the former vividly bruised, though happily not cracked. But the runs still came, the target approached, the clouds darkened, the tension was unbelievable, wickets fell and the crowd gave voice to thrilling disbelief. Barrington, Jim Parks and Close succumbed to Griffith and if ever his arm was purposefully bent, it was surely now. England were 203–6 and all four results were possible.

In a blur of arms and legs, Hall accounted for the two Freds, Titmus and Trueman. Eight were needed from the last over, bowled by Hall. Two runs came from the first three balls. Derek Shackleton, recalled by England at the age of 39, found his ageing respectability was not quick enough between the wickets. He was run out from the fourth. This meant that Cowdrey, his right arm in plaster, had to come out, padded like an ice-hockey goalkeeper, for the last two balls of the match. He stood, massively and gratefully, at the non-striker's end while off-spinner David Allen somehow hung on at the other. Phew. An incredible game, but a draw – and one which you would have thought even the most hard-hearted would have crossed the road to watch.

At Bourda in Georgetown, Guyana, in 1967–68, England, who were one up in the series, managed to get away with another mind-boggling draw with their last pair together. It was a six-day match and the West Indies set the pace from the start. Garry Sobers and Rohan Kanhai both reached 150 in the West Indies first innings. Boycott then made a hundred for England and Tony Lock, flown out as a reinforcement, made his highest Test score of 89 in this last Test. On the sixth day, England had either to bat all day for a draw or to score 308 to win. I cannot remember a tenser day's cricket as England fought desperately to hold on to the series.

The pitch was badly worn, which helped the spin of Gibbs and Sobers. They bowled 71 overs between them that day, taking all nine wickets to fall, although Sobers had picked up John Edrich bowling fast at the start. With Gibbs taking the other four, England lost their first five wickets for 41. It looked all over. It was then that Alan Knott joined Colin Cowdrey. Gradually, with ever-increasing confidence, England were given something to hope for. Cowdrey, elegant, purposeful and assured while making good use of his pads to play the spin, and Knott, small, impish, resourceful, seemingly risky and twinkle-toes all at the same time, now put on 127 and ate up the minutes as well, which was more important. Then Gibbs, with his umpteenth lbw appeal against Cowdrey, at last enlisted the umpire's assistance.

The spinners raced through the tail, leaving the final pair of Knott and Jeff Jones together for the last, agonising few minutes. Jones had to face the final over of the match, bowled by Gibbs. Before the over began, the two batsmen met in the middle of the pitch. I later asked Knott what they talked about. 'Talked about?' he replied. 'We sang the first two verses of "Land of My Fathers".' It worked. Somehow Jones survived a hail of lbw appeals. If ever there was a time for a home umpire to give way to the urge to favour his own side, this would have been it. As it was, Guyanese umpire Cecil Kippins kept shaking his head until the very end and England won the series.

Draws like these two are worth waiting a lifetime for, and perish the doubters.

D

DRS

As more money has come into big cricket in recent years, the importance of making as sure as possible that correct decisions are made by the umpires has become paramount. At the top level of the game, players are living in a highly competitive, winner-takes-all atmosphere. A number of unpleasant things have crept into the game as players continually try and push the Laws to their limits and shade the odds in their favour. Umpires are being put under relentless pressure by bowlers and fielders doing their utmost to gain an advantage, no matter whether it is fair of unfair. I hope now that umpires feel that the Decision Review System (DRS) is working for them and not against them. The bottom line surely is that if a greater percentage of decisions are now correct, DRS must be greatly to the game's advantage.

As we live at a time when electronic technology rules the world, it is not surprising that it has come to encompass cricket too. Once, there were two umpires out in the middle on their own and their decisions stood. Everyone knew that mistakes were bound to be made, human nature being what it is, and the players accepted this as part of the game. At a time when tradition was increasingly being brought into question, electronic aids were seen as a way of improving the decision-making process and when they became available, they soon established a foothold. We now have Hot Spot, Snicko, Hawk-Eye and the rest trying to find out the truth. The on-field umpire makes the initial decision and if either the batsman or the fielding side question the decision, they signal to the umpires, who then pass the buck to the third umpire in the pavilion. He studies the television replays in slow motion to see whether electronic wizardry can confirm or deny the onfield umpire's original decision. This is what is called the Decision Review System, or DRS for short.

When it was introduced, it had an uncertain start. The on-field umpires, wrongly as it happened, instinctively felt that they were being turned into Aunt Sallies and made to look fools. At first, they must have felt great embarrassment when their decisions were overturned, although the way of DRS, especially with lbw decisions, has been to give the benefit of the doubt to the umpires rather than the batsmen, as the Laws have always insisted. Now, when an umpire in the middle has said not out, DRS falls over backwards to try and let the original decision stand. In the early days, if the umpire had said not out and the ball was shown to be hitting the outside of the leg or the off stump hard enough to remove a bail, the umpire's decision was still allowed to stand. Equally, if in identical circumstances the original decision had given the batsman out, this decision would also have been allowed to stand. The umpires were being given a margin for error, which still stands, although the margin is now smaller than it originally was and in time may be cut down still further.

The game has benefited from DRS, although there will always be the backwoodsmen who insist that human error has always been part of the game and it should stay that way. When electronic aids were first used, there was reasonable doubt as to their competence. Could these aids produce accurate lbw decisions when the game was being played on a pitch with an uneven bounce? Was Snicko able to differentiate between the sound made when the ball hits the bat and when the bat itself makes hard contact with the batsman's own boot? And was it able to ignore the noise made when the bottom of the bat comes into contact with the ground, when, for example, a batsman is trying to dig out a yorker? The feeling then was that human incompetence was preferable to electronic incompetence, but these aids grew more efficient and now they are beyond doubt here to stay. After all, the game is made to look foolish if a batsman is given out and, before he has left the ground, the whole world can see on their television screens that he is not out.

Electronic aids were first used to try and eliminate the odd howlers that umpires inevitably make, but now DRS has crept irretrievably into the fabric of the game and the unscrupulous try to use it to their advantage if they can. DRS has sometimes adversely affected the rhythm of the game. If a batsman is out three minutes before the close of play, the batting side might appeal in the hope the time wasted in confirming the decision will mean that one less over is bowled before the close of play. We have seen, too, how electronic aids have shown that a batsman who has taken a couple of paces down the wicket and been hit on the pad can be out lbw. Before DRS, no umpire in his wildest dreams would have given a batsman out lbw when he was that far down the pitch, but the ball-tracking technology has shown it can be the correct decision. At times an opportunistic fielding captain will now take a chance when the situation

W.G. – the colossus who bestrode cricket in its early stages.

K.S. Ranjitsinhji, aka the Jam Sahib of Nawanagar, whose wristy strokes took the art of batting to new levels.

The not-so-tender trap. Harold Larwood purveys Bodyline at Bill Woodfull in 1932–33.

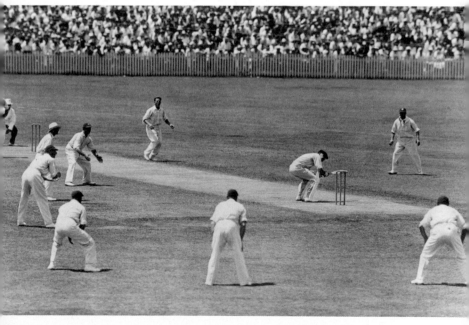

The 1984 vintage of *TMS*. Back: Tony Lewis, HB, Ray Illingworth, CMJ, Peter Baxter, Bill Frindall; front: Don Mosey, Trevor Bailey, Brian Johnston, Fred Trueman, Tony Cozier.

Dressed to kill for the first day of my final Test. A last chuckle with Tuffers.

Miss Paterson, my shrewd and
formidable first coach.

The young and the old. Denis Compton and Patsy
Hendren about to take on Surrey in 1936.

Denis Compton in front of the stumps, Henry Blofeld behind them. Eton v Forty Club, May 1956.

Above: An all-rounder of astonishing ability, Keith Miller only knew how to attack.

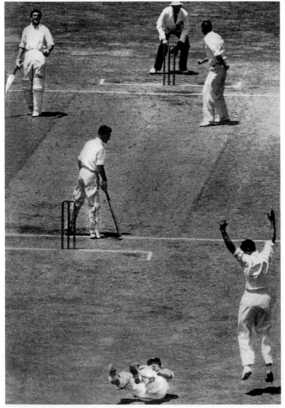

Left: Magic. Godfrey Evans catches a well-timed glance by Neil Harvey off Frank Tyson in Melbourne in 1954–55.

Miller was the most charismatic of Test cricketers. Hollywood, eat your heart out.

Alan Knott, predatory, agile and full of beans, enjoying himself immensely. The greatest wicketkeeper of them all.

Knotty at his best. Paul Sheahan of Australia gave him half a chance in 1968 – and regretted it.

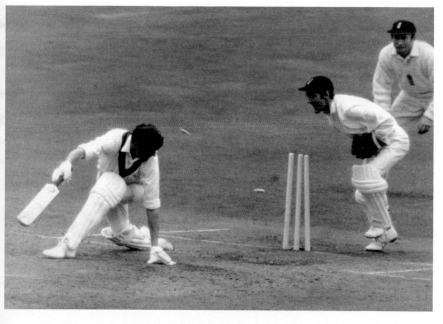

Perhaps the finest action ever. The immortal Fred Trueman in full cry.

Basil D'Oliveira remained wonderfully composed despite the political turmoil surrounding his career.

England v WI in 1966. Back: Geoff Boycott, Eric Russell, John Snow, D'Oliveira, Colin Milburn, Derek Underwood; front: Ray Illingworth, Jim Parks, Colin Cowdrey, Tom Graveney, Ken Higgs.

Colin Ingleby-Mackenzie, dapper, comical, polished and exultant after leading
Hampshire to the Championship in 1961.

Imran Khan bowling his inswingers with majestic certainty at Edgbaston in 1982.

The future prime minister of Pakistan holds aloft the World Cup in Melbourne in 1992.

Ian Botham on his way to an incredible 149 not out in an extraordinary Test match at Headingley in 1981.

In 1987, Botham publicises his Hannibal-inspired charity walk across the Alps.

warrants it and will ask for a review even though the batsman is well down the pitch.

There is at the moment one situation in which these aids are not only no help, but they also confuse an otherwise straight-forward situation. When a batsman is caught low down –at slip, say – and the fielder is sure the ball has carried and he has taken a fair catch, the batsman himself may be unsure as to whether the ball has bounced before going into the fielder's hands. He asks the onfield umpire for confirmation and he passes it on to the third umpire. He will now look at the replays, but the camera has a way of foreshortening these pictures and the replays tend to make it appear that the ball has hit the ground first. In this case, the batsman will be given the benefit of the doubt, although it is nearly always the wrong decision. Of course, batsmen have come to realise this happens and one or two may ask for a review even though they know for sure that it was a fair catch in the first place. I am sure that in time technology will come to terms with this.

E

BILL EDRICH

Bill Edrich, who was Denis Compton's partner-in-arms for Middlesex and England in 1947, was a less ethereal batsman, but the richest of characters and the most amusing of men, with a great knowledge of the game and how it worked. He was also, for a time, the head of a remarkable cricketing family which grew up around South Walsham in east Norfolk. Bill, a short man, was one of four brothers to play County Championship cricket and there were a number of occasions when a side of eleven Edriches took on the full Norfolk side – and often won. I once played for Norfolk against an Edrich XI at Ingham in north Norfolk and we lost that day.

The name was, of course, taken to even greater levels of distinction by Bill's cousin, opening batsman John Edrich, who also began his career with Norfolk before finding fame on the other side of the Thames with Surrey and then England, retiring with 103 first-class hundreds to his name. The family courage and determination was plain to see in John too.

While Compton was a product of Heaven, there was something happily earthy, man-made and heroic about Bill Edrich. He had a most distinguished war record in the RAF and no cricketer has ever had more guts. The more hopeless the situation, the more determined he became. He would take on any challenge, however hopeless it might seem. He was the bravest and most courageous of batsmen and a fearless player of the hook, with all its attendant risks. While Compton purred his way to 3,816 runs in 1947, Edrich's bottom-handed style produced 3,539 runs, most of them on the leg side, in the same season. The Edrich and Compton stands at the Nursery End of Lord's are the permanent memorials to the Middlesex Twins. Bill Edrich sometimes opened the bowling too, and off a short run was capable of considerable pace. He caught brilliantly at first slip, where his conversational powers and vibrant sense of humour also maintained a formidable standard.

Bill came to Middlesex in 1936, won his county cap the following year and in 1938 scored 1,000 runs before the end of May. He was a professional before the war, but afterwards played as an amateur and became one of the few who played for both the Gentlemen and the Players in their annual game at Lord's. He went to Australia with Walter Hammond's side in 1946–47 and he greatly impressed his hosts with the way he coped with rain-affected pitches.

He retired from Middlesex in 1958 and returned to captain Norfolk in the Minor County Championship from 1959 to 1971, when he was 55. I was lucky enough to play under him for the first few years. In 1959, Norfolk finished top of the Minor County Championship but, to Bill's great disappointment, lost to Lancashire Second XI, who had finished second, in the play-off. Bill's determination while batting, bowling – by then he had become an off-spinner – or fielding at first slip was as evident as it can ever have been.

He had a genius for getting declarations right and was never afraid to give the other side a chance if he felt it would in turn give Norfolk a better chance of winning. Captains today are seldom prepared to take even the slenderest of calculated risks; not so Bill. He was also more than skilful at conning the opposing captain into believing he had been given a good opportunity for victory and should go for it.

Playing under Bill Edrich was huge fun. He did not stand any nonsense either. I remember when we played Cambridgeshire at Lakenham, and I caught Maurice Crouch, their outspoken captain and opening batsman, behind the stumps for his second nought of the match. It was his first ever pair of spectacles. To start with, he was reluctant to leave the crease when the umpire's finger went up. Bill, beside me at first slip, speaking fluently and without repetition, left him in no doubt at all that the pavilion beckoned. Crouch, a farmer by trade, who was not given to seeing the other side of an argument, did not take long to realise he had to make the distasteful journey.

Then there was a match against Cambridgeshire, for whom the former Yorkshire and England left-arm spinner Johnny Wardle was playing. He and Bill had never been the greatest of friends, and in this match Wardle had been given out lbw to Bill and was also reluctant to move. He had his say, but once again Bill's oratory was altogether superior and he soon had him on his way too.

Bill was a great ladies' man and when he died, no fewer than five wives, past and present, turned up at his funeral. I dare say he would have been more proud of that than any record he achieved wearing his white flannel trousers.

F

FREDDIE FLINTOFF

Freddie Flintoff was born to take centre stage. Tall, blond, muscular, charming, there was more than just a touch of the Greek god about him. Cricket was his first love, but there was something about the young man even when he played for England's Under-19 side that suggested that cricket was only a starting point, a springboard. Greek gods are not two-a-penny in Preston, and it was soon clear that there was something special about the young Flintoff.

His cricketing career hit dizzy heights, particularly against Australia in 2005 and again in his last Test series in 2009. In between, there were periods of failure and it seems extraordinary that an all-rounder who was at one moment the best in the world could then go through periods when his form completely deserted him and he was lucky to be kept in the side, but there were reasons for this. As captain of England, he showed that he was one of those natural players who had never had to work out the problems that faced others, and that while instinct made him a remarkable player, it did not help him when he was captain.

Flintoff was an outstanding young player and captained the England Under-19 side in 1996 and 1997. The following year he made his Test debut against South Africa at Trent Bridge and it was obvious that he was a hugely talented all-round cricketer. He was soon being compared to Ian Botham – not a comparison that is always a help for a young player. It took Flintoff a year or two to settle in at the top level of the game. By the end of 2002 his Test batting average was 19 and his bowling average 47, but in the next three years, these figures improved to 43 with the bat and 28 with the ball. In the second Test against the West Indies at Edgbaston in 2004, he played a fine innings of 167, and one towering six over wide mid-on was dropped in the Ryder Stand by a spectator who happened to be his father.

Before the series against Australia in 2005, which was perhaps the pinnacle of his career, he had to fly home from the winter tour of South Africa for an operation on the left ankle which was to have an increasingly damaging influence on his career, though he was fit for the Ashes series. In the second Test against Australia at Edgbaston he broke Botham's record of six sixes in a Test match when he hit five in the first innings and four more in the second. He made a total of 141 runs in the match and took seven wickets, but even so, it may be that he will be longest remembered for his wonderful gesture of sympathy to Brett Lee, Australia's not-out batsman at the very end. Lee and Mike Kasprowicz had put on 59 for the last wicket and Australia needed only three more to win when Steve Harmison hit Kasprowicz's glove and he was caught behind. Lee sank to his knees in dismay and Flintoff went up to him and put his arm round his shoulders in a wonderful gesture of cricketing friendship. In the fourth Test, at Trent Bridge, Flintoff made a hundred as England won by three wickets, and his five wickets on the fourth day of the fifth match at The Oval helped England to the draw which enabled them to win the Ashes for the first time for almost twenty years.

It was now that he had a rather unsuccessful dabble with the England captaincy, a role he was never cut out for and which culminated in a 5–0 defeat in Australia in 2006–07. His ankle injury increasingly interfered with his career, although he had a good series against South Africa in England in 2008, with a memorable piece of bowling, 4–89, in the Edgbaston Test. The following winter in India he made exactly 100 in the first warm-up game, which was, strangely, his first hundred for England for four years. In February 2009, the Chennai Super Kings in the IPL bought him for a record US$1,550,000, but he was not successful and returned home early with a knee injury.

He announced he was going to retire from Test cricket at the end of the series against Australia in 2009 and it was remarkable how he kept going. In spite of all those injuries, he took five wickets in the Australian second innings at Lord's and no less a person than the former Australian captain Ian Chappell described this as the best spell of hostile fast bowling he had ever seen. Chappell captained Dennis Lillee and Jeff Thomson and knew a bit about Andy Roberts, Michael Holding and company from the West Indies. In the last Test, at The Oval, which was also his own final Test, Flintoff memorably threw out Ricky Ponting, the Australian captain, as England won the match to take the series 2–1.

Now to the other side of the man. Flintoff is a complex character who fought a more or less constant battle with his own demons during his career. This came to a head when he captained England in Australia in 2006–07. England had won the Ashes under Michael Vaughan's superb captaincy in 2005. Injury prevented Vaughan from taking the side to Australia the following year and, inexplicably in my view, the selectors chose Flintoff ahead of Andrew Strauss to take over. England lost all five Test matches and Flintoff seemed more and more out of sorts. His own form was poor and he was having trouble with that ankle injury, which will have done nothing for his peace of mind. He knew something was wrong with him and that he was unable to cope, but he had no idea what the problem was. According to Flintoff's 2012 documentary, *The Hidden Side of Sport*, it all became too much over Christmas when his side had already lost the Ashes. 'I was having a quiet drink with my dad on Christmas Eve and as we made our way home I started crying my eyes out. I told him I'd tried my best but that I couldn't do it any more. I couldn't keep playing. We talked and, of course, I dusted myself down and carried on. But I was never the same player again … Instead of walking out confidently to face Australia … I didn't want to get out of bed, never mind face people.' He did not know what the matter was and did not understand what was happening to him.

It is said that on that tour he was warned three or four times for inappropriate behaviour and for binge-drinking. At this distance, it seems obvious that something was seriously wrong with him, but it apparently did not occur to anyone at the time, for no serious effort was made to find what was amiss. For the 2007 World Cup in the West Indies, Michael Vaughan was fit enough to take back the captaincy and Flintoff was made vice-captain. England lost their first match, against New Zealand, and that evening several of the players drank in a nightclub until the early hours of the morning. This was only two days before an important game with Canada, and when they returned to their hotel, Flintoff decided to board a pedalo. It was reported that he had to be rescued when he fell off into the sea. When he later apologised for the incident, his version of the story was that he had fallen into the water while trying to board the pedalo in the first place, which seems really to come under the heading of 'splitting hairs'. The upshot was that he lost the vice-captaincy and was dropped from the side that beat Canada. Duncan Fletcher, the coach, revealed at this point that Flintoff had received a number of previous warnings about his behaviour. It apparently never occurred to him that these events were the symptom of a much more serious problem. Flintoff said, 'Throughout that World Cup, all I could think about was that I wanted to retire.'

It is sad that such a wonderful player's career should have been bedevilled by such things and it may seem unnecessarily unkind to dwell on them now. I am doing this because I think Flintoff was simply looked upon by those in authority as a naughty boy and no attempt was made to try and understand that all this was a reflection of a much deeper problem. Flintoff was the only one who appeared to realise that something was badly wrong and as a result he received no help.

It is extraordinary that Flintoff did not find out until 2012 that throughout his cricket career he had been suffering badly from bouts of depression. Even then, the discovery was made purely by chance. It was when he was making *The Hidden Side of Sport*, the documentary that also involved Ricky Hatton, Vinnie Jones and Graham Dott. 'Speaking to other people, I identified with how I felt and then I could sort it out, treat it . . . When you spoke to people, they'd talk about their experiences and how they felt. And I'd say, "That's exactly how I felt" . . . You have the weight of the world on your shoulders – fear, guilt, all sorts – for no apparent reason.'

When you take all of this into account, his cricketing achievements become even more remarkable. After finishing his Test career, he played some intermittent one-day cricket and began at once to throw himself wholeheartedly and immensely successfully into life in show business. At the moment of writing, he is a presenter of *Top Gear* on BBC1 and his list of credits over the intervening years is extremely impressive. He has, too, become a star in Australia, where he won their version of *I'm a Celebrity . . . Get me out of Here* and has made a name for himself on other programmes too. He has become a charming, most relaxed performer in front of the camera and seems, happily, to have discovered a medium which will hold all those demons at bay. This, at last, is a form of pressure with which Andrew Flintoff can cope. He is a great character, as this whole story shows, and I hope he will be on our screens for many years to come.

G

CHRIS GAYLE

Chris Gayle was the first thoroughly modern twenty-first-century international cricketer. A Jamaican, he is every bit as brilliant a striker of the ball as Viv Richards and Brian Lara. Left-handed, flamboyant, smilingly destructive, determined, outspoken and jolly, with a fierce inner resolve, Gayle knows his market value and is prepared to take on anyone who stands in his way. He came from a poor family in Kingston and soon realised that he had been born with a God-given talent. He has used that talent with an extraordinary single-mindedness to lift himself out of what threatened to be extreme poverty onto the ever-alluring platform of wealth.

Gayle's story is interesting. He has been a wonderful batsman, he stands tall and smiling at times, brooding behind his beard at others, but he has a mind like a safe-deposit box and does not easily let people near him either. He is very much a modern cricketer, as the game is swinging fast from two-innings Test cricket to all the different forms of the one-day game where lie the big financial rewards. I never got to know Gayle, but I always greatly enjoyed watching him play, and one could only admire his strength of character as he stood out so firmly for what he considered to be right for him. I would have liked to get to know him, but I do not think that would have been easy. However, he has been an extremely important figure in the development of the contemporary game.

Gayle was the second youngest of six children and as a teen-ager had been forced to work as a rag-picker to help the faltering family finances. Despite the rough circumstances of his early life, his unusual talent for cricket led him to the Lucas Club in Kingston. By his own admission, this saved him and he has acknowledged that if he had not joined Lucas he would in all likelihood be on the streets today. As an opening batsman who hit the ball murderously hard, he made an immediate impact and was soon playing for the West Indies Under-19 side. At the age of 19 he was in the Jamaican side, and within a year, in 1999, he was in the West Indies one-day team. Six months after that, he played his first Test match. In July 2001, he made 175 in the first Test against Zimbabwe in Bulawayo. At this time, Test cricket was still the pre-eminent form of the game and the arrival of such a remarkable batsman as Gayle gave the West Indies hope that one day they might again produce a Test side capable of competing against the rest of the world.

Gayle was finding that his approach to the game also produced great success in one-day cricket. In November 2002, he made three one-day hundreds against India and became only the third West Indies batsman, after Richards and Lara, to score 1,000 international runs in a year. Gayle could see that the one-day game was going to earn him a great deal more money than Test cricket. He was always on the look-out for a good deal and in 2005, he became involved in the first of a number of disputes with the West Indies Cricket Board (WICB). West Indies cricket was sponsored by Digicel and Gayle had a contract with a rival communications company and was dropped for the first Test against South Africa. He quickly realised that at this stage of his career he had to go along with the authorities and he ended his agreement with the rival company. He was reinstated for the second Test and then made a triple century in the fourth in Antigua.

Gayle was scoring runs with ease in both forms of the game, but gradually the lure of the shorter form and the financial rewards it offered seemed to concentrate his mind. In 2007 he made the first ever hundred in a T20 international, scoring 117 against South Africa in 57 balls. The following year, the Indian Premier League (IPL) began and Gayle, a prime target, was bought at auction by the Kolkata Knight Riders. He missed their opening games in the IPL because Sri Lanka were touring in the Caribbean. When he eventually arrived in Kolkata, a groin injury put him out of action and before the competition was over he returned to the West Indies, where Australia were about to begin a series. At this stage of Gayle's life, the demands of the WICB won the day.

He was back in India for the second year of the IPL and, although he had been made captain of the West Indies for their tour of England in 2009, he stayed in India until the IPL had finished and arrived in England only just before the first Test match. He was massively criticised for this and, to make matters worse, he went on to say during that tour that he did not want to captain the West Indies any more because of the pressures involved. To cap it all, he said he 'wouldn't be so sad' if Test cricket was superseded by T20. By then, it is probably fair to say that the money he was earning from the one-day game was speaking loud and clear. He was fast becoming a one-day mercenary. Even so, in December 2009 he scored a Test hundred against Australia in only 70 balls and a year later he became one of only four batsmen to score two triple hundreds in Test cricket when he made 333 against Sri Lanka. Don Bradman, Virender Sehwag and Brian Lara are the other three.

His relationship with the WICB became increasingly fractious and he did not play Test cricket again for nearly two years. In the IPL, however, he went from strength to strength, leaving the Kolkata Knight Riders for the Royal Challengers Bangalore. He was also signed by the Sydney Thunder in Australia's Big Bash and over the next few years Gayle played in just about every international T20 competition there was, including those in Zimbabwe, Bangladesh and Canada. In 2008, Gayle had been captain of the Stanford Superstars XI who played against England in a T20 game in Antigua, with the winners being paid a million dollars a man. Five of the West Indian players were persuaded by Stanford to reinvest their money in his companies and lost the lot when Stanford's fraudulent business empire collapsed. Gayle shrewdly took his money elsewhere, and it will have given him a useful start on his glittering path to riches.

It was Gayle who highlighted one of the biggest problems facing cricket in the West Indies, where the game has been perpetually strapped for cash. Small grounds, a low-income population and a side that did not win much kept sponsors, spectators and supporters away. The leading players received a pittance compared to those in more prosperous parts of the world, but with the emergence of the IPL and the other T20 competitions, they were given the chance to earn undreamed-of sums of money. Who could possibly blame them for grabbing the chance as they did? But their involvement in the IPL meant they were not available all the time for the West Indies. The WICB quite understandably refused to pick people who would play only when it suited them. This meant that a number of the best players in the Caribbean were not available for the West Indies, who could not do without their services if they were ever going to lift themselves back into contention with the best sides in the world.

There was no easy answer to this. Gayle's talents were badly needed, but his attitude was not. He was calm and in control as a player, but there was also an explosive side to his nature. He seemed to pursue trouble, but he knew what he was doing and it did not bother him. In 2006, he was in hot water for conduct which went against the spirit of the game in a Test against New Zealand. Later that year, in the Champions Trophy in India, he was fined after a run-in with the Australian Michael Clarke. The following year he was ticked off for publicly criticising the WICB, and it is fair to say that his success in both forms of the game perhaps made him feel that he was invincible. For example, when he expressed his preference for T20 over Test cricket while touring England in 2009, he was strongly criticised by both Garry Sobers and Viv Richards, but it did not seem to worry Gayle. He claimed that what he had said had been taken out of context and he refused to resign as West Indies captain.

In 2011 he was at it again, criticising the WICB and their coach Ottis Gibson, and he did not play for the West Indies for the next year. In April 2012, he reached an agreement with the WICB and he came back for one-day matches in the West Indies and in Florida. Then, in 2016, he started to chat up a lady commentator from Australia's Network Ten and asked her out for a drink while they were on air. Former Australian captain Ian Chappell's response to this was to try and persuade Cricket Australia to ban him from playing again in Australia. Another female sports journalist said he had been doing this sort of thing for years, while Gayle said it was a practical joke and a bit of fun. Then, late in 2017, he won a defamation case in Australia after being wrongly accused of exposing himself to a masseuse. Being the man he is, I doubt he lost a moment's sleep over any of these things.

Gayle is what you might call a bit of a lad. He is a wonderful player, and Graeme Swann told me that at England team meetings before playing the West Indies, 95 per cent of the time was spent talking about how to get Gayle out. Gayle was the man who really put flesh and blood on what is now known as 'player power'. He has made a lot of money by selling his wares to the highest bidder, which happened to be T20 cricket. You cannot complain about that. Many of today's players feel the same way as Gayle about where the game is going and the increasing importance of T20, but without having the courage to admit it. Gayle's guts and determination and his dramatic skills as a batsman, all of which had begun life at a pretty low level of existence in Kingston, have enabled him to lead the way in taking cricket to its new, modern frontiers. Gayle's attitude will inevitably have shocked the traditionalists, but he should not be pilloried, he should be congratulated.

G

ADAM GILCHRIST

No one has embraced the demands of both one-day and Test cricket better than Adam Gilchrist. Around the turn of the century, a great sea change took hold of the international game. The short form was moving towards the centre of the stage and, at the same time, its influence was affecting the way Test cricket was played. Runs were being scored much more quickly, and there were fewer of the old-fashioned batsmen able to bat for a day and a half and play the traditional long Test innings. Sides were now scoring 350 runs or more on the first day of a match. The game was altogether faster and surely, therefore, a much more inviting prospect for the paying public. Gilchrist was a pivotal figure in all this.

He opened the batting in Australia's one-day matches, but in the Test side went in down the order, mostly batting at seven. It was here that he changed things. Suddenly, at the fall of the fifth wicket, a new batsman emerged who from his very first ball went for his shots. Gilchrist was an extraordinary batsman. Not only did he have all the strokes and amazingly quick footwork and hands, but he also understood the importance of moving the game forward and taking control of a match. The irony has been that, although the increased pace of Test cricket provided much greater entertainment, the five-day game was – and still is – largely played out in front of empty seats, except for the Ashes series and most Test matches in England.

Gilchrist was perhaps the best wicketkeeper-batsman of them all. His strike rate in both forms of the game was remarkable and he became the first batsman to hit a hundred sixes in Test cricket. His 17 hundreds are the most ever made by a wicketkeeper in Test cricket. He is also the only batsman ever to have scored more than 50 in three successive World Cup finals, in 1999, 2003 and 2007. In the last of these, his innings of 149 made from 104 balls against Sri Lanka is reckoned by some to be the best one-day innings ever played. His 16 one-day hundreds are second only to Kumar Sangakkara, who went on to overtake Gilchrist's record of taking the most dismissals by a wicketkeeper in one-day international cricket. During his career, Gilchrist played in 96 Test matches for Australia and 287 one-day internationals and was vice-captain in both forms of the game. It is an incredible record.

When Adam was very young, his mother spent many hours throwing balls to him as soon as he could hold a cut-down bat. Cricket gripped the Gilchrist family and both Adam's brothers and his sister were completely hooked on the game. When he was about eight or nine, the family went to Shepparton, in Victoria, to do their Christmas shopping. As they were walking around, Adam saw a pair of wicketkeeping gloves in a shop window and from that moment his mind was made up. The first time he kept in a school match a return from the outfield hit the edge of the concrete pitch, bounced sharply and broke Adam's nose. Apparently, he only got over that when his father told him a white lie, which was that Rod Marsh had broken his nose in his first ever match as a keeper. Adam did not ask Marsh about this until they were both on camera recording Adam's *This is Your Life* programme. Rod kindly said that he could not remember the incident.

Gilchrist was born in New South Wales and when he was 13 his parents, Stan and June, moved to Lismore, where Stan runs the vibrant Northern New South Wales branch of the Lord's Taverners. My wife Valeria and I stayed with them a few years ago for a Taverners dinner and our bedroom window looked down on the net where Adam had practised his cricket. His family had made everything available to him that they possibly could and, knowing his delightful parents, it is easy to see where Adam gets his charm and his impeccable manners.

It is no coincidence that Gilchrist was perhaps the only cricketer of his time – he played for Australia from 1996 to 2008 – who consistently 'walked' when he knew he was out, and just occasionally when the umpire had already given him not out. His insistence on walking did not sit easily in the Australian dressing room, and in his autobiography Gilchrist wrote that he had 'zero support in the team' for doing this. Interestingly, he went on to say that he felt 'isolated' and 'silently accused of betraying the team. Implicitly, I was made to feel selfish, as if I was walking for the sake of my own clean image, thereby making everyone else look dishonest.'

This clean image was one part of Gilchrist, but on the field of play there was another, slightly contradictory, aspect to his performance. There were a number of angry outbursts and he was fined more than once for showing dissent at umpiring decisions. He also publicly criticised Muttiah Muralitharan's bowling action, not that he was alone in that. For doing so, he was ticked off by the Australian Cricket Board for making a ' detrimental public comment'. In the 2003 World Cup, Gilchrist accused Pakistani wicketkeeper Rashid Latif of directing a racist remark at him. Clive Lloyd, the match referee, absolved Latif from guilt and Latif then said he was going to sue Gilchrist, but nothing came of it.

Gilchrist has said that he owed a lot to his father, who had taught him how to bat in that net just below our bedroom. Father Stan spent much time trying to get his defensive technique right, but they would end every session playing attacking shots with a tennis ball, which may account for the grip Adam has always used, with his hand near the top of the handle. To hold the bat where he did and be able to play his attacking strokes so well shows that he must have extremely strong wrists.

Gilchrist is the most delightful and straightforward of men and this comes across strongly in the new career he has made for himself as a broadcaster. His views are fresh and immediate. He does not always hark back to his day, he does not shout at the microphone, as so many others do, and he expresses himself so charmingly you instinctively want to go along with his views. Gilchrist has the lightest of touches and has been an immensely engaging character in everything he has done, even if one or two umpires might not entirely agree. In his twelve years in the Australian side he was largely responsible for moving the game from its more sedentary past into the hurly-burly of the twenty-first century. There were others around at the time who gave him more than a helping hand, such as Freddie Flintoff, Brendon McCullum, M.S. Dhoni and Sanath Jayasuriya, but in my book Gilchrist was the guiding star.

G

GRAHAM GOOCH

Whenever I watched Graham Gooch stride out in his shining white helmet with his black moustache bristling, he always reminded me of the Pirate King in Gilbert and Sullivan's *Pirates of Penzance*. He deserved a mighty roll of drums. Few batsmen have filled me with such a sense of anticipation. When Gooch stood at the crease with his bat raised behind him, it was clear that he relished the challenge. It looked as if he was planning to execute the bowler. Even now, I can hear the crack of the ball hitting his bat in the first over of the day and racing away to the cover boundary. In Gooch's language, a half-volley was a half-volley and there was no messing about.

This may give the impression that he was a devil-may-care amateur without a worry in the world, but nothing could have been further from the truth. Gooch was the most dedicated of professionals who left as little to chance as he possibly could. No cricketer in my time has worked harder at his game and his fitness, and it was ironic that he should have found himself playing much of his Test cricket with David Gower, who was his opposite in just about everything. You would never have guessed from the way he went for his strokes and struck the ball that Gooch was not a natural extrovert. No professional has ever been more dedicated to the job of perfecting his art, both as a player and as a captain. He took the view that relentless hard work was the only way to improve, and if the England dressing room became a less humorous place under his leadership, the efficiency of its product definitely increased.

Gooch was a remarkable opening batsman. In a career which stretched from 1973 to 2000, he scored 67,057 runs in first-class and limited-over cricket, including 8,900 in Tests and 4,290 in ODIs. He is, too, one of twenty-five batsmen to have made more than a hundred first-class hundreds, and he also took 246 first-class wickets, swinging the ball quite sharply at just above medium pace. Added to this, he captained England with great singleness of purpose in 34 Test matches. These statistics, impressive though they are, inevitably tell only part of the story of a batsman who, at the wicket, was an irresistible spectacle.

Gooch's career was studded with some amazing pieces of batting. The innings I shall remember for ever was the century he made in the first Test against the West Indies at Headingley in 1991, when he was 37. I wonder if a better innings has ever been played. The scene needs setting. Age had just begun to break up the great West Indies team of the 1980s, but they were still the best around. Viv Richards was now the captain and the fast-bowling contingent of Curtly Ambrose, Courtney Walsh, Malcolm Marshall and Patrick Patterson was impressive enough. In a low-scoring match on an uncertain pitch, England had a first-innings lead of 25. In the next 452 minutes, Graham Gooch played the defining innings of his life. He stood up and repeatedly despatched the four West Indies fast bowlers to the boundary, mainly with fierce hooks and pulls, interspersed with some wonderful driving, straight and through the off side. When Carl Hooper came on briefly to bowl his off-breaks, there was a sublime moment when Gooch, who always looked to get onto the front foot, started to go forward, then went back, gave himself a bit of room and half-steered, half-cut the ball between slip and gully for four. He finished with 154 not out, scoring an extraordinary 61.11 per cent of England's total of 252. It was an innings that showed guts and determination in equal measure, as well as an impeccable technique on a pitch with an increasingly uneven bounce, and he never missed the chance to put away a loose ball. At the end of this fourth day, when the West Indies, needing 278 to win, were 11–1, he gave as modest an interview as you could wish to hear. It had been an innings which contained all the qualities of greatness, one of which was the humility he showed at the end of the day.

Gooch played another innings of immense character in Barbados in March 1981, in England's second innings in the third Test. On the second evening of this match, Ken Barrington, who was England's assistant manager, had died from a heart attack. Barrington was adored by the players and perhaps by Gooch most of all, for no one had helped him more with his batting and they had become close friends. The West Indies were in control of a match which for the final three days was played for many in a surreal world of shock and disbelief. England were left to score 523 to win. Gooch now produced his second Test hundred, making 116 out of 224 in a display that revealed not only great daring and skill, but also his extraordinary character. In Gooch's autobiography, written with Frank Keating, Gooch said, 'I thought of Kenny all through. "Make it count. If you get to 40, make it to 60; if you get to 60, make it to 80. Make it count, don't give it away." ... All I know is that my second Test century is one I will always treasure. It was all for Kenny. I hope he was proud of me that day.' It is hard to imagine a much more moving tribute. It said a lot about Barrington and a good deal about Gooch too. To feel as Gooch did and still make a hundred in a losing cause against Andy Roberts, Michael Holding, Colin Croft and Joel Garner reveals an iron will – and what an innings it was.

The other Gooch innings I must mention is, of course, the 333 he made against India at Lord's in 1990. Gooch, always modest to a fault, said sometime later about that innings, 'Yes, it worked out well for me, but more important we went on to win the match.' He had one piece of luck when he was only 36 and was dropped from a sitter behind the wicket. He then went on to bat for almost ten and a half hours, hitting 43 fours and three sixes. All his usual strokes were on display, of course, and it was a delight to watch him using his feet to the spinners. It was exhilarating and the largest score ever made at Lord's. To think that he then made a small matter of 123 in the second innings in just 113 balls shows what a phenomenal cricketer he was and how astonishingly fit he must have been.

During his long career, Gooch had a number of personal misfortunes and misjudgements to climb around, but his strong character enabled him to learn from mistakes and use them as a launching pad for further success. He first played for Essex in 1973 and immediately made his mark in county cricket. Two years later, at the age of 21, he was chosen to play for England against Australia in the first Test at Edgbaston. He batted at number five and was out for nought in each innings. He did not fare much better in the second match, when he made six and 31 and was dropped. It was three years before he got another chance. This was a chastening experience from which some players might never have recovered, but Gooch showed what he was made of and scored so many runs for Essex that the selectors had no option but to give him another go.

The biggest hiccup in Gooch's career came in 1982. He joined the rebel tour to South Africa, which had been set up principally by Geoffrey Boycott, and when the party arrived in South Africa, Gooch was made captain. This was apparently done because the players were not sure they wanted Boycott to captain the side. Gooch did not think he would be punished for going on that tour, or maybe the organisers had falsely persuaded him. He was at the peak of his form, unlike the other players, who were past their best. He came in for plenty of criticism and, like all the others, was banned from playing for his country for three years. He said, a trifle lamely, that the side was composed of professional cricketers and they had gone there simply to play cricket. This did not wash, of course, and as captain Gooch found himself constantly having to speak about things beyond the cricket field, as the expedition was a major publicity coup for South Africa in the apartheid years.

I am sure that Gooch had no idea that he was giving so much comfort to that regime, and perhaps the worst he can be accused of is being extraordinarily naive and unworldly. Nonetheless, it was a most unhappy episode for him and the effects lingered after he had returned to the England side, in 1985. He captained England for the first time in 1988, the summer when the side had four official captains during the series against the West Indies: Mike Gatting, John Emburey, Chris Cowdrey and Gooch, who was in charge for the fifth match, at The Oval. He was then chosen to take England to India in the winter, but the

Indian government refused to grant visas to the eight players with South African connections. The following year, in 1989, for the series against Australia, the captaincy was given back to David Gower, who promptly resigned after England had lost the series 4–0. The selectors returned to Gooch for the winter tours of 1989–90.

Before Christmas 1989, he was allowed to take another England side to India for a one-day competition. The Test-playing countries had officially decided to forgive players with South African connections. By then Micky Stewart was the England coach and he and Gooch had much in common as far as the work ethic was concerned. It is fair to say that the dressing room became a place of constant and serious hard work, at the expense of adventurous individuality. This spartan approach was bound to have a downside. There was one dramatic instance on the 1990–91 tour to Australia, when England played Queensland in a four-day match at the Carrara Oval on the Gold Coast. Just before lunch, Gower and John Morris were both out and afterwards Gower, who was not a good spectator, became bored and, accompanied by John Morris, who had made a hundred, slipped away to the little airport near the ground, where they hired a small aeroplane and persuaded the pilot to buzz the cricket match. This was more than Peter Lush, the manager, Micky Stewart, the coach, and Gooch, never Gower's greatest supporter, could put up with. They made an unnecessary fuss about the incident which should surely have been handled quickly, quietly and much less destructively. Gower, who had made hundreds in the second and third Tests, lost form badly for the last two Test matches and, needless to say, his relations with Gooch, which were often near breaking point, never recovered. After that tour Gower played only three more Test matches, while Morris never got another game.

Gooch may not have been the most original of captains, but he was always true to himself. He wanted England to win in his determined, yet selfless way. At times, it may be that he was too inflexible and too cautious in his views, but England's cricket would have been infinitely the poorer without him. Gooch has always been his own man in whatever he has done and, as far as I am concerned, I am more than happy to go along with anyone capable of playing as he did in that extraordinary innings at Headingley.

G

DAVID GOWER

David Gower was almost the epitome of a natural cricketer. He was a sublime, elegant and immensely gifted strokemaker in that willowy way which is so often the prerogative of tall left-handers. Yet, at the same time he could be infuriating. When he made runs, it was said that he displayed a laid-back genius; when he failed, he was accused of being detached and indifferent. In this, as I have written above, Gower was the antithesis to Graham Gooch, with whom he shared much of his career. Because of such different attitudes, these two supreme batsmen could only have viewed one another with deep suspicion.

Gower's batting was carefree and joyous, and on his day I can think of no one I have enjoyed watching more. He made everything look so easy and, as he stroked the ball effortlessly through the gaps in the field, he was hugely compelling. There was never a hint of hard work or careworn professionalism in the way he played, although to score 8,231 runs in Test cricket he must have needed strong mental application and a certain discipline, for no one scores that many simply by waving a magic wand. Yet Gower communicated enjoyment when he batted, if not when he was fielding, and he did not seem to have a care in the world, which was the measure of his genius.

Gower played in 117 Test matches for England and there are only six others who have played in more. I think it is possible to get a feel of the way in which he played cricket whenever you listen to him on television. There is more than a touch of humour in all that he says, just as there was laughter in those extraordinary strokes he played. I always got the firm impression that, yes, he was taking it seriously but not that seriously, thank heavens. Now, whenever he makes a comment on air, it is usually shrewd and it is as if he is making a suggestion rather than trying to lay down the law, which is the way of so many pundits. I find this as refreshing as one of those flashing strokes of his square of the wicket on the off side.

Gower's first ball in Test cricket spoke loudly of his huge talent and his approach to the game – and life as well, for the two almost always go together. It was the first Test against Pakistan at Edgbaston in June 1978 and I was lucky enough to be in the commentary box. England were 101–2 after bowling out Pakistan for 164. Liaqat Ali, who bowled left-arm fast-medium, ran in from the City End. His first ball to Gower was short and pitched on middle and leg. Gower positioned himself with quick footwork, swivelled and pulled the ball effortlessly between square leg and midwicket to the boundary in front of the Eric Hollies Stand. As I remember it, Gower just half-trotted a stride or two up the wicket before returning to his crease. His confidence, almost nonchalance, was extraordinary. It had been simply another ball in another day's cricket. He made 58 in that innings and his felicitous way of playing was highlighted by the contrasting approach of his partner, Clive Radley, who was on his way to a hard-working and eminently worthy five-hour hundred.

From time to time Gower's genius was let down by his personality, which was as carefree and uninhibited as his batting.

Cricket to him was always a game to be played for fun, but there were moments in his career when, in the interests of the side, he probably should have been able to rein in and discipline that genius a little more.

One of the most glaring examples of this happened when I was commentating on the fourth Test on the 1990–91 tour of Australia. About twenty minutes before the lunch interval on the third day, England lost their third wicket at 137 in reply to Australia's 386. Gower came to the wicket and scored 11 runs easily enough on a good pitch. With Gooch going well at the other end there was no reason why, on a typically easy Adelaide pitch, England could not have at least got up to the Australian total. Then Craig McDermott ran in to bowl the last ball of the morning session to Gower. It was shortish and on Gower's legs, and with an almost half-hearted swing of the bat, he gently helped it round to Merv Hughes fielding at deep backward square leg. It was as if Gower was giving him catching practice. If he had hit the ball properly it would have gone for six; if he had rolled his wrists over the ball while playing the stroke it would have gone along the ground. Gower sauntered off and Gooch could hardly contain his anger as he followed him in to lunch.

I wonder if the team management of Lush, Stewart and Gooch ever asked themselves if they ought to take some of the blame for this. When, as I have outlined in the piece about Gooch, Gower and John Morris hired that small aeroplane and buzzed the ground during the game against Queensland a week before the Adelaide Test, the team management, devoid of any sense of humour, went ballistic in their fury at these two players. (Coincidentally, both were born on 1 April. Maybe the date of his birth was Gower's secret.) Gower's subsequent loss of form for the last two Tests may have been attributable to the fuss that was made about this. Interestingly, Lush and Stewart were also in charge when Mike Gatting and umpire Shakoor Rana had their famous run-in while Pakistan and England were playing a Test match in Faisalabad in 1987. Gatting was publicly pilloried then, just as Gower was four years later.

Gower was one of those gloriously instinctive players who are unlikely to turn into good captains. Everything has come so easily to them that they have never had to face the problems that confront normal players. They find it hard to help their colleagues because they have never had to dissect their own game or rebuild it to iron out faults. For them, everything just happens, while the rest of us sometimes need a helping hand and guidance. Gower was captain of England for 32 Tests and never really settled into the job, winning only five of those matches, while losing 18. Having said that, in 1984–85 England won in India under his captaincy, which is never easy, and also against Australia in 1985. For all that, captaincy never seemed to rest easily on his shoulders.

Gower is a one-off and it seems unfair to apply the same rules to him as to everyone else. On the cricket field, he lit up the game as few other batsmen have been able to do. The languid strokeplay, the athletic saunter between the wickets, the lithe gazelle-like strides in pursuit of the ball in the field and the low, easy throw into the wicketkeeper's gloves (until towards the end, when his shoulder went on him) – all these things were a special part of the day whenever Gower was play-ing and were the reasons why people flocked to watch him. Frank Woolley, another tall left-hander, whom I never saw, reportedly had the same magical qualities when playing for Kent and England. I am sure he could infuriate too. The supremely elegant left-hander who tops this particular list was Garry Sobers, but I doubt he ever infuriated anyone. These mercurial left-handers are a precious breed, nonetheless, for they provide wonderful entertainment.

G

TOM GRAVENEY

On 19 and 20 January 1968, at Queen's Park Oval, Port of Spain, Tom Graveney took the art of batting as near to perfection as I ever saw it. In this first Test, he made 118 runs off the middle of the bat with a display of strokes which would have made the coaching book look to its laurels. His footwork, the basis of batting, was sweet, precise and balletic. This was Graveney in his second incarnation as an England player, when he scarcely even hinted at the shortcomings, mostly of temperament, he had shown in his first.

The bowlers that day were principally Wes Hall, Charlie Griffith, Garry Sobers and Lance Gibbs. By then, this formidable West Indian attack, which had carried all before it for a few years, was beginning to be caught up by Anno Domini. All three of the main fast bowlers no longer had quite the cutting edge they had brought to England in 1963 and 1966. But that cannot take away from Graveney's display that day.

Looking out onto the backdrop of the mountains of the Northern Range, with the flamboyant trees beginning, a little hesitantly, to burst into scarlet flower, it was a setting to match the innings. I was watching from the new press box close to the pavilion. After Graveney had moved from seven to 11 by driving off-spinner Lance Gibbs effortlessly through the covers for four, John Thicknesse of London's *Evening Standard*, sitting in the second row back, leant forward to Jim Swanton, in the first row, and asked, 'How early in a Graveney innings is it safe to say he will make a hundred?' Already he was batting that well. For the record, Swanton gave a rumbling non-committal reply.

I remember most clearly three moments in that innings. Graveney, tall and angular, was facing Charlie Griffith, whose recalcitrant manner, allied to his suspect bowling action, did not win him many friends. When he pitched short, Graveney, whose instinct always brought him onto his front foot, stepped forward and hooked him to the midwicket boundary. It was both imperious and dismissive. The pitch was slow, but all the same ...

He played this stroke two or three times, and soon after one of them Griffith let go a beamer, a full toss, which flew straight at Graveney's face. This is the most dangerous ball in the game and it has been outlawed. Graveney somehow managed to play the ball safely and when Griffith did not appear to overflow with apologies, he strode down the pitch with his bat raised like an executioner's sword. There followed a healthy exchange of views.

The third great moment from that innings was repeated two or three times and began with the stroke that had so moved Thicknesse. Gibbs was bowling his off-breaks from the mountain end of the ground. When he threw one up to the bat, Graveney leaned elegantly forward and gently, with perfect timing, stroked it away through a negligible gap in a packed off-side field. Two fielders turned to sprint after it but each time the ball would beat them to the cover boundary by two or three yards. It was delicious and exquisite – true artistry any gallery would have been happy to find a place for.

When Graveney had first come into the England side, the class, the skill and the expertise were all there, but something seemed to be missing. His temperament was the problem. When the going was really tough, Graveney sometimes did not seem able to handle it. I remember hearing Len Hutton talk about his batting in Australia on the 1954–55 tour. England lost the first Test in Brisbane and then won the next three. Graveney played in the second Test, scoring a total of 21 runs, and the pressure of a really tight match appeared to be too much for him. The last Test was played in Sydney, by which time England had won the Ashes and the pressure was off. It rained for two days and the match did not begin until the third. Graveney came back to open with Hutton and played a glorious innings of 111, which made Hutton furious. There was nothing much at stake and now Graveney was able to turn it on – where had he been when it mattered?

In 1960 Graveney left Gloucestershire, understandably in high dudgeon, after captaining the side for two years. His old-fashioned ideas had not always been popular in the dressing room and the committee decided to offer the captaincy to an unknown amateur, Tom Pugh, who had played in the same Eton XI as me in 1955. When Graveney heard that Pugh was being groomed to succeed him, he headed for neighbouring Worcestershire. He spent two years qualifying and then began the second and most glorious phase of his career. He fitted the scene at New Road, just as he was to do a few years later at Trinidad's Queen's Park Oval. In 1964, at the age of 37, he helped take Worcestershire to their first ever County Championship title, scoring over 2,000 runs that season. The lovely easy walk out to the middle, with the peak of his cap just as he liked it, pointing rakishly up at the tops of the trees, soon became as important a part of the New Road ground as the Cathedral looking down on it from the other side of the Severn.

I was lucky enough to get to know Tom Graveney reasonably well. In my first year at Cambridge, in 1958, he was one of two professionals employed by the university to coach the top twenty or so players in nets in early April. Tom was partnered by that delightful, red-faced, diminutive leg-spinner from Derbyshire, A.E.G. 'Dusty' Rhodes, who never played Test cricket but went on a Commonwealth tour to India and Pakistan and was a real character. Tom coached as he batted, softly with excellent timing, although there were times when I suspect we needed rather harsher treatment than he was prepared to give. I am not sure if, as happens with great players, he was able to understand the juvenile problems we had. I remember later on, after he had retired, commentating on Old England XI charity matches when Tom often played. Still with the same svelte figure, his off drive was angular poetry and his forward-defensive stroke made all of us shake our heads. Tom was always the most charming of men and our friendship, which began at Cambridge, lasted until he died. Whenever we met for any length of time, we invariably went back and relived that innings in Port of Spain.

G

THE GROUNDSMAN

No one is more important to a game of cricket than the groundsman. The state of the surface dictates any game. Most village and club grounds have only a part-time, volunteer, unpaid groundsman who is invariably a character – usually willing, always obstinate, seldom uncertain. As a breed, they do not take kindly to criticism and they are masters, too, at making excuses when things don't turn out the way they should have done. They know exactly what needs to be done when it comes to neutralising the main strength of visiting sides. They are loyal and keen, if a tiny bit dyed in the wool and salt of the earth, although if they are professional, they have to be prepared to take on board whispered advice from the committee room. Groundsmen have one of the game's more important keys in their pockets.

Their job is not an easy one. The reputation of a ground is often established by the groundsman and none more so, for example, than Trent Bridge, where for years the pitches were perfect for batsmen. For those who prepare the playing surface in more humble circumstances, the problems are essentially the same as they are for those in charge of Test and first-class grounds, although they do not have to achieve the same levels of excellence and, of course, they are free from the spotlight of publicity. They all have to work the best they can with nature, trying to adapt it to suit their needs and to thwart its worst excesses at either end of the scale. There has to be a philosophical side to their character – this is important for any groundsman – because when the elements have the upper hand, all they can do is hope to make-do-and-mend. Preparing cricket pitches is not an exact science.

When I was at school at Eton, our outstanding groundsman, Bill Bowles, produced excellent pitches which batsmen enjoyed more than bowlers. Bowles was a tall, stately man who rode around on a policeman's bicycle which seemed as upright as its driver. He had a lofty smile under a dark brown homburg hat and was always friendly in a distant and slightly superior way. When you saw him, you knew what you were getting, just as you knew it was safe to expect an even bounce on any surface he had prepared. You could play forward with confidence. In 1934, he founded the National Association of Groundsmen and in 1936 became the head groundsman at Eton. His advice was much sought after and he lent rather more than a helping hand at Trent Bridge during a mild crisis in the 1950s when soil from Eton found its way to Nottingham to try and help maintain its reputation for excellent batting pitches. He also steered the rugby fraternity onto the right lines with the surface at Twickenham. Bowles manipulated nature with considerable skill and know-how.

I have dealt elsewhere with perhaps the most remarkable groundsman of all, Cyril Coote, who masterminded Fenner's at Cambridge between 1935 and 1980, and was so much more than simply a groundsman. Cambridge has been an important part of the world as far as groundsmen are concerned. Flack is a Cambridge name and two them have gone on to become head groundsman at Test match grounds. Bernard Flack learnt his trade under the auspices of Cyril Coote at Fenner's, while on the other side of the parish Bert Flack looked after the sporting fields of King's College with no little skill, without being, at that time anyway, quite in Bernard's class.

When, in 1948, Lancashire needed a new groundsman at Old Trafford, they decided that Flack was their man and set off to Cambridge. They were in search of Bernard, the number two at Fenner's, but arrived instead at the door of Bert, a robust, moustachioed character with few doubts about himself, his job or anything else. He was a man who talked a formidably good game. It was not long before Bert Flack was installed at Old Trafford, where he was soon to become a national hero or an unmitigated rogue, according to choice, when he prepared the pitch which allowed Jim Laker to take 19 wickets for 90 in the fourth Ashes Test in 1956. In Australia, he has never been forgiven. Flack's defence was that while he had wanted to leave some grass on a surface that was not too well bound together, the day before the game began, the chairman of the England selectors, Gubby Allen, had taken a look at the pitch and had made the suggestion to Flack, with some emphasis according to the groundsman, that he should get rid of the grass. This he proceeded to do – and the ball turned square from early in the match, but Australia's two spinners, off-spinner Ian Johnson and the young leg-spinner Richie Benaud, were not in Laker's class.

After Flack had retired from Old Trafford, he would often return to watch Test matches there and regularly held court at the end of the day's play in one of the large hospitality tents on the practice ground at the Stretford End. He held his audience spellbound, even if many of them had heard the stories before. No matter if he had initially been the 'wrong' Flack, he was one of the game's great characters. He must be the only groundsman ever to have used a mixture of sand, marl and cows' intestines to prepare his pitches. Flack would pick up the intestines at an old abattoir across the road from Old Trafford. Hey ho.

The plum job for any groundsman is that of head groundsman at Lord's. In my time, the MCC have been splendidly served by Jim Fairbrother, the dearest and most unassuming of men and a wonderful groundsman, who was cut down before his time by cancer. He was succeeded by Mick Hunt, who did the job with great skill and high humour for thirty-four years. (In the commentary box, we had to be careful to pronounce his name with absolute precision. To our huge enjoyment, there were times when it dragged the distinctive Yorkshire tones of Fred Trueman into something of a pronunciational tangle.) Hunt's dark-blue all-weather shorts and his sunburnt knees were always a reassuring feature of a Lord's Test match – and his pithy comments too. He retired at the end of the 2018 season and he will be a hard act to follow. Lord's will be a poorer place without him.

Groundsmen come in all shapes and sizes and, like umpires, they are regular Aunt Sallies, because players, committee men and spectators are forever blaming them for inconvenient results. Theirs is a difficult job, and it's likely to get harder still. Harnessing the weather has never been easy, but in this increasingly competitive era, the unscrupulous will also be constantly trying to twist their arms to make them produce surfaces which favour one side or the other. They will also have to resist the attentions of the bookmaking fraternity, who never stop trying to shade the odds in their favour. Groundsmen all over the world have their different problems and I think the game is well served by those who prepare the surfaces at all levels of the game, and what enjoyable characters they usually are!

G

A GRUB

A grub crawls along the ground; its cricketing equivalent is an underarm ball which rolls along the ground towards the batsman. When I first played the game at the age of seven, grubs were an unpleasant fact of life. It was the only way some youngsters could get the ball down to the other end, but even at that age such a method was held in contempt. If anyone stooped so low as to bowl a grub in the third-form game at Sunningdale, Miss Paterson, the presiding officer, would deliver a scalding lecture. It was an insult to human nature.

Grubs would have remained at the nursery level of the game if it had not been for the Chappell family, for many years a central force in Australian cricket. At the end of the season in the post-Packer years in Australia there has always been an annual limited-over competition between three countries. In 1981 these were Australia, New Zealand and India. When Australia played New Zealand on 1 February at the Melbourne Cricket Ground, we had a really exciting game and, with one ball to go, New Zealand were eight wickets down and needed to score six to tie. Greg Chappell, the Australian captain, went across to his younger brother, Trevor, who was bowling the final over.

They spoke briefly and then Trevor Chappell had a word with the umpire, Donald Weser, who spoke to the batsman, Brian McKechnie, who had on twenty occasions played rugby football for the All Blacks. He was a strong man, more than capable of clearing the boundary ropes at the vast MCG. In the press box we were not sure what was happening. Then McKechnie took up his stance, Trevor Chappell trotted a couple of strides up to the wicket and, with great care, deliberately rolled the ball along the pitch to McKechnie, who could only block it. Behind the stumps, Rodney Marsh made plain his disgust that such a tactic should have been used, and Australian celebrations were at best muted.

The outraged reactions round the world were led by the New Zealand Prime Minister, Robert Muldoon. It was difficult to argue against his gut reaction that it was 'the most disgusting incident I can recall in the history of cricket'. It was an appalling blot on the sporting reputation of Australia. I hope that is the last we will hear about deliberate grubs.

G
GULLY

Cricket has a most idiosyncratic list of names for the fielding positions. My dictionary tells me that gully is a fielding position between point and the slips – which for the uninitiated raises more problems than it solves. The slips stand next to the wicket-keeper and for a fast bowler there may be as many as four. There is a gap beyond fourth slip until you come to another close fielder at about 60 degrees from the batsman, and that is gully.

He is positioned there to catch or stop the ball that comes off a thick edge of the bat or maybe even the middle. It is one of the most important fielding positions. The greatest catch I ever saw taken in the gully was at Lord's in 1956 when the Australian captain, Richie Benaud, was fielding there for Slasher Mackay (brisk medium-paced seamers), who was bowling at Colin Cowdrey. The ball was wide of the off stump and Cowdrey, coming half forward, smacked the ball at great speed off the middle of the bat. Benaud said that the ball was hit so hard that he only saw a blur, and yet his reactions were so fast that he caught the ball above his shoulder in his left hand. He was knocked to the ground by the force of the stroke and yet managed to hold on. Benaud's honed instinct had won the day. It was an outrageous catch.

It was in this same position, in the second Test at Lord's five years later, that I saw the worst dropped catch I can remember.

Australia were again England's opponents and Cowdrey was once more the batsman, but this time Alan Davidson was the bowler. Cowdrey fended away a lifter and the ball lobbed in a gentle arc to the massive figure of Peter Burge in the gully. Burge, normally eminently reliable, can't have picked the ball up in its flight. He raised both hands with the uncertainty of a couple of interjoining question marks. The ball hit him on the right shoulder and the subsequent silence spoke of the universal disbelief within the ground. It is a relief to find that established Test players are human after all, but both these two efforts were superhuman – at opposite ends of the scale. This drop pursued Burge for the rest of his life and he always told the story with much laughter, for no one saw the funny side of it more than he did. Gully is a position which has always produced wonderful entertainment and more than its fair share of sensational catches, and some great characters have fielded there.

H

HAT-TRICK

There is nothing more exciting in cricket than when a bowler takes a hat-trick – three wickets with successive balls. When the first two wickets have fallen in succession, the whole ground sits up. The fielding captain brings up a platoon of close fielders, has feverish words with the bowler, the spectators stop talking and the new batsman, who would not be human if he did not feel slightly intimidated, takes guard, looks round the field and settles over his bat. The crowd roars encouragement as the bowler comes in. If he now takes another wicket, the ground erupts; if not, there is a groan of disappointment and those at the bar go thoughtfully back to their drinks.

The name 'hat-trick' has romantic connotations too because, or so the legend goes, in the eighteenth and early nineteenth centuries, a bowler who took three wickets with successive balls was rewarded with a new hat – a silk top hat, I always like to think.

It is a rare moment, but one that is all too pertinent, especially for the batsman who is the third victim. I write this with some feeling, for I had the agony in my first game at Lord's, in the 1955 Eton and Harrow match, at the age of 15, of walking back to the Pavilion after I had been bowled first ball in our second innings by Rex Neame, an off-spinner. It was a walk which went on for ever. Although my departure had been accompanied by outrageous cheering, I did not realise I had been the third victim of a hat-trick until twenty minutes after I was out – which at least helped explain the outrageous accompaniment to what was for me a solemn journey. I had been padding up when the second man was out and had no idea it was to his first ball and that I should have been trying to stop a hat-trick. If I had known, I hope I would not have tried to play it from two paces down the wicket. It shows you what a forgiving man I am, though, for Rex Neame became a close and lifelong friend.

I had been a member of the *Test Match Special* team for forty years before I commentated on my first hat-trick, and even then I shared the experience with Jonathan Agnew. India were playing a Test match in 2011 at Trent Bridge, a ground where exciting events always seemed to take place whenever I was at the microphone. India were batting and Aggers was at least three minutes late when he reluctantly, but cheerfully as always, handed over to me, immediately after Stuart Broad had taken the wicket of M.S. Dhoni, caught in the slips by Anderson. In the very first ball of my stint, Broad had Harbhajan Singh lbw. Then Praveen Kumar walked out to bat. He took a careful guard. He had an anxious and rather furtive look around the field and, hemmed in by masses of close catchers, he took up his stance. Broad started in from the Pavilion End with the crowd baying for blood. It was the perfect ball. It was up to the bat and seemed to leave the right-hander a fraction. It burst through Kumar's tentative push and his off stump exploded behind him. I think I described it as a 'humdinger' of a ball and it was all of that and more.

I can remember watching other, less dramatic hat-tricks when the first two wickets fall at the end of the bowler's previous over and the third comes from the first ball of his next. Toby Roland-Jones took the other variation of this – one wicket at the end of the previous over and two at the beginning of the next – in the match against Yorkshire that took Middlesex to the County Championship in 2016. There was also an occasion in a county match when the bowler took the last wicket in the first innings and then took two wickets with his first two balls in the second – a sort of long-range hat-trick.

In 1963, I watched an immensely irritating hat-trick on Kent's ground at Blackheath, better known for rugger. Kent were playing Surrey, it was just after twenty past six and in the press box I was all written up and poised with telephone in hand to dictate the story of the day's play to *The Guardian*, I think. Surrey's left-arm spinner, Roger Harman, whose bowling was steady but without any particular guile, now proceeded to take a hat-trick in what turned out to be the last over. Of course, it meant a rewrite, for this was now the big story of what had been a pretty dull day's cricket. It took me a while to do and played havoc with my evening assignations. Sadly, new top hats are no longer distributed on these joyous occasions, although I would have questioned whether, in the circumstances, Harman would have deserved his.

I

THE INDIAN PREMIER LEAGUE

My one big regret in cricketing terms is that I have never watched an Indian Premier League (IPL) game live, although I love the television coverage and all the fun and drama the competition produces. Then, in April 2019, I found myself in India helping to make a BBC television reality show, *The Real Marigold Hotel*. We spent two weeks in southern India and on our journey to the north of the country, we stopped in Chennai for two nights. On the first, the Chennai Super Kings were playing the Sunrisers from Hyderabad at the Chepauk Stadium. Yet, try as we might, we were unable to gain entry so that we could add an IPL occasion to all the other delights of *The Real Marigold Hotel*. So near, but so far.

However, even though we probably did not get within two miles of Chepauk that evening, the atmosphere of the IPL embraced me in a way it had not done before. No Indian city ever gets within touching distance of coming to a standstill, but even so there were not many hearts and minds in Chennai that night that were not wrapped up in the unfolding events at Chepauk. The Super Kings were at the top of the league and, in the most thrilling of finishes, they beat the Sunrisers off the fifth ball of the last over. My bedroom window rattled from Chennai's collective shriek of jubilation.

The IPL was then coming towards the end of its twelfth year. Its popularity seems to grow and grow as it makes unbelievable sums of money for the Board of Control for Cricket in India (BCCI), who own the competition that has become cricket's most productive gold mine ever. If any of the eight current franchises had to be replaced, the queue to bid for the new franchise would stretch halfway round India. T20 is the game's answer to society's ever-decreasing attention span and its need for instant everything. While this new form of the game is seen at its best in the IPL, it is spreading fast and furiously. Australia have their Big Bash competition, which is just about as popular as the IPL, and in South Africa and the West Indies T20 competitions are happily swelling the coffers, if not on quite the same scale of munificence.

T20 is surely here to say, although the English authorities may not entirely agree, for they have come up with yet another hybrid version of the old game. In 2020, the England and Wales Cricket Board (ECB) will preside over The Hundred, a new competition involving a hundred balls for each innings, as opposed to the 120 in the T20 competitions. This competition will also feature franchises. In order to guarantee success, it may have to offer the players large sums of money, although no other country plays cricket during the English summer and therefore the important players may feel that a little bit of extra pocket money would not go amiss. But they might also feel they need a rest. The Hundred may struggle to make its mark mainly because the other competitions got there first and there is little difference between 100 and 120 balls. The players taking part in the existing competitions already receive sums of money that were once associated with international sports like golf and tennis – and also football. It has meant cricket has come bursting into the twenty-first century, but without having much of a clue as to where it goes from here.

The IPL was a brilliant concept and the Indians deserve great credit for the way in which they first thought of the franchise idea and then let it develop. They were swift to embrace the razzamatazz which normally goes with American football and they have put together a product which provides wonderful entertainment. Some may say it is sacrilegious, but as long as Test cricket is left alone, so what? I love both the clamour and the glamour, even if it isn't cricket – as we used to know it, anyway. If T20 ever ruled supreme, however, we would never again have the excitement of seeing a genuine fast bowler race in with four slips and a gully waiting for the edge. We would also see fewer of those lovely top handed strokes through the covers. Nonetheless, the music, the noise, the energy and enthusiasm, on the field and in the stands, is terrific and whenever a six is hit, the music blasts out and it seems as if the whole ground is about to fall in. That game in Chennai began at eight o'clock in the evening and on television it provided brilliant prime-time entertainment – in India and around much of the rest of the world. I think there is no point in being squeamish about it, for it is a fact, but I don't believe it will stop Test cricket remaining as the gold standard of the game.

The IPL came into being in 2008, the brainchild of Lalit Modi, an Indian businessman and cricket administrator, and the tournament was successfully run with much help from Andrew Wildblood of the International Management Group, the company founded by the American Mark McCormack. The franchise format has worked brilliantly, with hopeful owners bidding for the privilege of ownership. The money they pay then has to be handed on to the BCCI during the ten-year period of ownership. Colossal amounts of money are then brought in by the sale of television rights, by general sponsorship, and by the sponsorship of individual teams. Teams bid for their players in the auction that precedes the competition each year, when there is a strict upper limit to the amount the teams may spend.

The competition is carefully policed and two teams, the Chennai Super Kings and the Rajasthan Royals, were suspended for two years after being found guilty of being involved in an illegal betting and match-fixing scandal. Remarkably, the co-owner of the Royals, Raj Kundra, who is married to a Bollywood actress, and Gurunath Meiyappan, the son-in-law of Narayanan Srinivasan, who was president of the BCCI for three years and then chairman of the International Cricket Council, were both banned from cricket for life for their involvement in this corruption by a committee headed by a former Chief Justice of India.

Other suggestions of corruption have been fully investigated too, but in a country where betting is illegal it is surely impossible to say with absolute confidence that the IPL is completely clean. The Indian authorities are doing what they can to see that it is and they are helped by the fact that it would be madness for players to jeopardise the big payments they are now receiving. Also, by dealing with these two important figures as they did, others may now have second thoughts about going down a similar path. Another team, the Pune Warriors, were suspended because the owners were unable to pay their dues to the BCCI.

The way in which the IPL has tried to stamp out corruption and maintain its standards has been impressive. I fervently hope that the IPL, and T20 in general, can peacefully co-exist with Test cricket and indeed that both can thrive off their startling differences.

I
COLIN INGLEBY-MACKENZIE

Colin Ingleby-Mackenzie was the Bulldog Drummond of the cricket field. He was debonair and dashing, an extraordinary throwback to the Edwardian era at the same time as being a man who was at the vanguard of the modern era. As a player and as captain of Hampshire in the 1950s and 1960s, he was certainly a reminder of the old-fashioned amateurs and their modus operandi in the early days of the century, but without any of their accompanying pomp and ceremony and with a much more highly developed sense of fun. He laughed at both cricket and life, and yet to be able to do both successfully, he took the trouble to understand exactly what he was laughing at.

Ingleby-Mackenzie was an Old Etonian to his core without ever being self-conscious about it. In many ways he was a descendant of those hirsute noblemen who had run the game a century before, and yet in the dressing room he was definitely one of the boys, and in time, of course, the leading boy. If it had not been for his determination and insistence, first as a committee member and then as president, ladies might have had to wait longer before they were allowed to become members of the Marylebone Cricket Club. Stuffy tradition was anathema to him. Working or playing for Ingleby-Mackenzie must have been great fun and the results were generally good too.

Ingleby-Mackenzie started as he was to go on. He left a trail of laughter behind him at Eton, as well as some tales of remarkable deeds of derring-do on the cricket field. His two years of National Service in the Navy probably left some of the ships rocking dangerously with laughter too. He then turned his attention to cricket with Hampshire at the same time as working for Slazenger, who produced sports equipment and who were happy to give him the time off to play cricket. Then, in 1958, when he took on the captaincy of Hampshire, he was claimed by the insurance world in the City of London. For Hampshire, he had played for some years under the captaincy of Desmond Eagar, who sensibly allowed his rumbustious new recruit to be himself while gently grooming him to take over the captaincy. In the City, he was lucky to have another ex-cricketing mentor, Bryan Valentine, who was himself a great character and had batted for Kent and on a few occasions for England. In the bowler-hatted insurance world he, like Eagar, was happy to let Ingleby-Mackenzie do it his way and everyone reaped the rewards.

His cricketing ability looked more hit-and-miss than it actually was. He was a gambler by nature and batting became an extension of his character. If he had been a bat-and-pad-close-together sort of chap, he would have been a much more consistent run-scorer, but a much less exciting person and maybe a hopeless leader of men. His captaincy of Hampshire was based on taking calculated risks. Ingleby-Mackenzie took Hampshire to their first County Championship title in 1961. In a year in which enforcing the follow-on was forbidden, in the hope of making county cricket more entertaining, Hampshire won ten of their matches after their captain had made a calculated declaration, giving his opponents a realistic chance of victory. He therefore kept them interested in the chase to the point where they were prepared to lose wickets in pursuit of victory. The follow-on was restored for the 1963 season.

His side understood the qualities of their captain, which as well as his humour and calculated risk-taking included great loyalty to his players, which inspired the trust and loyalty they showed him in return. Ingleby-Mackenzie's famous obiter dicta soon became well-worn clichés. Nonetheless, he told an over-serious television interviewer that he attributed Hampshire's success in 1961 to 'wine, women and song'. On another occasion, he was asked if there was a curfew for the players when they were staying in hotels for games away from home. 'I like them to be in bed by half past nine,' he replied. When the interviewer said he thought this was a bit early, Ingleby-Mackenzie replied, 'Well, the game starts at half past eleven.' As this shows, he was always determined that the cricket he controlled should be fun and that the dressing room should be a joyful place. Umpires were sometimes persuaded to take a transistor radio out to the middle with them so that he could listen to an important horse race in which he will have had a sizeable bet. Ingleby-Mackenzie was a great and kind human being. He was always unhappy when he had to drop a player from the side, and never for a moment was he mean or arrogant.

He was a great deal more clued up about all that was going on than one would have thought from his happy-go-lucky approach. As far as tactics were concerned, he would shrug his shoulders and simply say, 'Roy Marshall and Leo Harrison do all that.' His genius as a captain lay in his skill in being able to assess risk and calculate the odds when it came to declarations.

Having said all that, he had under him some extremely able players who were good enough to take advantage of the opportunities provided by his adventurous and unorthodox form of captaincy. There was also his own flamboyant batting, which sometimes served Hampshire brilliantly when they most needed it. In 343 games, he scored 12,421 runs with 11 hundreds and an average of just over 24, which does not remotely reflect the value of a batsman who was prepared to take on any situation, whatever the risk.

One of his greatest innings was played against Essex at Cowes in the Isle of Wight at an important moment in Hampshire's bid for the Championship in 1961. Coming in at number six in the second innings, he made 132 not out in 140 minutes to win the match. Three years earlier, an innings of 107 in 88 minutes had brought victory against Kent, while a few weeks later he had made a hundred against Somerset in only 61 minutes – after reputedly being up all night. It would have been lovely to think that someone with this approach might have been asked to captain England. If he had, however, there would have been too many doubters and cynics who would never have stopped reminding the world how often Ingleby-Mackenzie suffered from injury during the week of Royal Ascot.

I played for Norfolk against Hampshire at the old Northlands Road ground in Southampton in the first round of the Gillette Cup in 1965. Hampshire won easily, but Ingleby-Mackenzie's presence and captaincy made it a far-from-gloomy occasion. I had the luck to stay in for nearly half of Norfolk's innings and the chatter and the laughter and the sense of fun orchestrated by the Hampshire captain kept everyone on their toes and made sure that in spite of the impending heavy defeat, it was memorable and terrific fun. I also played for Jim Swanton's Arabs on their tour of Barbados in 1966 under Ingleby-Mackenzie's captaincy. Our flight was delayed at Heathrow to enable our captain to get there in time after a heavy night in a gambling club in Berkeley Square. He was, by the way, rumoured to have been one of the last people to have seen Lord Lucan. When we landed in Barbados at the start of the tour, a local television reporter asked him on the steps of the aeroplane what he thought about his side. Without a moment's pause, our captain said, 'We have no weaknesses except the manager.' Jim Swanton did not mind having his leg pulled – as long as it came with the right social credentials.

In Barbados, we had a difficult tour against some very good sides and Ingleby-Mackenzie's indomitable brand of captaincy made sure it was all the greatest of fun, just as he did years later in his two-year term as president of the MCC when, with his chuckling good humour, he persuaded the doubters and the dinosaurs that it was time to admit lady members to the Marylebone Cricket Club. Colin Ingleby-Mackenzie was truly a man for all seasons.

K

IMRAN KHAN

Any emperor would have been pleased to look like Imran Khan. It is appropriate, therefore, that as the age of emperors has passed, Imran should have become prime minister of Pakistan. It is the culmination of an extraordinary career and, being the man he is, I am sure there will be more to come. Imran was born a Pashtun, a tribe originally found around the north-west frontier of Pakistan. He was educated mostly in England and became one of the most important cricketers of his generation. He also had film-star good looks and was a prominent figure in the top levels of London society before becoming a powerful and sincere politician.

He was a wonderful natural fast bowler who was genuinely quick and able to swing the ball in late to right-handers more or less at will. He was first educated at Aitchison College in Lahore and then moved to the Royal Worcester Grammar School, before going up to Keble College, Oxford, where his life and his cricket took shape. He played for the university for three years and was captain in 1974, while his good looks coupled with his fascination with the English social scene ensured that he acquired a playboy image. At that time he was a mildly perplexing figure. It was as if he was aware that he was destined for greatness without quite knowing where to go out and find it. There was a tinge of shyness about Imran as a young man which can sometimes be sensed even today. He was a magnificent cricketer, but the game was only a temporary vehicle designed to help him find the path for which he was destined.

His cricket created a huge and important public awareness, especially at home in Pakistan. By the time he had finished his cricketing life in 1992, it was clear that politics would now claim him. Cricket had supplied him with what were in effect his gap years, enabling him to sort out his mind, to position himself for what he decided his ultimate path in life was to be. In 1995, he married the beautiful Jemima Goldsmith, the daughter of Jimmy, whose entrepreneurial good sense had turned him into one of England's richest men. She became a Muslim and learned Urdu and they had two sons. Their marriage lasted for nine years, by which time Imran had in every sense left the social life of London and was becoming increasingly immersed in life and politics in Pakistan. He has been married twice more to ladies from his own country.

Imran adored his mother, Shaukat Khanum, who died of cancer in 1985, and it was in her memory that he decided to raise the money to build a cancer hospital in Lahore. It was his original intention to retire as a cricketer in 1987, but he kept going in order to remain in the public eye, which would make it easier for him to raise the appropriate funds. When he finally retired in 1992, he feared that he would become a depreciating asset, which would make money harder to raise. He need not have worried. The Shaukat Khanum Hospital was opened in Lahore in 1994 and, of course, it gave him even greater celebrity in his own country. His intention was to make up-to-date cancer treatment available to the poor and this will have hardened his political ambitions. In 1996 he was able to form his own anti-corruption political party, which was slow to take off but over the years weathered the attacks on it, mostly from those who obviously feared the effects of an anti-corruption party ever being voted into power. His party gradually gained momentum until, in the election of 2018, it won more seats than any other. As it did not have an overall majority, he needed coalition partners to enable him to form a government and become prime minister.

Born with a remarkable natural talent for cricket, it was inevitable that he should captain Pakistan. He did the job intermittently between 1982 and 1992, but in those days there was a restlessness about him as he tried to sort out his future. I have little doubt that he saw himself even then as a potential saviour of his country. His finest moment on the cricket field came in 1992 when, under his captaincy, Pakistan won the World Cup, beating England in the final in Melbourne. By then, Imran was almost 40 and as a captain he was able to bring together a disparate group of players who had great talent but strongly differing views about the way the game should be played, about their colleagues and about almost every other aspect of life. Imran was able to make them all pull together for the common good.

I was lucky to watch much of his cricket and, strangely, one of my strongest memories is of his batting. Pakistan played the second Test on their tour of Australia in 1989–90 at the Adelaide Oval. Australia had a first-innings lead of 84 and then Pakistan lost their first five second-innings wickets for only 90. It was at this point that Wasim Akram joined his captain, Imran, and they put on 191 in one of the most exhilarating partnerships I have ever seen. It is seldom that two brilliant players both bat at their best at the same time. Although these two were known primarily for their bowling, they were both high-class batsmen. They each made a hundred, and while Wasim was the more extravagant, scoring 123 of the 191, Imran was no less assured and magnificent at the other end, playing what was truly a captain's innings as he made sure Pakistan scored enough runs to avoid defeat.

Imran was always a most commanding figure. If Pakistan were in the field, you knew within seconds that Imran was the captain and he batted with the same measured authority. There was never anything frivolous or unattractive about his cricket or his demeanour. Imran's patience as captain of Pakistan was severely tested in 1983–84. He had been suffering from a stress fracture and had been unable to bowl for Sussex in the previous English season. In spite of that, he was chosen to captain his country for their first five-Test tour of Australia. He was not fit to play until the fourth Test and then it was only as a batsman. He may have only played then because his deputy, Zaheer Abbas, who was probably no great admirer of Imran, was not making much of a job of the captaincy. There had been a farcical situation in Brisbane, where the second Test was played, when the news came from the Pakistan Board of Control that Zaheer had suddenly been appointed as the official captain. Within twenty-four hours we had the news that Imran had been reappointed by the same Board. Later, when the tour ended, the team returned home to one of those bouts of internal bloodletting that is sadly a feature of Pakistan cricket.

In Sydney, the venue for the fifth Test, the Pakistan side and several journalists were staying at the Sebel Townhouse on the edge of Kings Cross. David Bowie was also staying there and one evening Imran asked me if I would like to go up to a party Bowie was giving in his room. We went along and the singer was clearly in awe of Imran, who beamed sweetness and light on all present in his patriarchal way. Throughout his time in cricket and afterwards, when his political inclinations were gaining strength, we would meet in unlikely places and, no matter where, he was always a good friend. We met at breakfast once in Abu Dhabi at a majlis, a gathering of perhaps a hundred people in a vast room for an Arab breakfast given by a member of the Abu Dhabi ruling family who was also a great cricket lover. Politics were important but Imran still found time to come and have chat about life and cricket. On one occasion we met on a private cricket ground in Wootton near Woodstock. Our host persuaded him to take off his jacket and bowl a couple of overs after tea, off a longish run too. His natural inswingers were still there and it was extraordinary how he made an old ball dip in such a long way and so late in its flight. It was privately televised and I was doing the commentary, so for me these two overs were manna from heaven. Imran and I had a good laugh about it all afterwards, before politics and his two boys reclaimed him for the rest of the day.

For all his glitter in other directions, I shall always remember his extraordinary ability as a cricketer. There was more than something of an aristocratic lion in Imran as he ran in to bowl. He was tall, his run was controlled and every ounce of energy went into a lovely easy action and a predatory follow-through. Whether he bowled, batted or fielded, Imran never seemed to strain and there was a lithe grace about everything he did; his joints were wonderfully supple and he seemed to exude class and all its manifestations, such as rhythm, timing and unhurried positioning of his feet. Like all great players, he made it seem so easy. One only hopes that none of these attributes desert him while he tries to cope with what must be the supremely difficult job of being prime minister of Pakistan.

K

BARTON KING

Barton King has fascinated me all my cricketing life and has always seemed one of the game's most romantic figures. He played for Philadelphia from 1893 until 1912 and must have been one of the greatest ever fast bowlers. He was also the finest cricketer produced by the United States, where cricket was a going concern in the last half of the nineteenth century.

King was probably the first bowler to swing the ball significantly. He developed a delivery which he called the 'Angler'. It was a late inswinger which would move sharply in to the right-hander. He used it sparingly and with great effect. In 1908, Philadelphia toured England, playing first-class matches against the counties. His greatest performance came on a good pitch against Sussex at Brighton when he took 7–13 in the first innings. That year King finished at the top of the English first-class averages, with 87 wickets at 11.01 each – figures which only the great S.F. Barnes could have matched.

All this is impressive enough, but what made me never forget King was an extraordinary story told to me, I think, by one of the masters when I was about ten years old. King was playing in a club match in Philadelphia and the opposing captain, a good batsman, turned up late and in time only to bat at number eleven. As he came to the wicket, King sent all his fielders to the pavilion. He was about to run in to bowl when he saw the wicketkeeper still in place. King waved him away too, but then changed his mind and told him to stand twenty paces back and four yards to leg at a very fine leg slip. The non-striker asked him what a fielder was doing there. 'Oh, he's not a fielder,' came the reply, 'he is there to pick up the ball when the game is over and give it to the umpires.' King then ran in to bowl. The ball was fast, it swung in sharply, hit the outside of the leg stump and went straight to that one fielder, who threw it on to the umpire. No one was more delighted than Bart King. What a pity baseball came along.

K
KNOTT AND EVANS

No player is more involved in a game of cricket than the wicketkeeper. He is the lynchpin of the fielding side, usually the butt of humour in the dressing room and often laughably unorthodox with a bat in his hand. In every way, he is the joker in the cricketing pack.

In my experience, there was one wicketkeeper who had all these intriguing qualities and was perhaps the greatest of them all. His name was Alan Knott. He played his cricket for Kent for 21 years and for England in 95 Test matches between 1967 and 1981. I was lucky enough to have watched most of them.

I shall always remember a ready if determined smile, twinkling eyes under tousled black hair and quick, precise movements, the product of an uncannily sharp, anticipatory mind. Yet there was nothing devil-may-care about him. With Knotty, perfectionism and control-freakery formed a remarkable and happy partnership. Nothing was left to chance and yet he was always a joy to watch.

If the sun was shining, Knott usually wore an old washerwoman's white hat pulled firmly down over his head. It helped portray him as a cheeky figure of fun, but that could hardly have been further from the truth. Knott was immensely serious and single-minded about everything he did on the cricket field. He was fastidious in the extreme about what he ate, while his minute attention to cleanliness matched the care he took over his equipment.

I have two abiding memories of Knotty. One is of watching him keep wicket to Derek Underwood on a drying pitch. Pitches were uncovered until 1979. Although nominally a left-arm spinner, Underwood bowled at a brisk medium pace. On rain-affected pitches he was deadly and, for both Kent and England, Knott was his principal ally in destruction. In drying conditions, Underwood made the ball do everything but talk. From a good length, the ball would fly past the batsman's face or turn miles, lifting sharply at the same time, or maybe skid through low past the leg stump. Yet every ball that passed the bat invariably found the middle of Knott's gloves. If a catch or a stumping chance came his way, it was not wasted. At times it was like watching an Olympic gymnast at the peak of his form.

The other indelible memory comes from his batting. In 1977, England played Australia when world cricket was in a jittery state because of the determination of the Australian television mogul Kerry Packer to take control of the game. The third Test was played at Trent Bridge and it marked the moment when, after three years, Geoffrey Boycott ended his self-imposed exile from international cricket. Knott joined Boycott, who was finding the going tough, when the score was 82–5. Immediately, Knott's wrists, combined with his twinkling footwork and his imagination, got the scoreboard moving again in a manner which can only have irritated the Australians. He took the pressure off his partner, who worked his way through his own tricky period and went on to score his 99th first-class hundred, while Knott himself made 135 in his best innings for England.

If Knott was cricket's supreme wicketkeeping joker, for me, he had only one competitor when it came to skill, fun and entertainment: Godfrey Evans, who also played for Kent and England, in the immediate post-war years. As you will have gathered from my comments elsewhere, Godfrey Evans was my boyhood hero, sharing the position with Denis Compton. A man of indomitable energy and apparently made of India rubber, he stood up to the stumps to Alec Bedser, a sharp fast-medium, with a skill Knott would have envied and I doubt even he would have exceeded. Knott probably had the surer hands. He was balletic too, while Evans's athleticism was strident and robust, but his general ebullience was a real joy, even if he did not have quite the delicate touch of Knott.

There was one Evans moment it would be impossible to forget. England went to Australia in 1954–55 under Len Hutton's captaincy. Australia, put in to bat, won the first Test in Brisbane by an innings and plenty. By the time the second Test began, two weeks later in Sydney, England's Frank Tyson, a fast-bowling new boy, had been persuaded to cut his long run-up by almost half. The dividends were immediate: he took ten wickets in the match and England won by 38 runs.

The sides now moved on to Melbourne and the MCG for the Boxing Day Test. England batted first and it was only thanks to a remarkable innings of 102 by the young Colin Cowdrey that they reached 191. Brian Statham then took five wickets as Australia gained a first-innings lead of 40 when they were bowled out for 231. In their second innings, England were shown the way by Peter May, whose 91 took them to 279, leaving Australia to score 240 to win. At the end of the fourth day they were 75–2, with Neil Harvey, their most dangerous batsman on whom much would depend, 9 not out.

Tyson bowled the first over the next morning to the left-handed Harvey. He picked up a couple of runs and then played an authentic leg glance at a ball just short of a length. It went off the middle of the bat and Evans, with brilliant anticipation, moved two paces to his right and somehow managed to hold on to the ball in his right hand. He had moved so quickly that he took an extraordinary catch without falling over, which probably made it look easier than it was. This was such a body blow for Australia that they never recovered and were all out for 111, losing by 128 runs. Tyson took 7–27, taking his tally for the match to nine and to 19 for these two Tests.

For me, Evans and then Knott were irresistible behind the stumps. They were very different characters. Evans was the extrovert who took life, as well as cricket, head on. Knott was a more delicate precision instrument who was forever reducing the margin for error. As far as he could help it, nothing was left to chance.

These two encapsulated the full glory of wicketkeeping. Everyone has their own favourites and there are plenty to choose from. Sadly, in recent years the art of the wicketkeeper has been downgraded. In the modern game, wicketkeepers have to be all-rounders, dual-purpose cricketers. It is many years since national selectors simply picked the best wicketkeeper at their disposal. Nowadays wicketkeepers have to bat – and pretty competently at that. Knott's impetuous, idiosyncratic batting brought him five hundreds for England, and if he had been around today, he might just have fitted the bill. Evans's swashbuckling hitting, in character with a man who always seemed to go for broke, may have made his inclusion in modern times more problematical. Knott and Evans both kept wicket with a brimming sense of humour, although Evans's humour was the more extravagant and Knott would have been hard-pressed to keep up with him after the close of play.

K

VIRAT KOHLI

Virat Kohli's character has enabled him to grab hold of both Indian cricket and India in a way that maybe even Sachin Tendulkar, a different and more reserved character, could not manage or, indeed, would not have wanted to. The game there needs to be led by a figure who is himself a rare phenomenon: charismatic, good-looking, in every way his own man, larger than life, inhabiting a rarefied world of his own and whose image is everywhere, in the newspapers, on the billboards, the radio and television, on the lips of everyone and permanently in the general consciousness. Kohli has performed this function admirably, for he has conquered not only India, but the world. Success at cricket, truly the national sport in India, brings with it a huge feeling of national and personal identity and a comforting sense of security.

Kohli is the most compelling of cricketers in both attitude and style. His very presence takes hold of you as he comes out of the pavilion. He is a magnificent strokeplayer; he has enormous self-confidence; his punched defensive strokes make the fielders fear what will come next; he will take on any challenge and he is no mean slip fielder. Although Kohli is very much a free spirit in the way he plays the game, his flair and skills are constantly being honed and controlled by a remarkable mental process. By his own admission, long hours in the nets do not suit him, for they do not help him to maintain the freshness that is so crucial to the way he plays. On the other hand, his mind is never still. He is a deep thinker about the game; he goes through extensive mental preparations for every match and every bowler he will face. He is always trying to make sure he sticks to what is a carefully thought-out plan.

Kohli scores his runs at a rare speed and they are the product of orthodox strokes, both in Test and one-day cricket. He is no slogger and he does not play the reverse sweep or the scoop over the wicketkeeper's head. 'I don't feel the need to play extravagant shots,' he says. 'The bowlers are bowling the same balls at me, so I score my runs with the same shots. Why should I try and play a shot that is not my strength?' For Kohli, batting is all about getting into the zone, and after the first ten balls of an innings he will know if he is there or not. 'When you're in the zone, your feet move, you leave the ball well, middle it beautifully, and you're not even thinking about the score . . . It's the calmest feeling in the world.' All this reveals strength of character and great determination, and it's easy to see how someone who thinks in this precise, analytical way would fit so well into the captain's shoes. Kohli was a great admirer of M.S. Dhoni's captaincy, spending many days in the slips beside him learning from him and working out for himself the reasoning behind Dhoni's decisions.

Cricket today is an extremely demanding game and Kohli is now the best and most important player in the world. It is easy to think of him as purely an instinctive batsman, and yet from what he says you begin to see how little even a player like Kohli, who has so much natural talent, is prepared to leave to chance. This also raises a question: do modern players think more about the game, or is it simply the fashion nowadays to let it all hang out, as it were? Jack Hobbs and Don Bradman – and W.G. Grace, for that matter – were surely every bit as technically complete as Kohli, perhaps even more so in the corridor of uncertainty around off stump. They must have worked out their way of playing just as precisely, but they would not have had to talk about it in an age when cross-examinations from the press would have seemed impertinent.

Virat Kohli was born in Delhi into a Punjabi family without any real cricketing background. His father was a criminal lawyer and gave his son, who at the age of three was already asking his father to bowl at him, as much support as possible. He took him to a new cricket academy in West Delhi when he was nine, where his coach later said, 'He oozed talent ... and I had to push him home after the training sessions because he wouldn't leave.' His father died in 2006 when Virat was 18 and only a month after he had made his first-class debut for Delhi. He was in the middle of a match against Karnataka and his mother insisted he should continue, and the day after his father's death, he made 90 and saved the game for Delhi. His coach Chetan Chauhan spoke glowingly of his attitude and determination, while his mother said, 'Virat changed a bit after that day ... His life hinged totally on cricket after that.' Virat himself said, 'The way I approached the game changed that day. I just had one thing in my mind, that I have to play for my country and live that dream for my dad.'

At the age of 19, he made his debut for India's one-day side. In 2011 he was selected to tour the West Indies, with some of the main players being rested, and Kohli played his first Test, at Kingston, and struggled throughout the series against short-pitched fast bowling. Later that year he was selected for India's tour of Australia and in the fourth and final match, in Adelaide, he made his first Test hundred. Kohli's progress from that point was amazing. He played both types of the game with equal facility and exciting runs poured from his bat. His statistics seem to be climbing happily upwards, although there were some low scores followed by moments of doubt which he soon overcame. He currently averages more than 50 in Test matches, ODIs and T20 internationals, and he was the quickest ever to 11,000 runs in ODIs.

After helping to steer India to the World Cup in 2011, he first captained the one-day side in 2013, although he did not take over from Dhoni permanently until 2017. In 2013–14, there were hundreds in 52 and 61 balls in a one-day series against Australia in India, a Test hundred in South Africa and another to save a Test in New Zealand. Man of the Match and Player of the Series awards rained down like confetti. Then came a big hiccup, in England in 2014, when he averaged 13.4 in ten innings and Jimmy Anderson kept finding his outside edge. His technique was questioned by none other than Geoffrey Boycott, who forcibly suggested Kohli needed to 'get back to basics' when negotiating that corridor of uncertainty. Kohli soon found the answer.

He then succeeded Dhoni as the Test captain for the first Test on the Australian tour in 2014–15, when Dhoni was injured, and Kohli proceeded to score a hundred in each innings. His 141 in only 175 balls in the second, on a worn pitch, was regarded by many critics as the best fourth-innings display they had seen in Australia. I had the luck to be in the commentary box at the Adelaide Oval and I shall never forget the power and certainty with which he hooked and cut Mitchell Johnson with the second new ball. Dhoni returned for the second Test in Brisbane, but retired altogether from the captaincy after the third in Melbourne. Kohli succeeded him and was in charge at Sydney, where he made 147 in India's first innings and became the only captain in the history of Test cricket to score a hundred in each of his first three innings in the job. He finished with a record 692 runs in the series.

Unlike Tendulkar, Kohli relished the task of captaincy. In 2016, he made 200 in a Test against the West Indies in Antigua and, rather surprisingly, this was the first time he had made a double century in first-class cricket. The greatest compliment of all came then from Viv Richards, 'I love watching Virat Kohli bat ... I love his aggression and serious passion that I used to have. He reminds me of myself.' There could be no greater endorsement than that. He quickly developed a taste for double centuries and, back in India, he hit 211 against New Zealand in Indore. Not content with this, he made two more in India's next two series, against England and Bangladesh, and by scoring double centuries in four successive series, he broke the record held jointly by Bradman and Rahul Dravid, who had done it in three successive series. It is surely now only a matter of time before he goes past Tendulkar's astonishing records in both types of the game – as long as he stays fit. At the time of writing, he has made a total of 66 Test and one-day hundreds, while Tendulkar reached 100.

Kohli is the most influential cricketer in the world today and at a time when the game seems to be lurching more and more towards the shorter form of the game, it is significant that he has recently gone on record on two occasions proclaiming the importance and the strengths of Test cricket. In an interview he gave to *Wisden*, he said, 'I think that if you really understand the sport, if you really love the sport, you understand Test cricket and you understand how exciting it is. I cannot explain to you the job satisfaction that you get when you do well in Test cricket, because you know how demanding it is.' He also thinks Test cricket should continue to be played over five days. This could hardly be a more ringing endorsement, coming from the most modern of modern players, and the game's administrators should take serious note of what Kohli says.

Indian cricket needs its game to be led by semi-regal figures like Kohli, Tendulkar and Dhoni, and the world game benefits enormously from their presence. In their different ways, their genius brings drama, excitement, unbelievable skill and wonderment to the game. The game of cricket also needs these players who are able to make the impossible seem, well, possible. No one does this more than the good-looking Kohli who, appropriately, has married an exceptionally beautiful Bollywood wife, Anushka Sharma, and there surely cannot be a more glamorous couple in India.

L

LUNCH(EON) AND TEA

The lunch and tea intervals have long been important fixtures in the pageantry of cricket. Those who run the game have always feared their digestive systems would suffer if the lunch interval should ever become a movable feast like the tea break. Being less important digestive hurdles, teas, rather like elevenses, have to fit in as and when they can. Regulations concerning the time of the tea interval are extensive, muddled and incomprehensible, while those concerning the lunch interval glare at us rather like a dyspeptic monarch from the Middle Ages. The battle lines are joined between an inflexible steak-and-kidney pudding and negotiable scones and doughnuts.

The luncheon interval made a lurch towards modern times when those last three letters were dropped. Players no longer have to muncheon their luncheon while washing it down with some puncheon. No other sport has needed to make such an official business of eating because of the sport's own structure. In a two-innings match, one side may have to spend the entire day in the field and it would be churlish in the extreme not to allow occasional refuelling.

The lunch interval lasts for forty minutes. In the old days, players would have put on their blazers before sitting down in serried ranks in the players' dining room. In the first-class game today, attendants bring easy-to-eat food to the dressing room so that players who have been in the thick of it can nibble away in peace. The others will still roll up their sleeves to take on board the daily roast in the players' dining room.

In my first years as a commentator at Lord's, the players' and the committee dining rooms were underneath our commentary box in the Pavilion, and they were presided over with friendly determination and occasional militancy by Nancy, a small, formidable lady who hailed from Ireland. Her absolute command was occasionally more convincing than her cooking. She would make Brian Johnston his daily lunchtime platter of lamb sandwiches, which when I was a beginner I sometimes had to bring up from the kitchen.

In those days the players' lunch at Lord's was a splendid ritual. There was an amusing routine with a definite pecking order, which I imagine came down from the days when the professionals were at last allowed to join the amateurs for lunch, although they probably still had to put up with the scrappy bits of the joint. There were special places for the players, the umpires and the scorers, who squeezed into the tiny table by the door. Corpulent scorers were not encouraged.

Nowadays the players' dining room is a more democratic transit centre, with players arriving and leaving with trays and glasses, and formality has disappeared. I am not sure how this would have appealed to Nancy, who was awarded the British Empire Medal (BEM) by John Major when he was prime minister. Thus was cricket's luncheon ennobled. Perhaps Nancy should have been awarded the EON. So many cricket grounds have their own Nancys who are such important supporting figures in the structure of the game.

The tea interval lasts for only twenty minutes and in the professional game is served in the dressing room. But in the world of grassroots cricket the tea interval is one of the main events of the day. Sandwiches, scones and cakes of all sorts line up for appreciation and consumption while the kettle boils. Cake competitions take place, no doubt inspired by *Test Match Special*'s ongoing love affair with comestibles of this nature. *TMS* once held a highly amusing competition between the best tea ladies in the land. The winner's cake did nothing for our cholesterol.

The tea interval is considered to be a more frivolous affair than the more stately lunch interval. There are many ifs and buts to be dealt with before players at the first-class level of the game can be sure of their afternoon cuppa. Happily, at the good old village level of the game, however, the tea ladies, as we have seen, still regularly flex their muscles between innings and tea, thank heavens, is still as important an event as anything that goes on out in the middle.

M

MANKADING

India's tour of Australia in 1947–48 resulted in a big victory for Australia, but it also introduced the game's most unfortunate method of dismissal. Vinoo Mankad was an excellent all-rounder who bowled orthodox left-arm spin. In their fifth match, against an Australian XI, Mankad was bowling and Bill Brown was one of the opening batsmen. The Australian XI needed 251 to win in quick time. With Mankad bowling, Brown, at the non-striker's end, was backing up most enthusiastically and was sometimes out of the crease before Mankad had delivered the ball.

In accordance with what was an unwritten law, but in the time-honoured way of doing these things, Mankad stopped in mid-action and held the ball against the stumps, to warn Brown not to do it again. He did not heed the warning and Mankad ran him out soon afterwards. There was nothing wrong with this, and Mankad's morality was not doubted. A few weeks later, in the second Test match, Mankad again ran out Brown, but this time without giving him a warning first. Although Mankad was within his rights, he was pilloried by the media and few people sympathised with him. Mankad may have felt that his 'legitimate' running-out of Brown in the Australian XI game had been warning enough. For all that, it was seen as a cheap and underhand dismissal.

I remember a similar dismissal at the Adelaide Oval during the fourth Test between Australia and the West Indies in 1968–69. In a most exciting, topsy-turvy match, Australia needed to score 360 to win. They were given a wonderful start by Bill Lawry and Keith Stackpole and it began to look as if Australia would reach this big fourth-innings target. The two openers both got out and the score was 215–2 when Charlie Griffith ran in to bowl to Ian Redpath. He was into his action when he sensed Redpath was backing up too far, so he brought his right hand down and broke the stumps. Redpath was out of his crease and the umpire had no option but to give him out. Griffith had ignored the still-accepted practice of warning the batsman first. This produced great excitement, outrage and accusations of opportunistic cheating – water off a duck's back to Griffith, I am sure. The match ended in a draw, with Australia reaching 339–9, but what if Redpath had not been run out? Australia went on to win the fifth Test in Sydney and the series 3–1, so they will have felt justice was done, although the incident left a nasty bruise on cricketing relations between the two countries for quite a while.

This most unsatisfactory form of dismissal has happened on only four occasions in Test cricket and is always accompanied by howls of protest. The defence invariably states that it is within the Laws of the game, which is true, while the prosecution screams that it is not within the spirit of the game, also true. But it is not easy to decide whether the batsman, in his enthusiasm not to miss a run, is trying to steal an unfair advantage or is merely being caught up in the moment and being careless. Many believe in sticking to the time-honoured but unwritten rule that the bowler should first warn the batsman by stopping in his action and holding the ball over the bails but not removing them. This done, the bowler is fully within his rights to take the bails off the next time he catches the batsman at it.

In 2017, the Marylebone Cricket Club (MCC), who are the owners of the Laws of cricket, decided to make it clear that this unwritten code of conduct was no longer applicable and that the bowler was entitled to run out a batsman for backing up too far without giving him any previous warning. Maybe they felt that with the increase in limited-over cricket, especially Twenty20, when the financial stakes are huge, batsmen would increasingly try and steal an unfair advantage by backing up too far. It is easy to follow their thinking. But there is another important point in the Law governing this dismissal. The bowler is not allowed to remove the bails until the ball is live, which happens as soon as the bowler is into his actual delivery process and his arm is on its way to releasing the ball.

This was particularly relevant in the recent dismissal of England batsman Jos Buttler by Indian off spinner Ravi Ashwin in the Indian Premier League (IPL) in March 2019. I have looked at countless replays of the dismissal and there can only be considerable doubt as to whether Ashwin had begun his delivery process: in my view, more than enough doubt for the umpire to have given the benefit of it to the batsman. From where the umpire is standing, looking down at the crease in case it should be a no-ball, it is impossible for him to judge when, precisely, the bowler begins his delivery. This, therefore, should be a decision for the third umpire to take when he has seen the full replay and is in a position to make this judgement. Buttler, by the way, has previous in this respect, for he was run out in the same way in a one-day international at Edgbaston against Sri Lanka in 2014. With Buttler it is an excess of enthusiasm rather than a deliberate attempt to steal an unfair advantage. He must watch himself.

A dismissal in this way is never going to meet with everyone's approval, but it is necessary to have it in the Law book in order to keep the batsman honest. It cannot be the job of the umpire to try and decide whether the batsman is trying to gain an unfair advantage or is merely being careless. It is the batsman's job not to cheat and not be careless either. I would like the necessity of the bowler warning the batsmen first brought back into the game and set down officially in the Laws. Then we will all know exactly where we are and dismissals of this sort would not leave the bad taste they currently do. The warning should be officially noted by the umpires, who would inform the scorer, and then it would be up to the players and no one would have cause for complaint.

M
THE MATCH REFEREE

The match referee is the disciplinarian who was brought into existence to ensure players at international level uphold the standards of the game. They have to watch every ball of a Test match or one-day international and make certain the game's code of conduct is adhered to. The umpires report to the match referee, who will then act if the umpires point their finger at something a player may have said or done, or the way in which he has behaved. The match referees are able to fine or suspend players and to deliver finger-wagging lectures to any wrongdoers.

Match referees are invariably former players, which is both a strength and a weakness. They know better than anyone what is likely to be going on out there in the middle. They are also, in a sense, poachers-turned-gamekeepers and naturally feel protective of their own. They probably believe that strong cautionary words will do the trick, but sadly one gets the feeling that players today are inclined to bow their heads and promise not to do it again, but as soon as they are out of the room, they shrug their shoulders and life goes on as before. To be effective, I think a match referee has to be prepared to make himself unpopular with the players and must look to have a higher profile than most match referees do at the moment. It is their duty to leave the players in no doubt as to what is expected of them and be willing, if controversy looks like breaking out, to be a target for some of the fire directed at the umpires. I get the impression that match referees are not strong enough or outspoken enough, with a tendency to shelter behind the umpires rather than to take the lead themselves. If match referees were tougher, I believe it would make the umpires' job easier.

There is a great need for match referees to be stricter than they often are, not only in what they say but also in the punishments they hand out. Cynical players don't worry much about penalties unless they really hurt. Although the idea of red cards should surely have no place in cricket, I believe the time has come for the match referee to be given the power to send a player off, either for a period of time or for the rest of the match. It would cause an outcry to start with, but once players realised that it was a serious threat, I believe behavioural standards would improve. In an age when rewards for winning continue to grow, no player will be regarded kindly by his peers if he is sent off, thereby reducing the team to ten men. However distasteful it may seem, I believe the threat of the red card would be a big deterrent, although there is one big *but*.

In the times in which we live, it seems that no opportunity is missed to accuse opponents and their supporters of racism and any other sort of ism. This makes a match referee's job infinitely harder and on these occasions politics immediately come into play, and as soon as they do, the match referee has been bypassed, for the issue, whatever it is, has then effectively been taken out of the hands of the officials at the game. This happened at The Oval in 2006 when England were playing Pakistan. Darrell Hair, the Australian umpire, did what he considered to be right and penalised the Pakistan side for ball-tampering and at once the situation became politicised, with the R-word being thrown around. Much the same happened in Adelaide in 1998–99 when Ross Emerson no-balled Muttiah Muralitharan for throwing when England were playing a one-day game against Sri Lanka. Rather than illustrate a need for firmer match referees – for by the time both incidents had happened it had passed beyond the reach of the match referee – these incidents serve only to throw a light on the way of the world today. These are just two examples of the minefield international cricket has become for the game's officials.

M

MCC AND LORD'S

The Marylebone Cricket Club (MCC) and Lord's Cricket Ground, which the club owns, are virtually synonymous and, for me, both names have always had a magnetic ring to them. For more than a hundred years, the MCC controlled cricket from Lord's which, with its magnificent Pavilion, is the game's holy temple. The Trinidadian writer C.L.R. James sort of puts his finger on it in *Beyond a Boundary*, maybe the best cricket book ever written. Writing about the Olympic Games, he says, 'Olympia was not a city. It was a combination of Canterbury Cathedral and Lord's situated in a remote part of Greece.' He is putting the Olympic Games, Canterbury Cathedral and Lord's Cricket Ground on more or less the same footing, and there can be no more distinguished description than that. It settles the argument –if there ever was one. There is, too, something more than faintly ecclesiastical about the Lord's Pavilion, which is the magnificent centrepiece of the most famous cricket ground of all. I know I am biased, but is there another sporting holy of holies to compare with it?

The MCC first made an impact on me in 1948 when I was eight. My father was a member and at some point in the early spring his bright red membership booklet would arrive on the breakfast table in a pretty important-looking envelope. He would open it, pull out the gleaming card, set it down on his pile of opened letters and move on to the next. I never felt this was respectful enough. I hoped he would run his hands over it, open it and have a quick glance through that year's fixture list, perhaps with a slight bow of the head. I once plucked up courage and asked if I could look at it. Reluctantly, he passed it to me and I still get the same slight feeling of awe when, more than seventy years later, my own membership card comes through the letter box and I hold the new card for the first time. Which, as I write, it has just done for the sixtieth time. I can remember feeling the same twinge of excitement from my initial sighting of that extraordinary red card as I did when I first walked through the Grace Gates at Lord's with my mother and father in 1948. The card and the Gates are for me in the same bracket.

That day, 26 June 1948, will always remain as my most incredible cricketing memory. In Australia's second innings, after Arthur Morris and Sid Barnes had given Australia a good start, Morris was out. I was sitting with my parents on a rug on the grass between the boundary rope and Q Stand, where we had our seats. Q Stand has now become the Allen Stand, in memory of former England captain G.O.B. 'Gubby' Allen, who ruled the game of cricket for so many years with an Edwardian panache and firmness of touch. Morris's departure was the moment we had all been waiting for. He was politely applauded up the Pavilion steps by a crowd anxious for what was now to come. My father made sure I was looking at the front of the Pavilion as an increasing crescendo of applause burst out. I can remember a green baggy cap bobbing up and down as its wearer came down the steps. My heart stood still. This was Don Bradman, whose cricketing fairy tale of high scores I had already eagerly devoured from newspapers, magazines and books, for even at the age of eight I was an avid cricket reader and knew that Bradman should really be on a pedestal. Then this small and rather elderly-looking (for me) man came out of the Pavilion gate and walked briskly to the middle.

I could see already he was going to brook no nonsense from the bowlers. We settled back on our rug to watch him hit the ball sharply and shimmy up and down between the wickets. One ball I shall never forget. Alec Coxon, a Yorkshireman and a fastish bowler, was playing what turned out to be his only Test match. With an energetic run-up, he bustled in and bowled one short of a length to Bradman, who swivelled and pulled the ball between midwicket and mid on. The outfield was fast and, wonderful to relate, it was coming straight towards us. Sadly, there were two or three people on the grass in front of us, but happily they had not attended fielding practice recently and they did not completely stop the ball, which trickled on a foot or two – and there it was, almost in front of me. Not knowing whether or not I really should, I turned to my mother who, seeing my dilemma, bless her, said, 'Go on.' I leant forward and actually touched the ball. My father, who may not have spotted the romance of the moment, almost brushed my hand off the ball before picking it up and underarming it back across the rope. I still think it was about the most exciting moment of my life. It is so sad that these days sitting on the grass is no longer an option. It was fun, it was intimate and you almost felt you were a part of the game.

This is not meant to be a history lesson, but Thomas Lord, inevitably a Yorkshireman, had three cricket grounds in rapid succession, all close to each other in north-west London. The present Lord's was up and running by 1815, a year which also saw the battle of Waterloo, and it became the headquarters of the Marylebone Cricket Club. Lord's and I have grown ever more closely associated, first as a spectator and then as a player, before I moved on to the commentary box.

I first played there in 1955 when, as a 15-year-old, I kept wicket for Eton against Harrow. It was an ignominious start too. In our second innings I was the third victim of a hat-trick, the grisly details of which are recounted elsewhere in this book. Things improved, though, and the following year, keeping wicket for the Public Schools against the Combined Services in their annual two-day game, I found myself going to the wicket much too early on the first day, when we were 71–6. We finally achieved 214, by which time I had managed to slog my way, against some pretty inaccurate leg-spin, to 104 not out. I reached a hundred when we were nine wickets down, and how could I ever forget the thrill of waving my bat to acknowledge what applause the modest crowd could muster. When I walked off at the end of the innings a few minutes later, the members in front of the Pavilion stood to me – an amazing honour and a moment which was over much too soon. As I walked through the door into the Pavilion, one elderly member shuffled up to me and said, 'That was the hundredth hundred I have seen as a member at Lord's.' It was one of the few times in my life I have found myself lost for a word. There was no easy answer to that one and I pushed on.

Three years later, in 1959, I managed to creep into a less than distinguished Cambridge University side. We played a three-day game against MCC at Lord's and for the second time in my life I was thrilled to be playing against Denis Compton, in what turned out to be one of his last first-class games. In our second innings, I managed to score my only first-class hundred, and when an uppity, edgy cut brought me to three figures the great man walked forward from slip and shook me by the hand. Life does not get much better than that.

Another powerful memory for me from Lord's came in 1963 when, sitting in the Warner Stand, I watched Ted Dexter make 70 magnificent runs against Frank Worrell's unbeatable West Indies side. In appalling light, against some of the fiercest fast bowling I have ever seen, from Wes Hall and Charlie Griffith, Dexter smote the ball to all parts of the ground in a breathtaking exhibition of strokeplay. I can still hear the crack the ball made as it left his bat that day. Little did I think then that, nine years later, I would actually be sitting in the radio commentary box which was just behind me as Dexter batted that day.

I made my first live broadcast for the BBC from Chelmsford over the Whitsun weekend in May 1972. Four days later, I received a letter asking me to join *Test Match Special* for two limited-over games England were playing against Australia, at Lord's and Edgbaston at the end of August. For the previous ten years I had been using the press box at the top of the Warner Stand to cover games at Lord's for various newspapers, but I had never penetrated the holy of holies, the television and radio commentary boxes at the Pavilion end of the stand that housed such luminaries as John Arlott, Brian Johnston, Richie Benaud, Jim Laker and the others. At just after ten o'clock on the morning of 26 August 1972, I tiptoed my way in. It was a nerve-wracking moment – actually it was the most terrifying moment of my life – pushing through the door into the inner sanctum of *Test Match Special* for the first time. There I was, apparently on level terms with Arlott and Johnston, Norman Yardley and Freddie Brown, Trevor Bailey and Jack Fingleton – and later in the day we were joined by the momentous figure of Jim Swanton when he came to do his close-of-play summary.

It was difficult to believe it was actually happening. The moment I shall never forget came when John Arlott handed over to me for my first ever spell of commentary. I am certain I have never been so nervous before or since. Somehow I struggled through the next twenty minutes. I am not sure, but I think my first summariser was Norman Yardley, the kindest of men, who would have made it as easy for me as he could. My great comfort was that it was Lord's and friendly territory. I knew the ground well and the names of all the different corners of it – much better than I knew the names of the players.

That day was the most surreal of my life. I think if it had been any other ground but Lord's, it would probably have been my last broadcast. As it was, I suppose those who mattered felt that I had shown just enough promise to take another chance with me. I am sure it was a close-run thing. I think it was Lord's that saved me. That was, incidentally, the only time I ever commentated from the old box in the Warner Stand, and the only time I ever commentated with Norman Yardley and Freddie Brown, both gems in their different ways. The next year we had moved to the west turret of the Pavilion, which became our happy home until the turn of the century, when we had to move to the new space-age and, dare I say it, rather uncomfortable Media Centre at the Nursery End.

The MCC's influence over the game has waned since then, as first the Test and County Cricket Board (TCCB) and then the England and Wales Cricket Board (ECB) took over the running of domestic cricket. But the MCC still own and preside over the Laws of the game. Cricket is a game which has always had 'Laws', as they were called when originally drawn up, rather than 'rules', a fine point about which devotees of the game are rightly passionate.

The distinction between the terms once caused a heated discussion in London's High Court which I was lucky enough to hear. England players Ian Botham and Allan Lamb, a trifle opportunistically perhaps, were suing Imran Khan for libel. The famous advocate George Carman was acting for Imran, and he was not a cricket fan. The intricacies of the game were a mystery to him, and when he was cross-examining the former umpire Don Oslear, a real stickler for tradition, there was a most entertaining clash. Oslear insisted on talking about the 'Laws' of the game, while Carman continually referred to them as the 'rules'. Each time, Oslear, clearly feeling that Lord's was about to crumble, corrected him with some emphasis. Carman, who got most things right, did not enjoy this experience but, to his great irritation, was unable to find a telling riposte. The judge, Mr Justice French, was if anything more confused and it all made for a delightfully jolly Gilbert and Sullivan sort of interlude.

The MCC not only ran the game in England, but for many years, before the TCCB took over in 1968, they selected the England sides which toured overseas. These England teams played as MCC in all but the Test matches, when they became England. Like all governing bodies, the MCC often came in for criticism. They were accused, not unreasonably, of failing to move with the times and being too traditional in their approach to modern life. For example, when they eventually decided to elect lady members, they were well into injury time. But over the years they have been most dutiful guardians of the game. They have been tested too and never more so than by the Packer revolution, which keeps cropping up in these pages. The MCC will, I hope, always be there to prevent the game falling off the cliff, and the club will remain as the worthy and competent guardian of the greatest cricket ground of all.

M

MENORCA CRICKET CLUB

Cricket keeps turning up in unlikely places. Great Britain ruled Menorca for more than seventy years, almost entirely in the eighteenth century; Nelson had a house there; and the island has one of the biggest natural harbours in the world – all three facts not being unconnected. It seems improbable, though, that local Spaniards on a day off from the bull ring would eagerly embrace cricket. Nor have they, yet the island possesses a beautiful cricket ground which is as much a part of village-green England as you could wish to see, and there is a thriving club to go with it. It is a happy coincidence that it is legitimately entitled the MCC.

Nearly thirty years ago, two great friends, Andrew Manners and David Sheffield, who live on the island, decided that it badly needed a cricket ground. The club had put up with a rather primitive set-up before these two found a collection of small fields, with those charming stone walls, near the village of Biniparrell in the south of the island. Bulldozers dealt with the walls before an army of volunteers helped pick up the stones that covered the whole area. Grass was laid down, an artificial pitch was put in place, a watering system was installed, flowers and trees were planted round the boundary and a pavilion was built, with a highly effective bar beside it. They were up and running.

Their season now runs from March to November as club sides from England queue up to get on the fixture list. For six weeks in midsummer the ground is let to the island's hotels, who organise their own competitions, which helps settle many of the club's bills. The ground is also used for a pop concert each year with at least five bands doing their stuff and this also keeps the bank manager smiling. The club is shrewdly run.

The Menorcan side is made up of bustling estate agents and British expats reluctant to leave their playful years behind them, as well as some visiting Brits. Sadly, the locals have not yet joined in, but they no longer scratch their heads in amazement, partly because of the profit motive and partly because they love to see foreigners enjoying their island, even if some of their heathen habits are inexplicable.

One of the island's most distinguished players, well into his seventies and only recently retired as a participant, once kept wicket for Canada, which not everyone has done, before coming to Menorca. Graham Byfield has owned a house on the island for years. He is famous as an artist and has published a number of books featuring cities such as Oxford and Cambridge, Amsterdam and Barcelona, and has just finished drawing Singapore. His books are illustrated with wonderful drawings of important buildings and other places which have caught his imagination and have helped to set the character and atmosphere of these cities. They are brilliantly done. It was Graham who set the height of this particular bar which has also been jumped over by another notable wicket-keeper batsman, Jack Russell, of Gloucestershire and England. Graham has been as much a part of Menorcan cricket as Andrew Manners or David Sheffield, although these days all three are confined to their deckchairs. The cricket is always jolly and never soporific.

The other MCC, based in the neighbourhood of Marylebone, has sent a side to this amazing ground and the Lord's Taverners have also made their presence felt. Not long before writing this piece, I dined on the island with a former president of the Taverners. The extraordinary Nicholas Parsons has been a regular visitor there for many years and when he flew in this time, at the age of 95, he was as sprightly and charming and delightful as ever. The evening when we all dined in a hitherto most agreeable restaurant, with Nicholas and his wife Annie and several others, he had to wait, not just a minute, but ninety of them for a glass of orange juice which was so elusive that, although much talked about, it never put in an appearance. Having waited all that time, Nicholas then delivered a resounding *coup de grâce*. 'This is the worst service I have had in the last ninety-five years,' he declared, thumping the table and smiling with telling emphasis. Happily, this is very much the exception and not the rule, which is just as well, as lovely Menorca is about to become a new home for Valeria and me.

M
KEITH MILLER

Keith Miller was pure Hollywood. He mixed glistening, movie-star good looks with a devil-may-care Australian zest for life, an outrageous charm and an astonishing ability as an all-round cricketer. During the Second World War he was mostly stationed in the east of England as a pilot in the Australian Air Force and he was as brave as they come. After the war, as a fast bowler, he joined forces with Ray Lindwall in one of the great fast bowling partnerships. As a batsman, he was a wonderful strokemaker who took on every bowler he faced, no matter how desperate the situation. He only knew how to attack and everything he did on the cricket field was indelibly stamped with fun.

His figures suggest that he was not quite a Garry Sobers or a Jacques Kallis, but in my book he was up there with both of them. In 55 Tests he made 2,958 runs with seven hundreds at an average of 36.97 and took 170 wickets at 22.97. These are certainly modest figures for someone who is so highly rated, but it is always invidious to compare players from different eras. Miller, who lost a good chunk of his career to the war, would have played in more Test matches than he did – some of them against weaker opposition – if he had been playing in the modern era. The instinct, the style, the attitude and the execution with bat or ball or in the field was irresistible. It was evident that he played the game for his own enjoyment, which was surely one of the reasons he fell out badly with his immediate post-war captain, the relentless Don Bradman. There was something metronomic about Bradman, both as a man and as a cricketer. Miller's flair would have excited him; his unpredictability and his attitude must have maddened him.

Richie Benaud, who played under Miller's captaincy for New South Wales, went on record saying that he was the best captain Australia never had. For a long time after his retirement, Bradman ran Australian cricket virtually single-handed and there was no one who would dare disagree with him. It was Bradman's dislike and distrust of Miller that prevented him from ever captaining his country and forced him to play his final years under one of Australia's worst captains, Ian Johnson. After the fourth Test in Australia's first ever tour of the West Indies, in 1954–55, Miller with some justification told Johnson that he couldn't captain a team of schoolboys. Australia had made 668 and the West Indies were 147–6 in reply after Miller had taken two wickets in an over. Johnson immediately took him off and Denis Atkinson (219) and Clairmonte Depeiaza (122) began their record seventh-wicket stand of 347. Miller made three hundreds in that series, which Australia won 3–0, and in the fifth Test his 109 came after he had taken 6–107 in the West Indies' first innings.

Miller, named appropriately after those two fearless aviators Keith and Ross Smith, who were halfway through the first ever flight from England to Australia when he was born, made his Sheffield Shield debut for Victoria at Adelaide in 1939. In South Australia's second innings he ran out Bradman – a fitting start to their stormy relationship – and in the return match in

Melbourne he hit his first hundred. The war came next and Miller, flying out of England, graduated from Beaufighters to Mosquitos and on one occasion was playing football within an hour of a nasty crash-landing after an engine had caught fire. His enthusiasm and energy knew no rules and in training he flew his plane down the straight at both Ascot and Goodwood, but his commanding officers were happy to make allowances. Once, returning from a raid in a Germany, he made a detour on the way home to catch a glimpse of Bonn, the birthplace of Beethoven, his favourite composer. Bradman would not have enjoyed that either.

He was back on the cricket field in 1945, scoring two hundreds in the 'Victory' Tests between England and Australia. It was at this point that he took up fast bowling, because the Australians were one short in that department. At the end of that summer, he made 185 for a Dominions XI against England at Lord's, scoring his last 124 runs in 90 minutes, hitting a six that crashed into the top turret of the Pavilion, which is still the nearest anyone has ever come to emulating Albert Trott's feat of hitting the ball over the present building, which he succeeded in doing off the Australian Monty Noble's bowling in July 1899.

When England toured Australia in 1946–47 he teamed up with Ray Lindwall, who was fast and steady, while Miller was also fast but more erratic, although at times the more dangerous of the two. It was on the tour of England in 1948 that Miller and Bradman again locked horns. The Australians played Essex at Southend and made 721 on the first day. It was murder and Miller, going in with the score 364–2, showed his displeasure at what was going on by allowing himself to be bowled playing no stroke at his first ball, from Trevor Bailey, and exclaiming as he left the crease, 'Thank God that's over.' Bradman's more solemn retort was, 'He'll learn.' I am not sure Bradman got that right.

When Miller took on the captaincy of New South Wales, he was a good deal more organised than some people expected. He was famous for saying, when New South Wales took the field and discovered they had twelve fielders, 'One of you eff off and the rest scatter.' They will have known where they had to go. The crowds loved Miller and his matinee-idol image as he walked back to bowl, tossing back his mane of black hair as he went. He was always cheerful and dashing, there was not a mean bone in his body and he played the game and lived life by his own rules. In a world which had just come through nearly six years of war, Miller was the antidote the public wanted. He was someone, too, who never forgot people who had befriended him, be they gatekeepers at cricket grounds, stewards at race-courses or waiters in his favourite restaurants. He was friends with everyone no matter what their station in life was. He was the perfect hero.

I was lucky enough to get to know him. We first met in 1959 when he played a one-off match for Nottinghamshire against Cambridge University. I opened the batting for Cambridge and faced him with the new ball. In the first over he bowled a quick leg-break which took everyone by surprise and produced a loud chuckle from the great man. He batted at number five and made a hundred thanks to me dropping him off a skyer at deep midwicket when he had made 65. Years later, I found the scorecard of that game and when I asked Keith to sign it for me, he scrawled across the top of the card 'Well dropped, Henry'. He brought with him to Trent Bridge for that game a former Miss Victoria, who sat beguilingly in the ladies' stand for three days and turned just about every head in the ground.

After he retired as a player in 1956, Miller came across to England each year until 1974 to write about the game for the *Daily Express*. He had caught the owner Lord Beaverbrook's eye as well. No one was better value in the press box, although he seldom turned up in time to see the first ball of the day. In later life, he was struck down by illness, but kept going as only Keith Miller would. Even in a wheelchair he was as cheerful and full of life as ever. In his old age, the MCC commissioned his portrait to be painted, which now hangs in the Pavilion at Lord's where two other Australians have their portraits: Fred Spofforth, the demon fast bowler, and Don Bradman, who might not have been pleased his old adversary was hanging in the same hallowed precincts. It gave Miller great pleasure that his picture was there and, in spite of all that old age had inflicted on him visually, it was still the unmistakable figure of cricket's greatest matinee idol.

In his last years, Paul Getty would fly Keith over to England for the summer and he was a most agreeable fixture at Getty's wonderful cricket ground at Wormsley. In 2003, when it was clear that we would be lucky to see him in England again, I arranged a lunch at an hotel in St James's in London. Keith and his second wife, Marie, joined Colin Ingleby-Mackenzie, another kindred spirit, Johnny Woodcock, the cricket correspondent of *The Times* who also lived the life, and me for a wonderful lunch where we spent nearly four hugely enjoyable hours walking this way and that down memory lane.

It was the last time I saw him and it was wonderful to hear the old wartime pilot say yet again that he could not abide the way modern cricketers complain of pressure. 'They don't know what pressure is. When you look in your rearview mirror and see two Messerschmitts, that's pressure.' Even the Don might have agreed with that.

M
MY FIRST COMMENTARY BOX

The *Test Match Special* (*TMS*) commentary box I joined in August 1972 was a very different place from the box I left in September 2017. The constantly rolling evolutionary process of life itself has affected *TMS* just as it has everything else. The pace and tenor of society is reflected inside the commentary box as it is out on the field, where events now take place in a style, at a speed and in a format that would have been unthinkable fifty years earlier.

At Lord's, on 26 August 1972, England played Australia in the second of three matches in the first ever official limited-over series. The *TMS* team was John Arlott, Brian Johnston, Christopher Martin-Jenkins (CMJ), Norman Yardley, Freddie Brown, Trevor Bailey, Jack Fingleton and Henry Blofeld. Jim Swanton came in at the end of the day for another of his close-of-play summaries and the scoring was done by the ever-immaculate hand of Bill Frindall, aka the Bearded Wonder. For me, it was rather like being asked to go out and face Trueman and Statham with the new ball, with Jeff Thomson and Dennis Lillee coming on as first and second change. Michael Tuke-Hastings was in the producer's chair, which he preferred to sit on in Broadcasting House rather than down the road at Lord's. I was thrown in at the deep end.

I do not think there is anything new to be said about John Arlott and Brian Johnston who, in their different ways, were both supreme broadcasters. What fun they were, although Arlott was more of a help in my early days as far as the ins and outs of commentating were concerned, for I think Brian felt that one should work it out for oneself. Of course, Brian's insatiable sense of humour set a wonderful tone for our box. Arlott's red-wine moments have become as much a part of the legend of *TMS* as Brian's leg-over moment and I hope they will never disappear as such.

That first limited-over match at Lord's was sadly the only time I ever shared the box with Norman Yardley and Freddie Brown, both of whom went out of their way to be as kind and as helpful as possible. Norman was charming in an understated way and, if he disagreed with you, he did so in apologetic terms. He was also a wine merchant in Bradford, although, sadly, I never explored his shop. Freddie Brown was unapologetically robust and forthright and, to me, the man I always thought he was, having closely followed the progress of his England side in Australia in 1950–51. No one could have fought harder or more heroically and enthusiastically for a lost cause, with that white cravat tied randomly round his neck. On *TMS*, he said it as it was.

Jack Fingleton was a pithy, irascible Australian with a splendid and resonant chip when things were going badly for Australia. He did not take defeat easily, but he was great fun to work with and he kept me on my toes all right. When I had first met him in Australia, at the WACA ground in Perth in 1968–69, he said with a healthy twang, 'Blofeld, why don't you take those marbles out of your mouth?' It was a statement, not a question.

I think Trevor Bailey tended to disapprove of young commentators and perhaps felt that he alone could find the true path to eternal enlightenment. You only had to spend a short time on air with him to see how he must have got on the nerves of the Australians, especially in that home series in 1953, when England won the last Test at The Oval and took hold of the Ashes for the first time since the Bodyline series in 1932–33. Trevor would have approved of Bodyline, even if he would never have admitted it.

I hardly knew CMJ in those days. He was a few years younger than me: tall, spare, light-haired, a little shy, with a permanently surprised look of wide-eyed innocence (looks can deceive). The most charmingly unpunctual man I have ever met, he was always scrupulously polite, if a trifle apprehensive that I was about to try and lead him down the paths he had been told to avoid. I think he felt I was a little too near original sin for comfort. He was always a wonderful commentator. Unlike some who, at times of uncertainty, have been able to make it up with conviction, you always knew when you listened to CMJ on air that he was telling you the truth in those lovely modulated tones. If I had one complaint about CMJ as a commentator – and I say this with confidence, knowing he had many about me – it was that he was seldom as funny on air as he was at the dinner table.

Unlike many of us in the box, CMJ was a carefully selective drinker who had a reluctant thirst. Alan Gibson could hardly have been more different in this respect. He was a truly brilliant commentator, in the Arlott class, but he was handicapped by an insatiable thirst and any attempt to quench it was like painting the Forth Bridge – get to one end and you had to start again at the other. It may appear that John Arlott was similarly afflicted, but there was one subtle difference: Arlott knew when to stop.

The only time Alan and I commentated together was in the limited-over match at Edgbaston that year. I think he also took a dim view of new, young commentators. Sadly, his commentary career ended soon after this, but later we became good friends when he wrote the most enchanting match reports on county cricket for *The Times*. These essays – for that is what they were – were really 'A Day at the Cricket' rather than dutiful reports. He would bring in all sorts of extraneous characters, to whom he gave brilliantly chosen nicknames. The only trouble with meeting Alan Gibson for a glass of beer during the lunch interval was that one seldom saw any more of the cricket until after tea. He was the dearest and most delightful man, and what a joy it was to have known him.

There is not much left to say about Jim Swanton either. He was a big man with a stately walk and a bearing which any significant member of the clergy would have envied. He was a passionate friend of cricket who made a point of upholding the highest standards of the game on and off the field. For many years the cricket correspondent of the *Daily Telegraph*, he was a commentator for the BBC before becoming perhaps the best close-of-play summariser they have ever had. He had a great knowledge of the game and a strong sense of himself. As a writer, he was always more than readable, if not quite a purveyor of cricketing prose in the Cardus/Woodcock/Atherton class.

Our scorer, the Bearded Wonder, was an extraordinary phenomenon. The two previous *TMS* scorers, Arthur Wrigley and Roy Webber, had both died during the 1960s and Bill Frindall, a national serviceman who had been demobbed a short time before, applied for the job. He went on to develop the new system of scoring his two predecessors had invented. Bill was very bright, with a great love for cricket and the statistics which are such an important part of the game. He was also blessed with the most exceptional copperplate handwriting. Anyone who has seen his scoreboards will know what extraordinary works of art they were.

Bill was very much his own man, with his own way of doing things, and he did not readily concede that there were other ways of achieving the same objective. He felt he ruled the roost and this was never more evident than when he arrived at the start of the day, a long time before anyone else. When setting up his stand in one corner of our box, he would spread himself in such a way that one sometimes felt one was jolly lucky to be allowed to squeeze in beside him and commentate. It was Brian Johnston who immortalised him when he began to call him the Bearded Wonder and created a larger-than-life scorer. Bill considered this new appellation to be a great accolade.

He was a mine of information and supplied us with all sorts of statistics, which at first he would write down on a piece of paper and hand to us. Then he persuaded Peter Baxter, our splendid producer, that it would be simpler if he was given his own microphone, so that he could join in whenever he felt he had a relevant statistic. After this, the statistics grew more and more frequent and occasionally, one has to say, they were not particularly relevant. Bill joined *TMS* in 1966 and when Arlott departed in 1980 he became the longest-standing member of the team – as he was always more than happy to remind us. He was a useful bowler himself, who played much cricket for charity.

M
MY LAST
COMMENTARY BOX

Forty-six summers later, I was the only man left from that first team, although Geoffrey Boycott was partly involved because we were commentating on his batting at Lord's in 1972. It was not only the occupants of the *TMS* box that had changed, for the game we were describing had been stood on its head in the intervening years.

Upheavals had come thick and fast. We began with the Packer revolution, which took limited-over cricket to new levels of significance with coloured clothing for the players, white balls, black sightscreens and everything else. Poor old Test cricket was left hanging on for dear life. Then, in the twenty-first century, Twenty20 (T20) burst on the scene, at first as a slightly scary firework and then, swiftly, as an all-consuming blaze. It was invented in England, but then, for culpable reasons, England lost control of it. India grabbed hold with both hands and unleashed it on the world as the Indian Premier League. T20 spread like wildfire and we lived in a brave new cricketing world.

I spent my last day in the *TMS* box commentating with Jonathan Agnew, Simon Mann, Fazeer Mohammed, whose lovely lilting voice comes from Trinidad, Ed Smith, Geoffrey Boycott, Phil Tufnell, Vic Marks and Alison Mitchell. The scoring was in the hands of Andrew Samson, who was by a distance the best ever at that demanding job, though a drunken spider would have envied his handwriting. Sitting behind us all, in his tenth year in the producer's chair, was the avuncular figure of Adam Mountford, who had taken over from Peter Baxter in 2007.

I often wonder if have met a nicer man than Jonathan Agnew, who was almost as big a pushover for Brian Johnston's repertoire of nicknames as I was myself. His words, even the harshest, have always a charm and often a smile around them. He tells it as it is and when you listen to him, his reliability jumps out at you. Aggers is a peacemaker who does not care for the rough and questionable incidents that occur from time to time both on the field and off it. Nonetheless, he will convey them faithfully, if with a slight reluctance. He is a brilliant and effortless interviewer who does his homework and seldom uses notes. Above all, he is a good listener who, time permitting, will always allow an interesting conversation to develop rather than doggedly work through a list of preordained questions.

He was, of course, a fine fast bowler both for Leicestershire and on three occasions for England. Some people cite Aggers as an example of how these days the commentary team is filled only by former Test cricketers. This is nonsense, because before he became the BBC cricket correspondent in 1991 he had done a lot of work for BBC Radio Leicester, where he had most successfully cut his teeth. He came to *TMS* because of his broadcasting ability, although obviously his cricketing prowess was a help. With Aggers at the helm, *TMS* will always be in an impregnable position, for no one will maintain standards more wholeheartedly or fight our corner harder.

Simon Mann is known affectionately as Grumpy by an ever-decreasing number of elderly BBC employees, for it was a nickname at the start of his BBC career. He began as a *TMS* commentator in Zimbabwe in 1996–97. He had to put up with my selfish behaviour on the last day of the first Test in Bulawayo when I went on by myself for well over an hour and, perhaps more surprisingly, we have been good friends ever since. This has been chronicled in the entry on Zimbabwe right at the end of the book. He is another immensely reliable commentator who does not often allow himself oratorical flourishes but gives you a precise and extremely good-natured account of what is going on. He is wonderfully accurate and has never been known to confuse the fielder at mid on with the fielder at third man. Grumps is versatile, for he can turn his hand to commentating on football and anything else that comes his way and he brings the same qualities to everything he wraps his tongue around.

I always feel that Ed Smith, a relative newcomer to *TMS* who was spirited away to become the chairman of the England selectors, should have been called His Elegance, for there is more than a hint of stateliness about his demeanour as well as his walk. He was a considerable batsman with Kent and Middlesex, and briefly for England. He has an unusual cricketing brain and was a splendid commentator, although he was ideally suited to have been his own summariser as well. His theories about the game and its intricacies were always fascinating, even if they occasionally prevented him from keeping us up to date with minor details such as the score. But then none of us give the score enough. Ed loves the beauty of the game and when describing, say, a scintillating late cut (not often seen these days), he would salivate in his sophisticated way. It was a pleasure to hand over to him after my final spell of commentary that day at Lord's. In his first year as a selector, he backed a number of hunches which came off, even if he was rocked onto his back foot by a resurgent West Indian pace attack in the Caribbean in 2018–19.

Cricket has never had a much more jack-in-the-box character than Phil Tufnell. As a player he was an outstanding bowler and more than just a bit of a naughty boy off the field. In the commentary box, he is a character transformed and has shown that he is probably the most natural broadcaster of us all. His knowledge of cricket goes without saying, his sense of timing is immaculate, his turn of phrase is alternately light, refreshing, pungent and pertinent, and he is a master of the pause, which can be so important – something other people, myself included, often fail to understand. Tuffers is always a bundle of fun in the box and I shall never forget the day when he failed to arrive at Lord's because one of his guests the night before had backed her massive four-wheel-drive through the wall into his living room. It could only have happened to Tuffers.

I go back further with Vic Marks than anyone else in the box on the day I left. Vic and I first joined forces for *TMS* in India in 1984–85, when he was a player, and he became the best summariser I ever worked with. As an off-spinner who could more than just bat, Vic played for England in six Test matches and 34 ODIs. It is interesting how, in the summariser's chair, occupants who have only played a handful of times for their country bring an entirely different perspective to the job compared with those who have played in perhaps a hundred Tests. They look at the game from the position of players who were clinging on for dear life in the hope of establishing a firm grip on things. They understand the fears and apprehensions of newcomers to a side better than their more distinguished colleagues and, in Vic's case, are able to get it across in a highly digestible form.

Of all the summarisers I worked with, Vic was the best at reading a game. During a day's cricket there are moments when the advantage between the two sides begins to change. Vic was brilliant at spotting these moments before anyone else. He always talked a lot of sense and even when England were sinking out of sight, there was never anything mournful about his tones. However gloomy the outlook, that irresistible and slightly cheeky chuckle was never far away. It is never anything but a complete pleasure to run into Victor Marks, in the box or out of it.

Geoffrey Boycott has never been a man beset by self-doubt. He is deeply convinced that whatever he says in the *TMS* box is the right solution, whatever the problem may be. It was the same when he batted: he never had a shadow of doubt that he was on the right course, even though his progress might not have pleased everyone. Undoubtedly he has lent *TMS* a sharper cutting edge. This can bring its own difficulties, for when a person believes that the only two courses of action are 'my way and the wrong way', it is not necessarily the best lead-in to fruitful and interesting conversation. But forthright views and a strict singleness of purpose, which in his case has sometimes seemed to mean self rather than team, has great merit in a world where people in important places are forever changing their mind. Geoffrey's views can never be discounted and much of the time are correct. The only problem I sometimes have with them is that, when expressed in such clinical fashion, they can take the romance out of the game, which I would like to think is an essential ingredient at any level. Geoffrey can make cricket seem slightly robotic, but he played in 108 Test matches and scored 8,114 runs with an average of 47.72. With those figures, you are fully entitled to all your views. In his own way, he was a wonderful opening batsman for England, just as, in his own way, he is an extremely important ingredient of *TMS*.

The first lady commentator to join our team was Donna Symmonds, now one of Barbados's leading lawyers, who made her first appearance when England were touring the West Indies in 1997–98. She then commentated on the World Cup in England in 1999 and was back with us the following year when the West Indies came to England. Her success in the legal field took her away from sports commentary, but happily she has recently returned to the box. Cricket is in her blood and she has a wonderful voice.

After the advent of Donna, it was simply a matter of time before another lady came to join us. She was another most accomplished broadcaster, Alison Mitchell, who came to *TMS* for the first time in 2007, having already made her name working across almost the full sporting spectrum, on radio and increasingly on television. Alison has a pleasant voice and a nice easy way of describing things. As a notable sportswoman at Wellingborough School, cricket had not been her main game, but she has worked diligently and hard to understand the many intricacies of the game. She soon became an established commentator in both England and Australia, where having an Australian mother was probably a bit of a help, and in 2014 she became the first lady commentator to join the celebrated ABC commentating team.

While Alison led the way for the distaff side in England, she found important allies in Ebony Rainford-Brent and Isa Guha, both of whom are playing increasingly important roles for *TMS*, and both appear on our television screens too. As former England international players, they know the game inside out, and while Ebony has a charmingly authoritative way of putting her point of view across, Isa's easy, relaxed style has also won her many friends. With her ongoing interest in the development of ladies' cricket with Surrey at The Oval, Ebony is filling an important administrative role too. These three have, between them, become a most valuable part of the changing face of *Test Match Special*.

N

REX NEAME

This is a name associated more with beer than cricket. Rex had a foot in both camps, for he was a member of the brewing family who owned Shepherd Neame in Kent, and at Harrow he was an extraordinary schoolboy cricketer. He bowled well-flighted off-breaks, batted more than efficiently in the middle order and, as captain, he was a shrewd tactician. He was also the most delightful of men, always cheerful, and he would take on anything.

I must declare my own hand. In 1955, Rex took the only hat-trick there has ever been in the Eton and Harrow match at Lord's and I was his third victim – an unknowing one, as I have described elsewhere. Eton won the match, which softened the blow, but it was all a rather surreal experience. On the second day, Eton needed quick runs so that we could leave ourselves time to bowl out Harrow in their second innings. We made a good start to the morning and then wickets began to fall and in the dressing room we were scrambling to get ready to bat. Edward Lane-Fox was out and suddenly there was another scream and someone shouted to me, 'You're in, you're in.' I was in the back of the dressing room and snatched up my bat and gloves, shoved on my cap and set forth, not knowing quite what had happened. I passed an unusually po-faced Gus Wolfe Murray on the Pavilion steps and walked to the crease at the

Nursery End. I took guard, had a quick look round the field and settled over my bat.

Rex Neame, stocky and full of bounce, ran in from the Pavilion End and bowled, I think, round the wicket. The pitch was on the Tavern side of the square, with a short boundary. Conscious of our need for quick runs, I jumped out to this first ball and aimed my swing in the direction of the Tavern. I missed and heard behind me the ominous noise of the stumps being hit. I turned and saw my off stump was in a terrible state. As I trudged back to the Pavilion, I was confused. The ground had instantly erupted into frenzied cheering, which continued for most of what was an interminable journey. I knew it was not for me, but I could not think what had happened.

In the dressing room no one said very much – I don't think they even looked at me. I took off my pads, put on a blazer, tiptoed out of the Pavilion and walked round to the neighbouring Q Stand, now the Allen Stand, where my father and mother were sitting. When I arrived, my tall father uncoiled himself, looked round at me and said, 'You were a bloody fool to let him get a hat-trick!' That was the first I knew of it. If I had known, I hope I would have tried to play the hat-trick ball more circumspectly. For the record, I caught Rex behind the wicket in both innings. 'I never touched either,' he persisted throughout the rest of his life, but there's an Harrovian for you.

Despite everything, Rex and I became good friends and later we played quite a lot of club cricket together. He always managed to catch the eye of people who took touring sides to South Africa and similarly exciting places, where he would take some wickets and make a few runs, but he would only really hit mid-season form after the close of play, for he loved a party

– and he was not the only one. I remember playing with him for the Arabs, the nomadic side Jim Swanton founded in the 1930s. Rex was short and stocky, while Jim was big in every way and towered over him. I can remember the two of them having heated discussions about Rex's field placings. Jim always had strong views about such things, and so did Rex. It made for a lively exchange and, because of their disparity in height, they made an excellent comic turn.

As a boy, Rex was a remarkable all-round games player. He was principally an off-spinner and was in the Harrow XI for four years and captain in the last two, 1954 and 1955. He later played four games for Kent and a total of ten first-class matches, but he did not have great success at this level. If he had looked more the part, the family brewery of Shepherd Neame would undoubtedly have been prepared to give him the time off to play for Kent, but I am not sure that, being more in the mould of an old-fashioned amateur, he really took to the rigours and discipline of the first class game. As it was, he was a good club cricketer and was much in demand. He was also someone who enjoyed both his cricket and the life surrounding it.

Nothing gave him more pleasure than when his son, Jasper, won a place in the Harrow side as a leg-spinner. Rex was always excellent company and, as far as I was concerned, the greatest of friends. It was desperately sad that he should have perished at the relatively young age of 72. I only wish that the photograph of that hat-trick ball had not been so prominently displayed whenever I went to his house.

N

THE NIGHTWATCHMAN

The nightwatchman is a lower-order batsman promoted, at the end of a day, to protect a recognised batsman from having to play out the last few minutes, perhaps in bad light. If a wicket falls with, say, fifteen minutes of the day left and there are still some specialist batsmen to come, a tailender with a reasonable defensive technique may be sent in so that they remain for the next day. In recent years, this job has been done for England by Jimmy Anderson.

This is not a process favoured by all captains. For example, Steve Waugh, after captaining Australia for a year or two, decided it was not the way to go. Why not? Well, if a nightwatchman manages to get out before the close of play, as sometimes happens, it means that one of the specialist batsmen will be forced to take his place. On the other hand, if he survives until the close of play, the likelihood is that he will soon get out the next morning, handing the fielding side a useful early psychological advantage.

On six occasions in Test matches the nightwatchman has not only hung on the next morning but has gone on to make a hundred. The most remarkable example of this came when Australia were playing Bangladesh in Chittagong in 2006. Jason Gillespie came in to bat when Matthew Hayden was out just before the end of the first day's play in the second Test, with the score 67–1. Gillespie proceeded to bat for 574 minutes, facing 425 balls and hitting 26 fours and two sixes in his innings of 201 not out. He put on 320 for the fourth wicket with Michael Hussey, and Australia won by an innings and 80 runs. He has been giving Australian batsmen tips about how to play a long innings ever since.

Mark Boucher, the South African wicketkeeper, scored two separate hundreds after he had come in as a nightwatchman, although he was really a capable lower-middle-order batsman. He made both hundreds in 1999, against Zimbabwe and England. Another notable nightwatchman, who made 105 against India in 1977, was West Australian Tony Mann. His father, Jack Mann, was the chief winemaker at the Houghton vineyard in the Swan Valley and he won many awards for his renowned Houghton White Burgundy, a wine much enjoyed by his nightwatchman son.

The nearest an English nightwatchman has come to making a hundred was Alex Tudor, against New Zealand at Edgbaston in 1999. He was most unlucky because his partner Graham Thorpe's arithmetic was all over the place and he hit the winning four when Tudor had reached 99. I remember Tudor's innings extremely well because that was my first Test match back in the commentary box after a more-than-tricky heart-bypass operation earlier in the year. It was an appointment I came close to missing.

N

NO-BALL

The no-ball law added a splendid moment of drama and excitement to the game – until it was changed in 1963. The no-ball law is there to prevent the bowler gaining an unfair advantage and bowling from less than the official twenty-two yards. The change was that the no-ball would now be judged from the position of the bowler's front foot rather than the back foot.

A batsman cannot be out to a no-ball and therefore it allows him a free hit. Before 1963, when the position of the back foot was all important, the batsman heard the umpire's yell of 'no-ball' as the ball left the bowler's hand and therefore had time to change his stroke and to try and slog the ball for six. Now that the no-ball is called on the position of the front foot, the batsman cannot hear the umpire's call until the ball is well on its way. This does not give him enough time to change his stroke, unless it is a no-ball bowled by a spinner, a much less frequent occurrence.

The law was changed in order to try and eliminate 'draggers'. They were bowlers who brought their foot down behind the return crease but then dragged the toe and did not let go of the ball until the toe was some way over the bowling crease, and just occasionally the batting crease as well. They were bowling, therefore, from a distance which was in some cases much shorter than the official twenty-two yards.

This change has sadly taken some of the fun out of the no-ball. One moment of excitement it does produce is when a batsman is bowled or caught off a no-ball and is, of course, not out. It is frustrating for one side and exhilarating for the other.

There are a number of other reasons for the umpires to call a no-ball, such as breaking the regulations concerning field placing. Those calls tend not to lead to excitement but instead merely puzzle spectators as to why they have been made. Another more sinister reason for the call of no-ball – and by the square-leg umpire too – is when he considers that the bowler is not bowling but throwing, and also when a short ball goes over the batsman's shoulder.

I was present on two occasions when bowlers were called from square leg and both were highly charged. In 1960 at Lord's, Geoff Griffin, the South African fast bowler with a most suspicious-looking action, was called eleven times for throwing during a Test match in which he took a legitimate hat-trick. The game ended early on the fourth day and the two teams then played an exhibition match to entertain a big crowd. When England batted, Griffin came on to bowl at the Pavilion End. Syd Buller, a most experienced umpire, was standing at square leg. He now relentlessly no-balled every ball Griffin delivered, and to finish the over he had to bowl underarm. This ended Griffin's Test career. It was a public and embarrassing execution and it would not have been allowed to happen on the field like that today. After three more seasons of first-class cricket in South Africa, Griffin retired to run a hostelry which he named 'The Bent Arm Inn'– there was nothing wrong with his sense of humour.

The other occasion was many years later, in 1998–99, when England were playing Sri Lanka in an ODI in Adelaide. With his extraordinary action, off-spinner Muttiah Muralitharan, who took an incredible 800 Test wickets, was perhaps the most controversial bowler of all time, and it was claimed by many throughout his career that he threw the ball. Muralitharan was born with a bent right arm and also had a double-jointed right wrist. His action was going to look pretty strange in any event, but it was difficult to dispute that it did look as if there was a kink in his arm at the point of delivery. There were furious debates as to his legality, but shortly before this 1998–99 series in Australia, cricket's governing body, the ICC, had pronounced that his action was legitimate. At the Adelaide Oval, Ross Emerson, a fearless umpire and no stranger to controversy, called Muralitharan from square leg in his second over. The Sri Lankans, led by their captain, Arjuna Ranatunga, left the field and suddenly Adelaide became embroiled in a most unpleasant confrontation. Ranatunga was furious because of the ICC's recent decision about Muralitharan's action. Rumours were also circulating that this was a premeditated decision by Emerson, who had waited until Muralitharan's tenth ball before making his call from square leg. Ranatunga's immediate demand was that the game should be called off, and it was only after telephone calls had been made from the ground to the Sri Lankan authorities in Colombo that play continued. I cannot remember a much nastier atmosphere in a cricket match when play did restart.

Emerson had called Muralitharan for throwing in Brisbane three years earlier, and as this was the first time he had umpired Murali since, he would have said he was simply confirming his previous decision. At Brisbane, Emerson had called him seven times. At least Emerson was true to himself when he called Murali three years later in Adelaide, although one can only wonder why he waited until his tenth ball. Murali had also been called for throwing by Darrell Hair in the Boxing Day Test in Melbourne in 1995. It is impossible not to feel that Emerson and Hair, both umpires who enjoyed controversy, may have been deliberately drawing attention to themselves. After the Griffin incident years before at Lord's, it was extraordinary that umpires were allowed to make these public executions. A quiet word in the pavilion would have been the more satisfactory answer.

I would like to add a small personal snippet to the Muralitharan saga. There was about a week between the Perth and Adelaide Test matches on that 1998–99 tour. I had been asked by the former Australian wicketkeeper Barry Jarman, who lived in Adelaide and was now a respected match referee, to spend a couple of nights on his houseboat on the Murray River. He and I had become good friends when he was the referee in a series in the West Indies. The third member of the crew was another match referee, John Reid, a former New Zealand captain. He came to the Murray River with his wife, Norli. It was early on in our voyage that Muralitharan cropped up in conversation. Barry had brought onto the boat a handful of videos of Murali's action. On both nights the three of us stayed up until the early hours watching these videos and the slow-motion replays. John was lucky that Norli was reading a good book.

When we began that journey, Barry Jarman was certain Murali threw, while John Reid did not think so. After two nights of intensive watching, none of us was able to say definitely that Murali threw. At the moment of delivery, it was difficult to be sure that the elbow was bent more than it was anyway.

It is worth saying, too, that no more charming, delightful and amusing character has ever laced up his cricket boots. I will reiterate again that I don't think it matters if spinners throw, because they are not going to injure a batsman. In any case, what Murali did to take as many as 800 Test wickets required spinning skill at the highest possible level, kink or no kink.

N

NURDLE

At first glimpse, 'nurdle' seems to be a word one should be careful about using, but it is harmless. It is a term used to describe a single and just occasionally a two, if the fielding positions allow it. A nurdle is essentially a nudge or a tickle which pushes the ball into a gap, enabling the batsmen to scamper a single.

Rotating the strike by the use of a nurdle or two is a good way of keeping the scoreboard moving and it also irritates the fielding side. It can be infuriating for a bowler who is trying to wage a subtle campaign against a particular batsman to find that a nurdle has produced a run which has taken him down to the other end, and the bowler has to start his campaign all over again.

In all the years I spent in the *TMS* commentary box, none of my colleagues enjoyed a nurdle more than Graeme 'Foxy' Fowler, the former Lancashire, Durham and England opener, who was such a good summariser as well as being a fine left-handed batsman. We had several interesting discussions about what constituted a nurdle and how to differentiate between a nurdle and a steer, and the other way round. Yes, it was deep technical stuff, and Foxy used to get quite excited about a really well-executed nurdle.

O
OBSTRUCTING THE FIELD

'Obstructing the field' is cricket's most complicated dismissal. It should be simple for umpires to decide whether or not a batsman has deliberately tried to prevent the fielding side from getting him out, but there are grey areas – in keeping with the game's character.

These days batsmen are surrounded by close fielders in a way which never happened at the time the Laws of cricket were first written. The batsman is allowed to protect his wicket if, once he has played the ball, it looks as if it may run back onto the stumps.

When there is the chance of a run-out, batsmen instinctively try to run down the line of the ball as it's thrown by the fielder at the stumps, in the hope the ball will hit the batsman and not the stumps. At what point does this become deliberate obstruction? It is not that simple.

It was in a one-day international against Australia at Lord's early in September 2015 that Ben Stokes was given out by Sri Lankan umpire Kumar Dharmasena for obstructing the field. Stokes was facing Mitchell Starc and had driven the ball back down the pitch. It bounced nicely for Starc and in one movement he threw the ball back at the stumps, with Stokes well out of his crease. While falling back into his crease, Stokes thrust out his left hand to parry the ball and may have prevented it hitting the stumps.

Stokes claimed that he did this because he thought the ball was going to hit him, but the replays show it was well wide of him. The Australians appealed for obstructing the field and, after looking many times at the replay, the third umpire, West Indian Joel Wilson, was happy that Stokes should be given out, and it is difficult to disagree with him.

I was on the air with *Test Match Special* at the time and we were all wondering what was going on when it suddenly occurred to me that the Australians must have appealed for obstructing the field. Stokes was visibly upset by the decision and it may well have been that what he did was an instinctive reaction, thinking the ball was coming straight at him. He may have been sure there was nothing deliberate about his reaction, but the more I looked at it, the more it looked as if the umpires had got it right.

It was a decision that caused much argument. In the end it comes down to a matter of interpretation, but I think the right answer was eventually arrived at without leaving a serious stain on Stokes's character. The trouble is the terminology: 'obstructing the field' implies deliberate malice.

It was a matter of opinion. What was it that triggered Stokes's instinct to make him stick out his left hand? We will never know, but the evidence strongly suggested that the action might have stopped him being run out. The dismissal of Stokes shows that giving someone out for obstructing the field is seldom an easy decision to make.

P

A PAIR (OF SPECTACLES)

Batsmen have nightmares about collecting a 'pair'. To be out for nought in both innings is bad enough, but to be out first ball in each innings and collect a 'king pair' is the nadir. For all that, it is more memorable to be out for a pair than for two low scores. A pair of spectacles makes for better conversation than scores of, say, three and one, and a king pair better still.

The most famous pair of all was made at The Oval in 1880 in the first Test to be played in England. W.G. Grace captained England and two of his brothers, Edward Mills and George Frederick, were also in the side. England batted first and while W.G. made 152, G.F., batting at number nine, was caught by Alexander Bannerman off William Moule for a duck. When England batted again, needing 57 to win, G.F. was promoted to open and this time perished when he was bowled by George Palmer for another duck. This happened on 8 September and the story became sadder still. That evening, G.F. drove in his carriage down to Hampshire and slept in damp sheets at an inn. He contracted pneumonia and died in Basingstoke on 22 September. It was not a happy last two weeks for poor old G.F.

Leading the field in Test cricket is the New Zealand fast bowler Chris Martin, who collected no fewer than seven pairs in his 71 Tests. He holds the distinction of scoring fewer runs, 123, than the number of wickets he took, 233, and he was also the only batsman in Test history to have been run out twice for nought without facing a ball.

Another famous pair is the one collected by Graham Gooch in his first Test, against Australia at Edgbaston in 1975. He went on to score 8,900 Test runs. The unluckiest batsman after G.F. Grace was Gavin Hamilton of Yorkshire, who played in one Test match, against South Africa at the Wanderers in Johannesburg in 1999, and was out for a duck in each innings and never played in another Test! I was in the commentary box during that match and described one of his ducks. What a wretched chain to have round your neck for the rest of your life, but I am sure those two innings made a good story for his after-dinner speeches.

King pairs, when a batsman is out first ball in each innings, are obviously much rarer. In Test cricket, there have been twenty-one instances of this happening. The most notable sufferers have probably been Dave Richardson, the South African wicketkeeper and for seventeen years first the general manager (cricket) and then, from 2012 to 2019, the chief executive of the ICC; Adam Gilchrist, Australia's wicketkeeper, who features elsewhere in this book; and Virender Sehwag, India's dynamic opening batsman.

As a personal footnote, I feel I must mention the day when I played in a junior colts match at Norfolk's lovely old ground at Lakenham in the early 1950s. The pitch was mown in the outfield and after I had succumbed in both innings without scoring and my side had lost easily, it was decided that we should be given a third innings. Soon afterwards I collected my third duck of the day – a pair and a half of spectacles.

P

MISS PATERSON

Miss Paterson was where it all began. In May 1947, when I was seven and a half, I went away to boarding school at Sunningdale. There, on the remote third-form ground perched perilously between the railway line and the raspberry cages, under the guidance of the redoubtable Miss Paterson, I took my first tentative steps as a cricketer. I had been told I would have to play cricket at Sunningdale. I was looking forward to it. A puny number-six bat, which looked more than anything like a piece of kindling for a log fire, had been tucked into my luggage.

The pitch was small, the stumps did not have bails, we wore shorts and did not have pads or gloves, and we played with a small-sized cricket ball, which I promise was as hard as a big one. I was not much good, but obviously some sort of seed had been planted and the process of watering it now made a gentle start. The following summer I was promoted in the second-form game – and, more significantly, on 26 June 1948, I found myself sitting with my parents on the grass behind the boundary rope in front of Q Stand at Lord's, watching the third day's play in the second Test against Australia. I cannot believe I would have been there if the game had not well and truly grabbed me. Miss Paterson already had something to answer for.

She could never have been anything else but a school-mistress. She had dark, inquisitive eyes which often seemed to reach into places others never discovered. She was robust, with a firm Suffolk brow, a sturdy nose and a set of front teeth which required a quick second look. Further down, she wore sensible stockings and even more sensible shoes. When she wrote on the blackboard, she formed her small Rs with an unusual loop at the top, just as Harrods write theirs. They were known as 'Patey Rs' and for some strange reason they raised strong feelings among us inmates.

I remember Miss Paterson as being a great enthusiast who was quick to encourage, whether presiding over the second-form or the third game. She was a good teacher, but if you stepped out of line, it was at your peril. She was tough but she had a sense of humour, albeit on her own terms, and she applauded if you hit the ball to the boundary – even if it was off her own sharp underarm bowling off a seven-pace run-up. No boy at Sunningdale who came under her jurisdiction will have forgotten her. I will never forget her because she was the first to show me the ways of cricket. I will never forget her front teeth either, for they seemed to have been designed to enable her to eat corn-on-the-cob through a Venetian blind.

P

KEVIN PIETERSEN

Even if it came along a year or two earlier, the Kevin Pietersen question was England cricket's own equivalent of Brexit. Pietersen, arguably the best batsman in the world, was a mercenary who came to England determined to play Test cricket and to earn as much money as he could from the game, no matter what. He had not been a popular figure within South African cricket; he then lived an uneasy life in the county dressing rooms of Nottinghamshire, Hampshire and Surrey, to say nothing of England.

I, and anyone else who saw them, will never forget three of his amazing innings. In 2005, with Australia making the running all along and England needing a draw in the final Test at The Oval to win the Ashes for the first time for almost twenty years, he made 158 and we got that draw. When South Africa came to England in 2012, maybe Pietersen had a point to prove – and he did so by making an astonishing 149 at Headingley. During that innings he passed 7,000 runs in Test cricket, reaching that landmark quicker than anyone else had done before him.

During that same match, he sent messages from the England dressing room to the South African dressing room telling their bowlers the best way to dismiss Andrew Strauss, his captain, among several other things. This became public news and he was dropped for the next Test at Lord's. He then officially, and with startling insensitivity, publicly reasserted his desire to play for England in all forms of the game, having retired from one-day international cricket earlier in the year. There were no rule books for Pietersen. Alastair Cook, by now the captain, was anxious to see him reinstated in the England side and Pietersen went to India under Cook in 2012–13. It was in the second Test, in Mumbai, that he played the third astonishing innings, of 186, effectively destroying the Indian spinners in a match-winning stand of 206 with his captain. England won the series.

The following winter, 2013–14, England went to Australia. They lost the Ashes 5–0 in a tour of unusual bitterness, during which Pietersen appeared to disrupt the cricket management of Cook and Andy Flower, the coach. That was the end of Pietersen, who was then banned by England, and any hopes he may have had of getting a third chance disappeared when his ghosted autobiography appeared later that year. He was not friendly about all those who he felt had stood in his way. He reverted to becoming a limited-over mercenary and even then showed he would never learn from his mistakes. When he was based in Brisbane, playing in Australia's Big Bash, he spent his time pronouncing loudly that Brisbane was just about the worst place he had ever been to.

These two paragraphs tell us pretty well all we need to know of the man. He was a prodigious batsman, but he was someone with a colossal ego that invariably pointed him in the wrong direction.

As a postscript, I remember speaking to Pietersen once. The evening after he had made that 186 in Mumbai, he was sitting on a sofa by the swimming pool at the Taj Mahal Hotel when

I walked past him. I congratulated him on one of the finest innings I had ever watched. I also mentioned one extraordinary drive over mid off for six against Pragyan Ojha, the left-arm spinner. He managed a half-smile of acknowledgement, but did nothing to suggest he wanted to take the conversation any further. I have to say, though, I have never seen anyone hit a cricket ball as he did. If the rest of Pietersen's life had been as principled as his bat was when he drove that six over mid off, I dare say he would have broken just about every batting record there was. This was not only another example of why cricket can be such a true reflection of life, but also of why Kevin Pietersen was never likely to have anything more than a temporary foothold in the game. When I met him a few years later, he was playing for Piers Morgan's side in a village in deepest Sussex. He only scored a couple of runs, but he was charming in a rather remote and distant way.

P

THE PITCH

The condition of the strip of turf on which a game of cricket is played, the pitch, is immensely important. Over the years, the authorities have forever been trying to orchestrate its condition to make the game more entertaining and also to thwart the weather.

The ideal is a firm pitch which at the start of a match assists strokeplay at the same time as allowing bowlers to find pace and bounce. Then, as the game goes on and it becomes worn – I'm talking about a two-innings match played over three, four or five days – it will begin to help the spinners. But nowadays, by and large, pitches have become flat, boring and predictable. The main reason for this has been the sadly inevitable decision to cover all pitches from the elements. Spectators pay to watch cricket and so the elements need to be held at bay. Since the Laws were changed in 1979 and pitches have been completely covered, batsmen and bowlers no longer have to learn the technical skills needed to cope with drying pitches and the game is the poorer.

Batsmen are not the only ones to have suffered. Because of the covering, finger-spinners have effectively been turned into stock bowlers. They now toil away without ever being given the chance to bowl on a drying pitch, where occasionally they would be rewarded with the sort of figures that make life a little more endurable. This carrot has been withdrawn mainly in the interests of commercialism. Sponsors are naturally not happy if whole days are lost while the pitch dries after heavy rain. Grounds that have the necessary equipment also cover the outfield, so that a start can be made as soon as possible after rain. It makes sense to do everything one can to guarantee play, for this makes it more attractive to the paying public. It also means the corporate-hospitality facilities will be in greater use, but all this has come at quite a cost to the game itself. It has been robbed of some of its most intriguing aspects.

In the uncovered days, when a hot sun beat down on a wet surface it turned it into a 'sticky' on which bowlers would make the ball jump all over the place. Batting became almost impossible and only those with sound techniques could hope to survive for long. Bowlers also had to learn how to get the best out of such conditions. A sudden storm followed by sun would completely change the game and produce some extraordinary and dramatic cricket.

In 1928–29, in the third Test at Melbourne, Jack Hobbs and Herbert Sutcliffe opened the second innings for England on a surface which rain followed by a hot sun had made virtually unplayable. Not only did they cope, but they put on 105 for the first wicket using techniques which would be double Dutch to present-day batsmen. Thanks to them, England went on to score 332 to win the match by three wickets when no one thought they had much more than an outside chance of reaching 100.

Another of the more dramatic demonstrations of the joys and frustrations caused by a drying pitch happened in the first Test between Australia and England at Brisbane in 1950–51. Australia were bowled out for 228 on a good pitch on the first day and Freddie Brown's England side were rubbing their hands. During the night, the heavens opened as they can only in subtropical Brisbane. There was no play on the second day and on the third a start was not made until after lunch. Under a hot sun, 20 wickets then fell for 102 runs. First, England declared their first innings at 68–7, after which Australia declared their second at 32–7, leaving England to score 193 to win – and they lost by 70 runs. In England's second innings, Len Hutton was held back to number eight in the hope the pitch would have eased by the time he came in. It had not, and his 62 not out was an innings to rival those of Hobbs and Sutcliffe twenty-three years before. These extraordinary adventures no longer happen and the game is the worse for it, even if the coffers hold more money as a result.

There is another thing too. We now live in an age of drop-in pitches, which are helping to take another important and fascinating variable out of the game: the fact that all over the world, pitches in different countries naturally have their own characteristics which visiting batsmen and bowlers have to learn to cope with if they are going to be successful. Drop-in pitches were pioneered by Kerry Packer when he set up his own form of international cricket in 1977 in opposition to the traditional game. In Australia, where this revolution took place, Packer and his World Series Cricket were not allowed to use the traditional cricket grounds. As a result, other sporting venues requisitioned. To make sure these had pitches appropriate for the needs of the best players in the world, the pitches had to be artificially produced elsewhere and then dropped into the centre of these grounds. Now, they are increasingly being used in Test grounds and unfortunately the drop-in pitches do not replicate the innate characteristics of the natural pitches they have replaced. The WACA ground in Perth had probably the fastest and bounciest pitch in the world. A new ground just across the Swan River has now replaced the WACA and any chance it may have had of producing pitches with similar characteristics will have almost certainly disappeared with the decision to use drop-ins.

Sabina Park in Kingston, Jamaica, was another fast pitch, but this has slowed down considerably, not because of drop-in pitches but probably because of new and maybe inadequate methods of pitch preparation. Fast pitches need constant rolling and heavy rollers themselves are not found on anything like as many grounds as they once were. Motorised rollers do the job these days, while in the past the heavy rollers were pushed and pulled by platoons of ground staff, who have also disappeared in most places. I wonder if the motor rollers are either as heavy or as effective.

Pitches generally are more anodyne and characterless, and this trend is unlikely to change. Cricket needs all the money it can get and although the situation today is much better than it was, administrators obviously do not want Tests to end even earlier than a great many are already doing thanks to the influence of the limited-over game. Make the pitches more sporting and Tests would be ending in two days. The techniques needed for Test cricket are being sacrificed at the altar of the shorter, more instant form of the game. The poor old pitch may never have been left in peace, but, alas, no one in their right senses is going to urge a return to the 'bad' old days of the past, when pitches were uncovered and open to the elements. Nowadays, bowlers need to hope that incompetent groundsmen will come to their aid.

P

THE PRESS BOX

I joined the Fourth Estate with terrific enthusiasm in late May 1962 because it looked as if it might release me after two and a half years' bandage in the City of London. This passage to freedom had come about as a result of my first meeting with John Woodcock, the most able and distinguished of all the cricket correspondents of *The Times*. He held that office from 1954 to 1987. Wooders, as Brian Johnston had already dubbed him, was to become my greatest friend from all the many worlds I have inhabited and he remains so to this day. I know of no one shrewder, funnier or braver, for his life has been tormented by, among other things, a pair of extremely painful hips which are continually being replaced and have left him in constant pain. Nevertheless, he was often to be found walking with a dog, usually a beloved spaniel, at his side. No one gave better advice than Wooders, no one watched a day's cricket more carefully – he would invariably pick up points all his competitors missed – and no one enjoyed a party more than he did. I don't think it would have been possible to have had a better or more loyal friend.

In December 1975, we were both staying at the Weld Club in Perth while covering a remarkable Test match between Australia and the West Indies. At dinner on the second night of that game, we decided we would drive out to India for the

England tour which began the following November. Once planted, it was a seed which flourished and we soon persuaded three other intrepid souls to join us, one of whom wanted to drive us there in his glorious 1921 Silver Ghost Rolls-Royce. One of the others bought our back-up car, a gleaming new yellow Rover, and on 6 October 1976 we set off on the most remarkable and memorable journey of my life, which we completed in forty-six days.

The press box when I began in 1962 was very much an old-school affair. The leader of the pack was the *Daily Telegraph*'s Jim Swanton, whose booming voice meant cricket almost as much as John Arlott's exaggerated Hampshire tones. He was a terrific friend of the game, no one knew its history better, and in the 1930s he had founded his own nomadic cricket club, the Arabs, which still has an impressive cast of players and a good fixture list. In the press box, I soon realised that one had to tread delicately if Jim was there. Writing time began in the box around the tea interval, after which he discouraged conversation – and laughter too.

Another regular was Michael Melford, the son of the actor Austin Melford, who worked for the *Daily Telegraph* and the *Sunday Telegraph*. He spent much of his time studying the form book and there were few shrewder judges of a horse. Mellers (Brian Johnston again) was probably the only gambler I have ever met who consistently and profitably out-thought the bookmakers. He was the dearest of men and he understood cricket and rugby as well as he did horses. He was a writer with his own unmistakable way of making a point, but it was never done unkindly. He was also extremely drole, with a genius for producing quiet but telling and amusing one-liners.

John Clarke, a large, genial fellow, wrote for the London *Evening Standard*. When he wore his brown homburg, John looked more like Inspector Maigret than Rupert Davies managed to do while playing the inspector on television. John was a man of resolutely fixed habit who wrote easily about the game, even if some of its intricacies remained a mystery to him. His opposite number on the London *Evening News*, Lyn Wellings, was dynamite. He was a thin, wiry man who had bowled fast for Oxford University and briefly for Surrey. He not only loathed the cricketing establishment, but was deeply suspicious of them too and never wasted a chance to have a go at the authorities. Although he knew the game extremely well, he made a business of taking the alternative view. I always got on well with him, but you never knew when the next explosion was coming and there were occasions when someone or something would upset him and he would shout the roof off.

The doyens of the Sundays were Ian Peebles of the *Sunday Times* and Alan Ross, who wrote for *The Observer*. Peebles, a Scot, had bowled leg-breaks for England before the war when Don Bradman was at his most prolific. He was a charming man, with a huge twinkle in his eye and the sense of humour which should be, and often is, the natural prerogative of leg-spinners, who sometimes return figures which would make them suicidal if they were unable to laugh. Ian was a wine merchant, too, an occupation which is also probably helped by a sense of humour. I met Ian when I was at Eton, for his sister had married Claude Taylor, who was a master there and taught me so much about the mechanics of batting, as well as the actual beauty of the game which he loved more than anything. Ian Peebles would play for Claude when he brought his own team along to play Lower Sixpenny, the Under-15 side which was where all young cricketers hoped to make their mark when they arrived at Eton. His bowling was getting a bit creaky by then, but his good cheer and encouragement was unforgettable. His humour was never far away when he wrote and he was also a most interesting thinker about the game and a shrewd observer.

Alan Ross was an extraordinary character who wrote beautifully and his writings went far beyond the confines of cricket. For many years he was the editor of the *London Magazine*. A more than useful cricketer himself, he won a wartime Blue at Oxford University. Alan was a poet, too, and a considerable literary figure and he brought a formidable intellect to the task of describing cricket matches. He was always the most delightful of companions and in his younger days had been one of the set that used to be seen with Princess Margaret. For the record, Alan Ross was the man who actually wrote, when describing the batting, not the bowling, of New Zealander Bob Cunis, that 'his batting, like his name, was neither quite one thing nor the other'. Several others have claimed authorship, but Alan was the first to write these words, in *The Observer*.

Another wonderful character to grace the press box in those far-off days was Brian Chapman, who was the cricket correspondent of the *Daily Mirror*. Brian was a considerable journalist who had for a time edited the *Daily Express* in Manchester. He was the most able of writers and could turn his hand to any style of writing that was needed. He had a lovely turn of phrase. At that time the three principal writers for the popular press were Chapman, Charlie Bray, who had captained Essex and wrote for the *Daily Herald*, and Crawford White of the *Daily*

Express. All three were splendid characters and none of them teetotallers. Bray, as captain of Essex, had put Yorkshire in to bat at Leyton in 1932, only for Percy Holmes and Herbert Sutcliffe to put on 555 for the first wicket, the first-class record. As journalists these three hunted together. Bray would come up with the idea, White would do the legwork and Chapman, a superb journalist, would write them off the page in between mouthfuls of gin and Dubonnet.

Alex Bannister of the *Daily Mail* was another familiar face in the press box at that time, until he was surprisingly succeeded for a few years by the brilliant and charming Ian Wooldridge, who became a good personal friend. Another extraordinary performer was Clive Taylor, a delightful man who, like Chapman, had the genius of being able to turn it out for any newspaper in whatever style it required and who died distressingly young. There was Brian Scovell of the *Daily Sketch*, who is even older than me and whose cricketing life still goes on. The *Daily Mirror* was later looked after in some style by Ian Todd, who had been one of the press party on my first tour, to India in 1963–64. His great friend Chris Lander ('Crash') was also his chief adversary because Lander did duty on behalf of *The Sun*, the *Daily Mirror*'s greatest rival. Their partnership in opposition began when Ian Botham's memorable activities caught the attention of the red tops. As Lander was a great personal friend of Botham, he had what might be described as a foot in the door. Lander heroically accompanied Botham on a number of his extraordinary walks in aid of leukaemia. Both Lander and Todd were great fun and found it difficult to refuse a party.

John Etheridge, one of the longer-standing members of the present press box, now serves *The Sun* with distinction. Michael

Atherton has become a more than worthy successor to the position at *The Times* once held by John Woodcock, as were his two immediate predecessors, Alan Lee and Christopher Martin-Jenkins. Scyld Berry now reigns supreme at the *Daily Telegraph*, having taken over from Derek Pringle at the *Daily* after years of service with the *Sunday*. Berry has noble support from Nick Hoult, who spends much of his life arranging the thoughts of Geoffrey Boycott, Michael Vaughan and any other cricketing celebrity his papers may use. He does it brilliantly too.

When an England side goes on tour, part of the press box is as pleasantly full of familiar faces as ever, although for many years now I have been across the way in the commentary box.

Q
QUESTION TIME

Cricket is a game which lends itself to trick questions. I was once asked by John Woodcock, who was making a point about the cosmopolitan nature of the game, to name a Greek, a Chinaman and a one-eyed Norwegian who had played Test cricket. I was unable to come up with any of them and the question has haunted me ever since, even though I have now managed to find the answers. As the trio played 32 Test matches between them, I ought to have done better.

Ellis Achong, whose parents were fully fledged Chinese, was born in Trinidad and played six Test matches for the West Indies as an unorthodox left-arm spinner. It was Achong who first bowled the unorthodox left-arm spinner's googly which, because of its inventor, became known as the 'chinaman', or so one theory goes. The second was Xenophon Balaskas, who had Greek parents and was born in Kimberley in South Africa. He played nine Test matches as a leg-spinner between 1930 and 1939, and three of them with the third member of this unusual group, 'Buster' Nupen.

Nupen, the most interesting of the three, was born in Norway in 1902, and when he was only seven, he banged two hammers together and a metal splinter flew into his left eye, which had to be removed. He went on to play 17 times for South Africa as a fast off-spinner and captained South Africa in the first Test of the 1930–31 series against England, in Johannesburg. Nupen took 11 wickets on the matting in that match and led South Africa to a highly unexpected victory by 28 runs. After the match, Nupen paid tribute to the England captain, Percy Chapman, and said simply of his own performance, 'I am glad to have been of service to my side.'

Surprisingly, Nupen was considered such a poor bowler on turf that the South African authorities decided to persuade Hubert Deane to come out of retirement and captain the side for the next two Tests. The second Test was played in Cape Town on the first turf pitch to have been used for a Test match in South Africa. Nupen, still in the side, took only one wicket and was then strangely dropped for the third Test, when they were back on the matting. One can only wonder what the South African selectors were up to. H.B. 'Jock' Cameron captained South Africa in the fourth Test, on matting again, when Nupen was recalled and took nine wickets, but then he was dropped for the final match, when they again played on turf. (That was the match in which the start was delayed for twenty minutes because the bails were found to be too big.) It is extraordinary there should be such a difference between matting and turf that such a brilliant bowler on matting should not be worth his place on a turf pitch. I suppose it applied the other way round too.

Nupen is officially described as having been a fast-medium bowler, but there is a most interesting account of a conversation in a box at Lord's in 1959. 'Buster' Nupen introduced his son to Jack Hobbs, who said to him, 'Young man, you should know that your father was the most dangerous off-spin bowler the world has ever seen,' and a fellow sitting six feet away, with his elbow on his knee, said, 'I'll second that.' That fellow was Walter Hammond, who had been lbw to Nupen for 49 in the first innings of that first Test in 1930–31. Hammond had retaliated by bowling Nupen for one in the second innings.

Nupen and Balaskas played two Test matches together in this series and one against Australia five years later.

Q
A QUICK SINGLE

A quick single must never be confused with a short run. Quick singles are the result of enterprising and imaginative calling by the batsmen and are nothing like as hazardous as they often seem. It is important for batsmen to learn to judge when they can run between the wickets without any serious danger of being run out. A quick single is when the batsmen with good judgement go for a run which does not really seem to be there. With the wicketkeeper standing back, for example, a batsman may just drop the ball down in front of him and call for a run. The close fielders do not have to go far to pick up the ball, but if the striker's judgement is right and his partner is on his toes, the run is safe enough.

Quick singles are tactically important because they can upset the equilibrium of a fielding side. They also annoy both the bowler and his captain, and when players get upset funny things can happen. To try and stop these quick singles, the captain may bring his fielders in closer, opening up bigger gaps behind them which the batsmen can make good use of. Quick singles are a key part of a batsman's armoury and it is surprising how often players forget their importance, for they can be so disruptive for a fielding side.

Some batsmen are masters of quick singles. Graham Gooch was a fine example of this, realising they are such a good way of keeping the scoreboard moving, especially when the batsmen are being tied down by tight bowling. Also, by rotating strike in this way, a bowler is prevented from carrying out a plan of campaign against one particular batsman.

Then there are other batsmen who seem unable to learn what constitutes a single, let alone a quick single. It would be hard to imagine two batsmen further apart in character, approach and attitude of mind than Denis Compton and Geoffrey Boycott, but they had one thing in common: they were both appalling runners between the wickets. It was always said of Compton that his first call was nothing more than a basis for negotiation. Compton even managed to run out his brother, Leslie, in his benefit match for Middlesex at Lord's. Boycott had an overwhelming regard for his own safety rather than his partner's. If he felt *he* could safely reach the other end, that was good enough. On his return to Test cricket at Trent Bridge in 1977, after three years of self-imposed exile, Boycott succeeded in running out the local hero, Derek Randall, himself no mean judge of a quick single, in front of his home crowd. The difference between Compton and Boycott was that Compton was cheerfully unaware of what constituted a safe single and ran himself out at least as often as he ran out his partners.

There was a famous occasion in the second innings of the Test match in Christchurch in New Zealand in 1977–78 when it was felt in the dressing room that Boycott, the England captain, was batting far too slowly, ignoring the interests of his side. Ian Botham, on his first tour, was promoted and sent in at the fall of the second wicket with the specific instruction from the rest of the team and the management to run his captain out. It took him two balls.

R

RANJITSINHJI

Cricket has never known a more romantic figure than Kumar Shri Ranjitsinhji. Ranji played for England in 15 Test matches, all against Australia, between 1896 and 1902, and from 1907 to 1933 he was the Jam Sahib of Nawanagar. There is much intriguing mystery about Ranji, who came by his title in curious circumstances, learned to play cricket in England and seems to have been an early victim of racism, in addition to inventing the leg glance and giving a new meaning to extravagance. He also cut a remarkable figure, which seemed to incorporate a combination of wealth, style, make-believe and Machiavellian cunning. He looked like a cross between a maharajah and a conjuror – which, with a bat in his hand, he was. Of all the batsmen from an earlier era, Ranji is the one I would like to have seen more than any other.

Ranji was the son of a farmer, and his paternal grandfather, Jhalamsinhji, was a cousin of Vibhaji, the Jam Sahib of Nawanagar. Jhalamsinhji was reputed to have fought valiantly in a battle on behalf of the Jam Sahib, but there are those who felt that this was only a story that suited Ranji's version of events. Vibhaji then disinherited his own son for trying to poison him and he had to look to Ranji's branch of the family to find an heir. Ranji now came strongly into the picture, but Vibhaji never completed the formal adoption. Although Ranji was for a time the ruler elect, his hopes faded in 1882 when one of Vibhaji's ladies at court had a son, Jaswantsinhji, who succeeded him when he died, changing his name to Jassaji. However, he died suddenly in 1906 and it was thought in some quarters that Ranji had plotted his death.

In amongst all this, Ranji, who had been disinherited after Jassaji was born, went to live in Cambridge in 1888. He failed the entrance exam to Trinity, but was admitted to the college as a 'Youth of Position' the next year. He was also a youth of considerable extravagance and the money he was allowed by the state of Nawanagar was not nearly enough. Ranji had played a little cricket in India and spent the next three years learning the game in Cambridge before playing for the university in 1893. By now his expenditure was seriously exceeding his income and he was unable to stay at the university for the following season. He began to play for Sussex and after two good seasons he was selected for England to play Australia in the second Test, at Old Trafford, in 1896. Ranji had not been selected for the first Test, at Lord's, because Lord Harris, who was the *éminence grise* at the home of cricket, objected to him on grounds of race. At Old Trafford he made a painstaking 62 in the first innings and then a remarkable 154 not out in the second in a game which England lost. Over the next few years, Ranji's batting was extraordinary. He scored most of his runs on the leg side and many of them from his famous leg glance, and there was a wonderful Indian sheen to his batting.

His principal coach when he arrived at Cambridge was Dan Hayward, the brother of Tom Hayward, who scored many runs for both Surrey and England. In those days Ranji tended to pull away from a fast bowler, which was not a particularly safe manoeuvre. He would move his back leg across to the off and to prevent this, Hayward pegged his right boot to the ground. With the right leg anchored, he was still able to move his front leg across to the off side and this allowed him to flick the ball away behind his legs. Ranji learned to play this shot to great effect. Hayward had, therefore, inadvertently helped Ranji invent his most famous stroke. His other two most productive shots were a lovely wristy Indian late cut – a stroke which has almost disappeared, for it is nowadays considered too risky – and the off drive, which he learned later than the other two.

By the end of 1896, Ranji had had scored 2,780 runs, including ten hundreds, and was top of the English averages. Ranji's style of play was completely new and shocked some of the older players. With his lithe figure and his supple and wristy strokes, he displayed a form of batting which had never been seen before in England. While all this was happening, Ranji stayed firmly focused on India and Nawanagar. He had set his heart on becoming the Jam Sahib and nothing was going to get in his way. In the end, his cricketing fame proved a great help to his ambitions in Nawanagar, which is one of the reasons both sides of his life were so inextricably entwined. He realised how important it was to make the biggest possible impact on the cricket field.

In 1897 he scored another 1,940 runs and suffered that season from poor health, but was ready to take his place in Andrew Stoddart's side for the tour of Australia in 1897–98. He began the tour well before falling ill and, although he played in the first Test, he was not fully fit. Even so, he made 175, at that date the highest score for England in a Test match. He went on to be England's most prolific batsman on the tour, scoring well over a thousand runs, though Australia won the series 4–1. On the voyage home he jumped ship in Colombo and went back to India, where he stayed for nearly a year in order to ingratiate himself as much as he could with all those who would help him in his quest for Nawanagar. He returned to Sussex in March 1899 and became the first batsman to score more than 3,000 runs in an English season. This prodigious form continued the following year, when he also passed the 3,000 mark. He was still pursued by financial troubles and was not helped by the death of one friendly source of income in India.

He was not quite so consistent in 1901 and had a poor series against Australia in 1902 when he was fully occupied in fighting off bankruptcy. The 1902 series saw the end of his Test career after scoring 989 runs in 15 matches. He went on playing for Sussex in 1903 and scored almost 2,000 runs. The following year he just passed that figure and was top of the national batting averages, although this was the end of his career as a full-time cricketer. He came back to play intermittently for Sussex in 1908, by which time he had finally been installed as the Jam Sahib of Nawanagar. Six months after Jassaji's death in 1906, the British administrators had decided that Ranji was the man to succeed him. His popularity as a cricketer, and his consistent networking in India with the powers that be, had paid off handsomely. He continued to turn out occasionally for Sussex and even suggested himself to the England selectors for the triangular tournament in 1912, but they declined his offer.

During the 1914–18 war, Ranji lost an eye, but not in France, where he was stationed for much of the first year. Most ironically, it happened when he was on leave in England in 1915. He was hit in the right eye by a shotgun pellet on a grouse moor he rented in Yorkshire. In 1920, he played three more games for Sussex, but found that it was too difficult with only one eye. He was also well into his forties.

In all, Ranji scored 24,692 first-class runs with glorious Indian inconsequence and finesse and made 72 hundreds. These were amazing figures, but his happiness was complete when his title, even if somewhat unscrupulously acquired, was officially upgraded to that of Maharajah. He died in India of heart failure on 2 April 1933.

R

REVERSE SWEEP

If ever there was a heretical stroke, it is surely the reverse sweep. It began life as a devil-may-care excrescence and has passed through acceptance to respectability, even if it has not quite yet gained admittance into the Pavilion at Lord's, or indeed into the MCC coaching book. In English minds, the reverse sweep made a bad start when, as played by Mike Gatting in Kolkata, it cost England the 1987 World Cup.

We live in an age when many boundaries are being pushed back. To that extent, the reverse sweep is a logical extension to the way of cricket as we knew it. It is a stroke for which bowlers are unable to set a field and therefore it has a surprise value. It has its dangers, however, and can produce top edges and wickets. Gatting found this out to his and England's cost that day at Eden Gardens when he top-edged a sweep against Allan Border and was caught by the keeper, Greg Dyer, running to square leg.

The reverse sweep is an exciting stroke for spectators. It goes against the natural order of things and fielders look as perplexed as everyone else when they find a right-hander turning into a left-hander and the ball scurrying away to where it is least expected. It has become less heretical nowadays because batsmen have learned to play the stroke at so many different angles and out of the middle of the bat. Since those early days, much thought has gone into the shot and the current generation of batsmen play it with a control which at first seemed impossible.

It has almost reached the stage where, if a batsman does not have the reverse sweep in his armoury, he is hardly qualified for one-day matches at the top level. Yet every time I see the reverse sweep played, I still cannot help but think, 'What ever next?'

R

JOE ROOT

Joe Root, like his predecessor as England captain, Alastair Cook, is an undemonstrative man. He emerged into first-class and then Test cricket more by a process of osmosis than with a Ben Stokes-like explosion. His class, composure and unusual talent crept up on us all and by the time he arrived in the England side, it was the logical end to an inevitable journey. Once there, he was quick to establish himself in his beautifully elegant but slightly fragile manner, both as a man and a batsman. It is a fragility that comes from his mildly schoolboyish appearance rather than from any weaknesses at the crease or in the dressing room. There are not many players I have enjoyed watching or commentating on in recent years more than Joe Root. I have never seen anyone hit a cricket ball more sweetly and few are blessed with such an easy and compelling classical style. There is something about his batting and his footwork that makes me think of Torvill and Dean on the skating rink. He seems almost certain to go past Peter May, more a showjumper than a skater, and end up as the best batsman England has produced since the war.

Root's first Test match was the final game in India on the 2012–13 tour and on returning to England he quickly established himself in the side. He made two useful scores against New Zealand at Lord's and then posted his first hundred in the

Test at Headingley. The Ashes were contested in the second half of the summer and after three small scores as Alastair Cook's opening partner, Root played a glorious innings of 180 in the second innings of the Lord's Test. The Root family almost took over that match, for his brother, Billy, who was playing for Yorkshire Second XI at the time, was one of England's reserve fielders. While Joe was batting, Billy took him out a glass of water and gave him a hug and later they were both on the field together again when Billy came on as substitute for Ian Bell. Not only that, but their charming parents were on hand to tour the broadcasting boxes.

There was little doubt that, as far as England were concerned, Joe was the chosen one and his route to the captaincy was secure. It soon became a surprise when he was out for a low score. He stood in the slip cordon alongside Cook and showed that he had a safe pair of hands. Young Joe Root, good-looking with a high forehead and fair wavy hair, was English cricket's blue-eyed boy and, with him in the side, the future looked in safe hands.

Root was never going to be more than a temporary opener, but there was some doubt over the best place for him in the batting order. Root himself has been determined to stay at four in Test cricket, but Trevor Bayliss, the England coach, would like to see him at three and there is always a strong argument that number three is the place for your best batsman. Interestingly, I write these words during the first Ashes Test in August 2019, when Root has gone in third, and with some success in the first innings. If he now adds runs regularly in that position, it may change his attitude. I am sure that this is the best place for him, especially at a time when England do not have an established opening pair and need at all costs to prevent one early wicket becoming two or even three.

In the early days, his looks belied his maturity and he emerged well from an unpleasant late-night incident in a Birmingham bar after a match in the Champions Trophy in 2013, a competition which was slotted in between the New Zealand and Australian series. He had been teased by his team-mates that he was too young to grow a beard and so put on a false one when, after a win, the team went to a neighbouring bar for a celebratory drink. For some reason, this upset Australia's somewhat pugilistic opening batsman, David Warner, who was in the same bar with the Australian side and had been drinking Jägerbombs. He tugged Root's false beard and then threw a punch which apparently glanced off Root's chin. Root's reactions were splendid, for he and the other England players promptly left the bar. Later, Andrew Gale, his Yorkshire captain, said, 'Joe couldn't fight his way out of a paper bag. He looks more like the Milky Bar Kid than Mike Tyson.' This incident made Root seem an even safer pair of hands.

Root also quickly became a regular member of England's one-day side and in this form of the game he was prepared to bat at number three. He was prolific in both forms of the game and in 2015 became England's vice-captain in an Ashes series England won 3–2. This was the final confirmation that Root would take over from Cook. With every match, Root was growing in maturity. His youthful looks may have given the impression that he was something of a greenhorn, but the added responsibility began to have an effect and his tally of runs continued to pile up.

Cook decided to pack in the captaincy after England's disastrous series in India in 2016–17, although he stayed on as a batsman. Root took over the captaincy and had the satisfaction of scoring 190 against South Africa at Lord's in his first Test match in charge. England beat both South Africa and the West Indies in 2017 and in my last summer before I retired from the box I had the joy of commentating on England's two victories at Lord's and Root's 190. I also had the questionable thrill of describing their huge defeat by South Africa at Trent Bridge. During the series against the West Indies, Root's fifty in the second Test brought him level with A.B. de Villiers's record of scoring a fifty in 12 successive Tests. The going became rather more difficult for Root after that when he took the side to Australia in 2017–18 and England fell in a heap, losing 4–0.

It is not always a good thing for an incoming captain to have the brooding presence of his immediate predecessor in the dressing room, although Cook will never have tried to interfere. Nonetheless, his very presence could have been slightly intimidating for Root, even though there was little he could have done to stem the tide in Australia. For all that, he unquestionably shot himself in the foot when he put Australia in to bat in the second Test in Adelaide. Was that a personal, last-minute decision made as he went out to toss, or was it a discussed decision? He did not have a good series with the bat and the pressure of the captaincy in a losing series probably had a lot to do with that. Root found out in no uncertain terms that Australia can be an unforgiving place for a losing captain. The early evidence showed that Root was not an adventurous captain who was prepared to take risks, even if it is not easy to take risks – Adelaide apart – when you are always coming from behind. Ian Chappell, a severe but shrewd judge, took criticism of Root's captaincy a stage further on Australia's Channel Nine, saying he was too defensive and was concerned more with defending runs than taking wickets.

A series in Australia is a tough proposition for an experienced captain and even though things went badly wrong, Trevor Bayliss, England's coach, said after the tour he was confident Root would improve as a captain. In 2018, Root was probably still a bit shell-shocked after the Ashes and he did not make another Test hundred until the last Test of that summer in England, against India at The Oval, having gone for three series without one. It was an emotional game for another reason too. Alastair Cook had finally decided to retire as a player and he made a triumphant hundred in his final Test innings.

In 2018–19 England won all three Tests in Sri Lanka, but then, surprised by the West Indies' fast attack, lost the series in the Caribbean 1–2. During the third Test at St Lucia, Root appeared to be abused by the fast bowler Shannon Gabriel and he was heard on the stump microphone to say to Gabriel in reply, 'There's nothing wrong with being gay.' This took the heat out of the situation, although the full exchange between the two players has never been revealed, and Root received much praise for the way in which he handled things. At the end of the match the two players shook hands. It was an incident which revealed Root's maturity and his ability to control himself and defuse a potentially dangerous confrontation. These are important qualities for a captain. Root may still have plenty to prove tactically, but mercifully for England, he is a brilliant batsman, the most likeable of men and, like Cook, without hang-ups or ego problems or any other distractions to divert attention from the business of playing cricket and winning Test matches. I think the evidence so far demonstrates that he is learning fast and that before long he will be showing the world how the job should be done – assuming, of course, that his players are up to it.

As a batsman, one minor criticism can be levelled at him, but only because he is so good. Early in his career, he acquired the habit of getting himself out when he had made about 50, either through a lapse in concentration or perhaps, without realising it, after allowing T20 mode to take over. While scores of around 50 are a long way from failure, it is hundreds, and big hundreds at that, which are significant in Test cricket, for they win matches or prevent them from being lost. Root is already showing that he has begun to get a grip on this, as his recent form has shown, and I am sure this is a sign that he has become more comfortable and confident as a captain. With all the cricket that is played today, he is lucky not to have to captain England's one-day side and I am sure he will learn from Eoin Morgan's splendid example in that more hectic province of the game.

I met Joe for the first time at Lord's, on the day of my retirement, on 9 September 2017. After doing a completely unexpected lap of honour around Lord's at the end of the final Test match against the West Indies, I was standing amongst the crowd who had gathered in front of the Pavilion for the end-of-series prize-giving, talking to Michael Vaughan. Suddenly I noticed Joe Root in a group a few yards away and told Michael I had never met him. Michael asked him to come over, and after shaking hands he asked me if I would like to come up to the England dressing room for a glass of champagne and instructed Michael to bring me up. Soon afterwards, I found myself walking up the steps into the Pavilion beside an Ashes-winning captain. We went through the Long Room, up the stairs and into the England dressing room, where Joe and the rest of his team could not have been kinder. Joe made a friendly speech of welcome and presented me with an England shirt signed by all the players, a memento of which I am extremely proud. It was a wonderful occasion and no one could have been more friendly and charming than Joe himself. It was an amazing gesture from a man I had met only a few minutes before and it made me feel quite certain that England's captaincy is in the right hands.

R

THE RUNNER

There is no more potentially comic figure in cricket than the runner – and what important and delightfully humorous figures they sometimes used to be. I have to use the past tense because sadly, for me at any rate, the ICC abolished runners in international cricket in 2011, which probably means that in time they will completely disappear at all levels. If a batsman is injured, it is surely both logical and reasonable for him to have someone else in his side to come out and run for him. It is very much in accordance with the spirit of cricket, and often a runner would add an element of high good humour to a game where the authorities take both themselves and the game increasingly seriously – I think, to the game's detriment.

When, for example, a star batsman who was taking his side to victory was injured, a substitute runner would emerge from the pavilion fully kitted out and dressed for battle. His job now was to run the injured batsman's runs for him. If the injured man was facing the bowling, the runner would stand in front of the square-leg umpire. The non-striker then had to remember that he would be called for runs, not by his partner at the other end, but by the padded-up substitute at square leg. It often took a big leap in faith for him to take this on board.

When the batsman played a stroke and his runner at square leg sensed a single, the runner would shout 'yes' and start off.

The non-striker, perhaps bemused by the direction the call had come from, might now start off a fraction late. Then, when well into his run, he would look up and see the batsman who played the stroke standing still. This could cause momentary panic and the non-striker would slam on the brakes, only to realise a moment later that his new running partner was already safely ensconced behind him at the end he had just left, albeit somewhere out by square leg. He would start off again, but because of the hesitation he would be in danger of being run out. This hopeless situation could become even worse if the injured batsman suddenly took it upon himself to run as well. In this case, there might be three batsmen on the move simultaneously, all shouting their heads off in a rare and seldom satisfactory cacophony. It has even been known for all three batsmen to end up in the same crease – in fact, it has happened not all that infrequently!

Of course, the mix up I have described is an extreme example, but it does show how the game could degenerate into comical chaos when a runner joined the fray, and was none the worse for it. The truth usually was that when a batsman needed a runner, he was so affected by his injury that batting became much more difficult and he did not last for long. (I am still trying to find out the longest partnership ever made in first-class cricket between two batsmen when one had a runner, which is not a statistic I have ever come across.)

Runners were not always pure farce, because they did fulfil an important, if temporary, role in helping the injured man to score a few more runs. In county cricket, runners took their duties pretty seriously, even though it could end in comical disaster. At lower levels, runners become increasingly chaotic and greatly entertaining and I hope they will continue to be used. In the old days in good old village cricket in Norfolk, I remember runners could get themselves into terrible tangles and made the afternoon much more fun.

S

THE SCORER

There is something splendidly antiquated about the traditional scorer. The idea of two people sitting, pen or pencil in hand, chalking up each run and its relevant details, as well as acknowledging the signals of the umpires, somehow doesn't fit with the high technical age in which we live. Of course, computers, laptops and iPads have all gradually become involved, but that nineteenth-century painting of a corpulent bespectacled scorer sitting at his small, round table with his pen – it should have been a quill – still looms large. But, of course, scorers are crucially important, whether they do the job electronically or with a good old pencil or, in the earliest days, by cutting a notch into a stick. The scorers have always been the game's official account-keepers.

It is actually in the *Test Match Special* commentary box that scoring has been taken to new frontiers. A new method of collating the details was first put together by the then *TMS* scorer Arthur Wrigley, who had scored for Howard Marshall, the BBC's principal cricket commentator before the war. Wrigley was then called away by the Great Scorer in the sky and his inventions were inherited by Bill Frindall. With a ferocious and mildly noisy single-mindedness, Bill tweaked and developed this new system. He published a number of books illustrating the system he had now put his own mark on, although Wrigley was perhaps the true inventor. The *TMS* method, thanks largely to Bill's books which eloquently spread the word, has been widely adopted, although there are probably many scorers at grassroots level who are still sitting in front of old-style scorebooks, pencil poised.

Scoring is not an easy job and even at the top level it causes tricky problems. The pace, the drama and the bustle of the one-day game has made the scorer's life even more complicated. I will never forget a 40-over John Player League match in 1984 between Northamptonshire and Kent at Tring. It was a match which Kent apparently won in an exciting finish.

The two official scorers were both delightful and elderly former county cricketers I knew well. The Northamptonshire scorer was Jack Mercer, who before the Second World War had bowled successfully and most economically with the seam for Sussex and then Glamorgan. Jack was also, rather improbably, a member of the Magic Circle and was not far from being stone deaf. He would have found it much easier that afternoon to produce a rabbit out of a hat than to come up with the correct score. His Kent counterpart was Claude Lewis, who had bowled left-arm orthodox spin for Kent. He had a quiet voice and therefore faced quite a job to make Jack aware of what he was saying. Claude had a charmingly laissez-faire approach to scoring and at moments of potential disagreement would throw up his hands, look at his partner and, with a shrug of the shoulders, say, 'Anything you say, mate,' which was no great help to accuracy.

For this match, the two scorers were sitting on their own at a rickety wooden table some way from the pavilion and, more pertinently, the scoreboard. They were old friends and, in spite of Jack's deafness, they happily reminisced in between scoring for most of the afternoon, but in the final few overs, a little anxiety crept in. They had both lost their way and looked feverishly at the umpires, the scoreboard and each other before collectively shaking their heads. When the last ball had been bowled, neither of them was sure who had won or by how much, but after much frantic adding-up, they agreed to tell the same story. Kent were named as the official winners by three runs. Most people agreed with the result, but there remains much discussion about the margin of victory.

S

SHORT RUN

The uninitiated may think a 'short run' is a crafty way of stealing a run without running the full length of the pitch. No such luck. A short run is something to be avoided because it is not allowed to count. If either umpire signals a short run, it means that one run will be deducted from the score.

A single run is when the batsmen complete one run as they run from one end of the wicket to the other. To complete the run, both batsmen have to cross the popping or batting creases, which are nineteen yards and one foot apart. When they run more than one run after the striker has played a stroke, they have to touch their bats down behind the batting crease at each end before coming back for the next run. They keep repeating this process if they want to run a third, a fourth or a fifth run.

The umpires will be watching closely as they touch their bats down behind the batting crease. If the bat is short of the white line of the crease or lands on the white line itself without crossing it, it is considered a 'short run'. The umpire makes the appropriate signal to the scorers and if, for example, the batsmen have completed three runs, one will be deducted. Similarly, if two runs have been completed, the striker will only be credited with a single. It is pure clumsiness on the part of the batsman concerned.

The most interesting short single I ever encountered came in a village match soon after the Second World War. Hoveton and Wroxham were playing neighbouring Coltishall and the vicar of Coltishall, who had won a Victoria Cross in the First World War, was one of the umpires. Hoveton and Wroxham were batting and the batsman played the ball on the leg side and he and his partner ran a single. Both batsmen clearly completed the single and were waiting by the stumps at each end of the pitch. The vicar was standing at square leg and he now proceeded to put the fingers of his right hand onto his shoulder and shout 'One short run!' to the scorers. Everyone looked rather surprised, but the vicar had no doubts and no one had the nerve to ask him what he meant. Maybe it was simply another instance of God 'moving in a mysterious way his wonders to perform'. I was told the scorers made the arbitrary decision not to deduct a single from the total.

S
SIGHTSCREENS

In recent times, sightscreens have generally grown larger, which in a splendidly obtuse way has made them less intrusive. In the old days, when they were smaller, if a bowler decided to change his line of attack from, say, over to round the wicket, the batsmen would wave majestically into the distance. Seeing the signal, the sightscreen attendant (if there was one), members of the fielding side or spectators would push the screen across until it was once again behind the bowler's arm. This process often produced moments of high humour. Sometimes the sightscreen obstinately refused to move. Not infrequently the pushers would ignore the batsman's precise instructions and push it either too far or not enough, at which point the spectators would chip in with fruity vocal encouragement. I remember one occasion at a county match – I think it was at Northampton's Wantage Road ground – when a corpulent assistant lost his hold on the sightscreen and fell into a spectacular heap.

Sightscreens are extremely important. They enable the batsman to have an uninterrupted view of the bowler as he runs up and of the ball when it leaves the bowler's hand. If there is sudden movement behind the bowler's arm, the batsman is bound to be distracted. The sightscreen can be one of the most attractive parts of the paraphernalia of cricket. As you drive through the country, shining white sightscreens are often the first indication you are passing a cricket ground. They are a most agreeable feature.

Of course, there are still sightscreens that have to be moved, these days by – one hopes – ever-alert attendants rather than casual helpers. The Pavilion End at Lord's has perhaps the most famous moveable sightscreen in the cricket world. Although Lord's and the MCC own the Laws of the game, the MCC are, as owners of the ground, a law unto themselves. The famous Lord's Pavilion, where the members sit and watch, stands behind the bowler's arm and a solid sightscreen would severely limit the joys of watching from the celebrated Long Room. There was a time when moveable solid sightscreens on runners were introduced there and if the bowler decided to bowl from the other side of the wicket, there would be a stampede in the Long Room as members ran across from behind the sightscreen to the area it had just left and which now offered watching room. If there was a left-hander and a right hander batting, this could happen as many as four times an over. When I was in the Pavilion, I always found it hysterically funny to see the elderly Duke of this and the Marquis of that doing the ten-yard dash.

The moment when the authorities at Lord's had rightly decided that sightscreens should become part of the furniture in the Pavilion was that amazing Test match against the West Indies in 1963. The weather was terrible and the light never good and Wes Hall and Charlie Griffith raced in and bowled with an impossibly dark background, which was made even more difficult for the batsman by members of the MCC wearing dark suits and returning from the loo. That was the match in which Colin Cowdrey had his forearm broken by Hall and Brian Close played a hugely brave innings in which he was badly bruised.

At first the moveable screens were solid, hence the turmoil in the Long Room. Then it was decided to experiment with see-through or diaphanous sightscreens. When they were installed, the members no longer had to move, even if the diaphanous screens allowed only quite a good view rather than a perfect one, but it was better than nothing and certainly better than galloping across the Long Room.

There is quite a romance to sightscreens.

Wicketkeeper Ian Healy runs to congratulate Shane Warne on his first ball in a Test in England. Mike Gatting remains incredulous.

The leg-break, the googly or the flipper? Only Warne knows. Surely the best bowler ever.

A wonderful moment: Freddie Flintoff consoles Brett Lee after England's two-run win at Edgbaston in 2005.

A pivotal figure in the modern game, wicketkeeper-batsman supreme Adam Gilchrist gets things moving at Old Trafford in 2005.

Michael Vaughan and his team celebrate at The Oval in 2005. His superb captaincy brought the Ashes home after 18 years.

Sleeves buttoned to his wrists as usual, Graeme Swann on the attack.

Swanny finding a bit of turn with Karen Clifton at a *Strictly* photocall.

Vaughan, such an elegant strokemaker, makes room to cut at Headingley in 2008.

Chris Gayle doing what comes naturally, slogging for six in Perth in 2009–10.

The reassuring sight of Andrew Strauss leading England onto the field, in Dubai in 2012.

Sachin Tendulkar lifted on high by the Indian players after winning the 2011 World Cup.

Virat Kohli working this one away to the off with clever improvisation in a T20 game.

I wonder if Kohli, the Indian captain, had one eye on Bollywood when this picture was taken.

The perfect approach, total control and determination. Jimmy Anderson at the point of delivery.

Ben Stokes at his vibrant best making 258, England's fastest ever double century, against South Africa in 2015–16.

Not usually given to emotional outbursts, Anderson enjoys taking his 500th Test wicket.

England captain Joe Root stands tall and gives a loose ball all it deserves.

An extraordinary Test career is over. Alastair Cook leaves The Oval for the last time in 2018.

A crucial moment in the 2019 World Cup final: Man of the Match Ben Stokes dives and accidentally deflects the throw to the boundary.

A piece of village-green England in the Mediterranean – the beautiful cricket ground in Menorca, the island that has become a new home for Valeria and me.

S

SLEDGING

Sledging surely goes against fair play and everything else that cricket is meant to represent. Mind you, this is an oldie speaking. Sledging is something that has probably gone on, in more modest form, for a long time, with close fielders yapping away at the batsman. In the best of all possible worlds, sledging should be considered unpleasant and unnecessary, but it has been allowed to establish a hold in the modern game because the authorities have never made a serious attempt to stop it. The irony is that these same administrators occasionally become squeamish about something they made no attempt to stamp out.

It was in the 1970s that it was developed to the extent that it became an important extra bowler for the fielding side. It was the Australians who brought sledging firmly into the second half of the twentieth century, although I am sure they will protest at this accusation. Ian Chappell was one of Australia's best ever captains and he was comfortable with this form of attack, although with such a talented side under him, he was a captain who should have needed it less than most.

Nonetheless, captains and bowlers have always tried to give the batsman every problem they can and it is difficult to say that sledging does not fit in with modern society. No one would agree with this more than Jimmy Anderson, who holds the palm for these things in the present England side. It is not only an Australian disease, for it caught on fast and has reached out to all sides at every level of the game. Like so much today, sledging may be out of bounds for one generation, but not for the one coming along behind.

The biggest worry I have with sledging is that it can become inappropriately personal, which is abhorrent. This is where captains and umpires have a responsibility they do not always accept. It is another example of players pushing the laws to the limit in the hope it will gain them an advantage, even if it is palpably 'not cricket'. Some players are immune to the barbs of sledging and no one more so than England's former captain Mike Atherton, as Allan Donald, Glenn McGrath and many other bowlers discovered to their cost. When McGrath found the edge of Atherton's bat in Sydney and the umpire did not give him out caught behind, McGrath made a point of asking Atherton why he had not walked, something most Australians are themselves congenitally unable to do. Atherton smiled, looked him in the eye and said quietly, 'When in Rome, dear boy.' The sequel to this story is amusing too, because Ian Healy behind the stumps was somewhat confused. A little later he said to Atherton, 'Mate, I don't get that. We're playing in Sydney.'

Andrew Strauss was another who was impervious to sledging, but these players are in the minority. On the other hand, young players starting their careers at first-class or Test level know it is something they are going to have to cope with. It is not easy to prevent the nasty comments that fly around these days from getting under your skin. Sledging has become a sort of modern bouncer that contemporary players must learn to

deal with, for it is not going away any time soon. Their parent-
age will be doubted, their courage mocked, their ability laughed
at, their right to be there at all thrown heavily into doubt and
on it will go. Best to ignore it, but not at all easy to do so.

S

BEN STOKES

Ben Stokes is a cricketer who would enhance any Guy Fawkes Night party. Everything is loud, colourful and possible, as well as being potentially explosive. You never know what is going to come next. The results have often been magnificent, but off the field his character has had a habit of leading him down altogether less attractive alleys. Although these two manifestations of Stokes's character appear to come from opposite ends of the spectrum, they both surely go back to the same gene. You are not going to have one without the other. On the other hand, he has just won England the World Cup, almost single-handedly at the end, and I dare say it was only because he is, to say the least, the unconventional chap that he is that he was able to pull it off in the final against New Zealand. If he had been a bat-and-pad-close-together sort of chap, his cricket would not have been able to reach the extremities it did that evening at Lord's.

When Stokes comes in to bat or his captain brings him on to bowl, we all sit up, and there are not many cricketers who have this effect. The flame is now under the touchpaper. Some of his displays have been breathtaking and unbelievable, but it is impossible to isolate them from what happened outside the Mbargo nightclub in Bristol in September 2017. This incident has, alas, come to define Stokes as much as his batting or bowling, and I fear it may be with him for life.

I have met Stokes twice: once in the England dressing room at Lord's and once in 5 Hertford Street, in Shepherd Market in Mayfair. This is London's premier, most fashionable and expensive watering hole, founded by the son of Mark Birley who invented Annabel's, once a supreme nightclub just round the corner in Berkeley Square. Hertford Street is in every sense a mile or two from the Mbargo in Bristol and I doubt Stokes learned any bad habits there. On both occasions I realised I was meeting a determined, self-contained man.

Stokes's career has been littered with remarkable performances on the field and craziness off it. He made his debut for Durham in 2009 at the age of 17 and bowled no less a batsman than Mark Ramprakash with his third ball. But trouble soon followed. In 2012–13, he went on an England Lions tour to Australia and, with three matches still remaining, he was sent home with Kent's Matt Coles after what were diplomatically described as 'two breaches of discipline'. The following winter he was back in Australia with the 2013–14 Ashes side and made his first Test hundred in the game in Perth. Later in 2014, he missed the World T20 tournament in Bangladesh because shortly beforehand in Barbados he reckoned he had a bad decision against him. When he returned to the pavilion, in his frustration, he punched a dressing-room locker so hard, he broke his wrist.

Stokes played an important part in England's victory over Australia in 2015. The moment I will never forget came on the first morning at Trent Bridge in the third Test match. Stuart Broad was bowling to Adam Voges (Voges (61.87) finished with the second-highest batting average to Don Bradman (99.94) in the history of Australian Test cricket among those who played a minimum of 20 innings). Voges came forward to drive a ball which left him a fraction off the pitch and sliced it to the right of Stokes at fifth slip. Stokes flung out his right arm and at full stretch held an incredible catch when the ball was almost behind him. Only Stokes could have taken that catch and it was another illustration of his unique talent. Drama, controversy and Stokes attract each other. It was later that summer, in the second game in the limited-over series, that Stokes was given out for obstructing the field, in the incident I have described in the entry on that rare form of dismissal.

One of my greatest regrets is that I did not see his 258 in only 198 balls against South Africa at Cape Town in 2015–16. It was the fastest double century ever scored for England and the second fastest of all time. It was an astonishing innings and there was nothing the South African bowlers could do to contain him. Comparisons with Ian Botham came thick and fast. I flew out to Johannesburg to commentate on the following two Test matches. When I arrived, I never seemed to stop watching replays of just about every stroke he had played in that innings or listening to the descriptions by those lucky enough to have been there.

Before long he was given the vice-captaincy of the Test side and not the least of the reasons for this may have been the hope that the added sense of responsibility would help to curb the less positive side of his nature. Stokes was now established as the most exciting cricketer in the world and it was no surprise when, in the Indian Premier League in spring 2017, he was bought for £1.7 million by Rising Pune Supergiant. Surely this should have increased this new sense of responsibility and there could now be no going back to his bad old ways. On 24 September that year, England beat the West Indies in a limited-over match at the County Ground in Bristol. Afterwards, the England players went out to celebrate and let their hair down and it was then that Stokes, in company with one or two others from the side, including Alex Hales, found his way to the Mbargo nightclub.

He was not selected for the Ashes series in Australia in 2017–18, even though the case against him was not heard until the following summer. In the 2018 IPL auction, he picked up another £1.4 million when he was bought by the Rajasthan Royals. He was chosen for the first Test against India at Edgbaston at the beginning of August 2018, but was in Bristol Crown Court when the second was played at Lord's. He was then acquitted of affray by the jury, so there was no legal reason why he should not return to the England side and he was back in the team for the remaining three Tests.

Stokes was chosen to go to Sri Lanka in November 2018 and played an important part in England's 3–0 victory, the first time England had won all Test matches in a series in the east. Stokes's approach on that tour received high marks from Trevor Bayliss, the England coach. We can only hope that the red-headed haze of anger which has consumed Stokes intermittently in his career has now been forever laid to rest, so that he can give full rein to his unique cricketing talents. If no one hopes that more than Stokes himself, I am sure England's cricket supporters will not be far behind.

In the end, Stokes won the extraordinary World Cup final against New Zealand, which I have described in detail elsewhere, almost by himself. But his form in the subsequent Ashes series was even more phenomenal. After Steve Smith had scored two hundreds, Australia easily won the first Test at

Edgbaston. In the second, at Lord's, it looked as if another fine innings by Smith might win the match for Australia, but England were saved by another extraordinary piece of batting by Stokes, who in the end took England to within a measurable distance of victory themselves with his magnificent 115 not out.

It did not seem possible he could do better than this, but in the third match, at Headingley, he did just that. After being put in to bat, Australia were bowled out for 179, but England themselves fell in a miserable heap on the second day and were bowled out for a derisory 67. Australia then made 246 in their second innings, leaving England to make a most improbable 359 to win. They never looked as if they would get near that target and their ninth wicket fell at 286.

It was now that Jack Leach, who had made 92 as night-watchman in the Test against Ireland at Lord's earlier in the summer, joined Stokes, who had made 61. Stokes now grasped both his bat and the moment. He produced a series of breath-taking strokes and, while the undemonstrative and courageous Leach defended his wicket magnificently, managing to score just one run in the process, he took England to a one-wicket victory in maybe the most remarkable Ashes match ever. Headingley had claimed the honour of playing host to that after Botham and Willis's famous victory in 1981, but surely those two players and that Test now have to take second place to Stokes in 2019. Two Tests remained to be played in the series as these words are written and one can only wonder at what may be lying just round the corner.

S

ANDREW STRAUSS

Even if he was not the most glamorous of batsmen or in any sense a dasher, there was something of the Boy's Own hero in Andrew Strauss. He was fresh-faced, a sporting star at school, he got on with everyone and was the sort of chap every mother hoped their daughter would marry, if she had not married Alastair Cook first. He was a fine opening batsman too, without any unnecessary frills or conceit, and but for cruel luck he would have scored a hundred in each innings in his first Test match, at Lord's in 2004. He made 21 centuries and 7,037 runs in 100 Tests, with an average of 40.9, in addition to 4,205 ODI runs. He was, too, an England captain who was led a merry dance by Kevin Pietersen, although in the end it was Strauss himself who appropriately had the last word there.

Strauss leading the England side down the pavilion steps was one of the more reassuring sights of recent years. With Strauss there, you did not expect things to go wrong, any more than you did when he took guard at the start of the innings, and he did not drop many catches at slip either. Strauss was born in South Africa, although his mother was English. His parents then moved to Melbourne for eighteen months before they decided to settle in Beaconsfield in Buckinghamshire, and he was educated at Caldicott and Radley, both traditional English schools. It is perhaps not surprising, therefore, that when, at the relatively late age of 27, he began to play Test cricket for England, there seemed to be something indisputably English about him. He was organised, in control, unemotional and without any outrageous streak – and yet always with a ready smile.

By the time he first stepped on the field for England, Strauss had already undergone a veritable character change. When he was a boy at Radley, where another England captain, Ted Dexter, was educated, Strauss had a reputation for being 'chaotic', 'scatterbrained' and 'gullible', and was even accused of hardly being able to tie up his shoelaces. He then went on to Durham University and neither there nor, in 1996, when he first had a summer contract with Middlesex, would anyone have accused Strauss of looking like a future England captain, except, maybe, the indomitable and shrewd 'Foxy' Fowler, the Durham coach and former *Test Match Special* summariser, who had much to do with Strauss's development as a cricketer and a man. Strauss's experience in an unforgiving Middlesex dressing room also helped the process of steering him towards a more organised life. Mike Gatting put his finger on it: 'We did take the mick out of them a bit [Strauss's great friend from Durham, Ben Hutton, grandson of Sir Leonard, was with him], but you only do that if you know the boys can take it. It was a hard dressing room, but a fair one, and they both handled it really well.'

It was greatly to Strauss's credit that he was able to adapt himself as he did. Two years later, Strauss went out to play Grade cricket in Australia for Sydney University, where they insisted on playing him in the third XI and he kept scoring hundreds. When he was promoted to the seconds, he failed in his first match and was promptly dropped. When Strauss wanted to know what was going on, he was asked with custom-ary Australian subtlety who he thought he was and told that county cricket was a 'load of rubbish' anyway. As Strauss went on to be part of three Ashes-winning teams and was captain for two of them, he rammed this one back down their throats. Strauss spent a number of years playing cricket in Sydney and Adelaide during the English winters. It was while he was in Sydney that he met Ruth McDonald, an Australian actress, whom he was to marry in 2003.

Strauss first played for Middlesex in 1998 and made a quiet start, but two years later he made his first hundred and topped a thousand runs for the next three seasons. In 2002, he took over the captaincy of Middlesex, a job he held for three years, and did enough to show that when the time came, he would be the right choice for the England job. There was no sign of his chaotic and scatterbrained past. Strauss made his ODI debut for England in 2003 in Sri Lanka and was chosen for the Test side the following year in place of the injured Michael Vaughan, for the match against New Zealand at Lord's. This was a remarkable debut, for he made 112 in the first innings, and when he had reached 83 in the second, and seemed certain to become the first Englishman to make a hundred in both innings of his first Test, he was monstrously run out by his captain, Nasser Hussain. To make his point, he made three Test hundreds the following winter in South Africa and finished with 656 runs in the series.

In the 2005 Ashes series, Strauss made 393 runs, which was an important contribution to England's exciting 2–1 victory and the return of the Ashes after eighteen years. One of my abiding memories of that series came when I was on the air in the fourth Test at Trent Bridge. Adam Gilchrist, such a dangerous batsman, drove at Flintoff outside the off stump and the ball flew off the edge, wide of Strauss at second slip. He took off and held a breathtaking catch in his outstretched left hand with his whole body off the ground.

In 2006, following injuries to Michael Vaughan and his official deputy Andrew Flintoff, Strauss was stand-in captain for the four-Test series against Pakistan, which England won 3–0. It was in the final Test of this series, at The Oval, that the two umpires, Darrell Hair and Billy Doctrove, penalised the Pakistanis for ball-tampering and the Pakistan side refused to return to the field after tea and the umpires correctly awarded the game to England. All sorts of protests by Pakistan led to endless negotiations and the result was changed to a draw in 2008. Then, in 2009, the original result was restored, and even if umpire Hair's manner at the time may have been less than diplomatic, there can surely be little doubt that the state of the ball had been altered.

The following winter, Strauss had to suffer a 5–0 whitewash in Australia in 2006–07, when he was vice-captain to Freddie Flintoff, with Vaughan again unavailable because of injury. Opting to give the captaincy to Flintoff rather than Strauss had been one or the poorer pieces of judgement by Duncan Fletcher, England's highly regarded Zimbabwean coach. Kevin Pietersen captained the side in India in 2008–09, another remarkable choice, though by this time the side was being coached by Peter Moores. Captain and coach fell out, the tour was a disaster and both were replaced. Strauss finally took on the captaincy and in the 2009 Ashes series he made 474 runs, over 200 more than any other England player, and England won the series 2–1.

Strauss then took the side to Australia in 2010–11 and as captain played a considerable part in helping England to a memorable 3–1 series win.

Strauss's last series as captain was in 2012 against South Africa, who won the three-match series 2–0. It will be remembered for Kevin Pietersen's behaviour in the second Test at Headingley. He himself made 149 in one of the great innings played at the ground, but as we have already seen in the piece I have written about him, he was then found to have sent messages to the South African dressing room making derogatory comments about Strauss, his captain, and then to the South African bowlers, telling them how best to get Strauss out. Pietersen was dropped from the side for the third Test after being asked to confirm he had not sent the messages, which he refused to do, which of course pointed to his guilt. After the third Test, Strauss decided the time had come to retire, and who can blame him if he was later caught using strong language about Pietersen in a television commentary box when he thought the microphone was no longer live?

Three years later, Strauss was made the full-time director of England cricket. He was soon in action, sacking Peter Moores, who had come back for a second spell as England's coach, and replacing him with the Australian Trevor Bayliss. Strauss's next act was to tell Kevin Pietersen that he would have no part to play in the immediate future of England's cricket, effectively bringing his controversial England career to an end. Whichever way one looks at this, Pietersen, who continued as a one-day mercenary, had no one to blame but himself.

It was a triumph for Strauss's strategic thinking and planning that England won the World Cup. Strauss made it clear when appointing Bayliss in May 2015 that he was extremely anxious to do something to improve England's poor showing in international limited-over competitions. The Champions Trophy in 2017 and the 2019 World Cup were both being played in England and, talking of Bayliss's appointment, Strauss said, 'His expertise in the shorter forms of the game will be vital.' And Strauss's judgement was brilliant.

Strauss's appointment as director of cricket looked like being a great success, but fate struck the unkindest of blows when his wife, Ruth, was diagnosed with cancer. In 2018, he resigned from his job and devoted himself to looking after Ruth and his two teenage sons. She returned to Australia for the last few months of her life and died at the very end of 2018. Andrew Strauss now spends his time running the charity which has been set up in Ruth's name.

S

STUMPED

Wicketkeepers will tell you that a stumping is the most exciting of all the dismissals in cricket. The wonderful moment when the ball smacks into the gloves of the keeper who, seeing the batsman's back foot is either raised or out of the crease, whips off the bails and, spinning round towards the square-leg umpire, screams an appeal. When the keeper takes the ball outside the leg stump, it can be even more dramatic, especially if he is standing up to the wicket to one of the quicker bowlers.

All eyes used to go to the umpire, but sadly the arrival of the Decision Review System (DRS) has robbed this moment of some of its suspense because these days the umpires on the field will almost invariably call in the third umpire to make the decision. All eyes now turn instead to the big screen to await his verdict. Even so, when out or not out flashes up, it is not quite so exciting as watching the square-leg umpire raise his finger. That moment of execution was terrific.

As I have said elsewhere, at an early age I became a devout disciple of Godfrey Evans. When he was standing up to Alec Bedser, who was on the quick side of fast-medium, my pulse rate was not the only one to be affected. Just occasionally there would be a flash of movement, the bails would fly and a triumphant Evans, with the ball in his gloves, would be appealing for a leg-side stumping. It was an unbeatable moment. I still get a great kick out of a leg-side stumping.

When I was at my preparatory school and had escaped the clutches of Miss Paterson of the third form, I kept wicket for the first XI. We had a brilliant orthodox left-arm spinner in the side, Edward Lane-Fox, who turned the ball appreciably, and I was able to devour stumping chance after stumping chance. In one match against a neighbouring prep school, I think I made seven stumpings in an innings, and what fun it was. The batsmen were floundering, well up the pitch, and it required no great skill on my part – and DRS would not have saved any of them. Hence my passion for stumping.

S

GRAEME SWANN

Cricketers come in all shapes and sizes, but in my time none has been better value for money than Graeme Swann, both on the field and off it. He was as good an off-spinner as England has produced, but he was also unlucky.

The start of his England career was delayed for much longer than it should have been as a result of the surprising misjudgement of Swann – as a man and as a bowler – by the England coach Duncan Fletcher, who did not get much wrong. But Fletcher's sense of humour failed him when it came to Graeme Swann's somewhat reckless and insensitive behaviour on his first senior tour, to South Africa in 1999–2000. Swann's other piece of bad luck, a progressive injury to his right elbow, brought his career to a premature end. He finished with 255 Test wickets when he might have had many more if he had been given a proper chance early on. As a result, I am not sure his bowling has received the credit it deserved.

When his injured elbow forced him to retire, Swann took the opportunity to stretch his wings, just as Andrew Flintoff had done before him. He joined *Test Match Special* in 2014 and added quite a sparkle to the commentary box. He and I also did about twenty two-man shows in successive Octobers and it was an unholy alliance that worked pretty well. Swann loved the stage and it loved him. He is extremely funny in an irreverent but delightful way. In 2018, he was an inspired selection for *Strictly Come Dancing* and formed a brilliant partnership with the South African dancer Oti Mabuse. Swanny's enthusiasm, boundless energy and obvious sense of fun made him hugely popular. There was something wonderfully infectious about his commitment and humour. He was no longer just the superb off-spinner who had taken so many Test wickets for England. He had moved confidently on to a bigger stage.

As a 19-year-old, Swann had been chosen to tour South Africa with Nasser Hussain's side in 1999–2000. As he would be the first to admit, the glamour, excitement and having a bit of money in his pocket for the first time went to his head. He was never likely to make the Test side, although he played in a solitary one-day international. He had been chosen as a highly promising youngster to give him the experience of touring. Swann is a colossal extrovert and found the opportunities, not to say the fleshpots, of South Africa, hard to resist. I dare say Hussain and Fletcher, both hard men, and neither of them known for their humour, took the view that if a young player was selected to go on tour with his country, he should be able to work out for himself what was expected of him. With a more sympathetic management team, Swann's early career might have taken a different course. As it was, he returned home from that tour as a reject and Fletcher, in particular, never changed his mind about the man or his bowling. It was not until Fletcher had been replaced in 2007 by Peter Moores, in the first of his two brief spells as England coach, that Swann was given another chance. Moores had played for Sussex and Swann had invariably bowled well against them.

After being selected for England's one-day side on a tour of Sri Lanka in 2007–08, where he was successful, Swann was picked for the tour of India the following winter and had an amazing start to his Test career. He was chosen to play in the match in Chennai, when he became only the second bowler to take two wickets in his first over in Test cricket. Gautam Gambhir was lbw to his third ball and Rahul Dravid to his sixth. There was no stopping him after that, and he went on to play a major part in three Ashes-winning series. Not only did he take 255 Test wickets, but his cavalier approach to batting brought England 1,370 useful runs. He also took 54 catches, many of them brilliant efforts at second slip, where he is still badly missed.

As the years passed, his right elbow gave him increasing trouble. Cysts that had formed in his elbow because of all the work it had had to do began to disintegrate and bone fragments destroyed nerves in the elbow. The effect of this was that Swann could not feel his fingers and as a result he had no control over the ball when it came out of his hand. He had a number of operations, including two in Minnesota where the American surgeon was the best in the business at this sort of thing. Swann says he had been reluctant to make himself available for the 2013–14 tour of Australia but that Alastair Cook, the captain, badly wanted his friends around him. This was the series in which England lost 5–0 and Kevin Pietersen caused chaos within the England party. Pietersen also appeared to have it in for Swann and was unpleasant about him in his autobiography. In our stage show, Swanny and I used to sit on either side of a small bookcase where Pietersen's book was prominently displayed. Each night, the first thing he did was to pick up the book and throw it dismissively off the stage. It always produced much applause and laughter.

On that tour of Australia, the crunch for Swann came in Perth. He told Cook he could not play in the third Test, but the captain wanted him in the side. As the feeling had now gone from Swann's right hand, he did not know where the ball was going and his bowling was all over the place, although he had the satisfaction of dismissing his bête noire, David Warner, twice in the match. When that game was over, Swann decided to retire and he left the party before the end of the series, which brought him a lot of criticism. His answer to that was that Andy Flower, the coach, had told him that with James Tredwell coming out as a replacement, there was no room for Swann and so he had to go home. Perhaps it was clumsily handled on both sides, but it was Swann who took the flak.

In nearly fifty years in the commentary box, Swann was one of the players I have enjoyed watching the most, whatever he was doing. His energy and enthusiasm were irresistible and, unlike several others, he always seemed to be enjoying himself. When these words are first read, he and I will be in the middle of yet another theatre tour.

T

SACHIN TENDULKAR

Maharajahs may have been abolished, but India should find a princely title for Sachin Tendulkar, for no cricketer has stamped the country more firmly onto the cricketing map of the world.

The most entertaining clairvoyant early in Tendulkar's career was that irrepressible Australian bowler Merv Hughes. When, in the 1991–92 series in Australia, Tendulkar made 114 on the hard, bouncy pitch in Perth, the graveyard of so many overseas batsmen, Hughes said to Allan Border, Australia's captain, 'This little ***** is going to get more runs than you, AB.' Border scored a small matter of 11,174 runs in Test cricket. Going from the ridiculous to the sublime, Don Bradman said that although he had never seen himself bat, he thought Tendulkar was a lot like him. He even asked his wife, Jessie, to confirm this, which she did. Both were ringing endorsements.

Tendulkar was one of those rare cricketers whose true excellence can not be measured in terms of statistics, which the man and his skills and the very simplicity of his method somehow seemed to make irrelevant. Even so, a total of 34,347 runs from 663 international matches – he made 15,921 runs in 200 Test matches and amassed a further 18,426 in 463 ODIs – is formidable evidence of a considerable genius. He also hit 100 centuries in international cricket and none of these figures have been overtaken. Do they make Tendulkar the best batsman of all time? I dare say Indians would deny Don Bradman, who averaged 99.94 in 52 Tests, his claim for the top spot. There are many people who would hand the accolade to Viv Richards, whose figures do not begin to tell of the way in which, without wearing a helmet, he destroyed a whole generation of extremely hostile fast bowlers. How boring it would be if there was ever a definite answer to the eternally beguiling question of who was the best.

Tendulkar's modest and undemonstrative approach to the job of scoring runs marks him out. As a person, he is as charming and natural and unforced as his strokeplay. The Don's batting was a trifle humourless and he took to the crease with him a metronomic majesty, an unassailable assurance and all too little romance. Viv never shirked a challenge and took up each one with a flamboyant, abrasive and extrovert flourish, which made him, in some ways, the most irresistible of the three. There was a powerful romance about Viv at the crease.

Where Tendulkar would undoubtedly top the poll is with his extraordinary modesty. He came into Test cricket at the age of 16 years and 205 days, a charming, unpretentious schoolboy whose mild diffidence gave the impression he was not really certain he should be there at all. Throughout his long career, Tendulkar's demeanour never suggested entitlement and this made him an even bigger attraction. There is still something of the schoolboy about him and his appearance has always retained that open, wide-eyed innocence. In some ways, like Bradman but not Richards, Tendulkar was a solitary man who kept himself to himself, and he did not enjoy milling crowds and being mobbed. His fame in Mumbai was such that he would take his car out in the middle of the night so that he could enjoy driving unrecognised through the streets. He was uncomfortable with the hysterical adulation he received everywhere he went – at home or abroad.

Of course, the art of batting came instinctively to him, but even so, there was something hesitant about his first steps in the game. His father was a prominent Marathi novelist and there was not a thread of cricket running through the family. As a young boy, Tendulkar's personality had a few rough edges to it. At school, he had what now seems to be the incongruous reputation of being a bully and was apparently quick to have a go at pupils when they first came into the school. He was then a keen follower of tennis and his hero was none other than John McEnroe. Maybe he was attracted by the raucous way in which McEnroe tried to bully the umpire and have his way on court. Young Sachin was first introduced to cricket in 1984 by his half-brother, Ajit, who may have felt it would be better if Sachin bullied the opposing bowlers rather than his fellow pupils. At his first opportunity in the nets, Sachin did not impress, but, given a second chance, he did well enough to be signed up for the local cricket academy, where he at once became passionate about the game. He soon moved on to a school which had a history of producing good players. It was not long before Sachin himself had acquired a considerable reputation as a young player, not only in school cricket, but also in Mumbai's leading club tournament.

Then, rather curiously, in 1987, he went to Chennai to train as a fast bowler, but Dennis Lillee, the great Australian bowler who was coaching there, had a look at him and told him he should concentrate on his batting. Back in Mumbai, in March that year, Sunil Gavaskar, Sachin's hero, gave him a pair of his own ultralight pads and consoled him for not winning a local cricketing award. 'It was the greatest source of encouragement for me,' was how Sachin later described it.

The following year, in 1988, Sachin scored a hundred in every innings he played and in a school game was involved in a record 664-run partnership with his great friend Vinod Kambli, who also went on to play for India. On that occasion Sachin made 326 not out, and this remained the highest partnership in any form of cricket until 2006, when it was beaten in an Under-13 match in Hyderabad. In this same year, he played his first game for Mumbai in the Ranji Trophy, against Gujarat. He made 100 not out and became the youngest Indian to score a hundred in first-class cricket. He was 15 years and 232 days old. Sachin went on to score hundreds in his first appearance in both the Deodhar and Duleep trophies, two other domestic Indian competitions. After all this, it was simply a matter of time before he found himself in the Indian Test side. That moment arrived the following year, 1989, when India toured Pakistan. In his first Test, in Karachi, he had made 15 before he was bowled by Waqar Younis, also playing in his first Test. Sachin made 215 runs in that series, for an average of 35, and he was not yet 17. Not bad for someone who only two years before was trying to become a fast bowler.

After that, he went from one mountain top to the next on that extraordinary record-breaking journey. No wonder he achieved god-like status in India. Being a normal young man without side, chippiness, hang-ups or obvious prejudices, he was the perfect role model. His example gave a generation of Indian youngsters massive hope both for themselves and their country. It is impossible to overestimate his importance to India and its people. What Sachin did was taken further by such players as M.S. Dhoni, Rahul Dravid, Sourav Ganguly and Virat Kohli, but without Tendulkar showing the way, their passage would not have been so straightforward.

There is neither the space nor the need to go through all Sachin's amazing performances, for the stories have been told so often. In spite of all this, he had to weather certain awkward moments in his career. Like some other natural and instinctive players, captaincy did not come easily to him. He had two tries with India and neither was a success. He first took on the job in 1996, when he was 23, and it did not work. He was not a natural leader. Tactically he had his limitations, and one of his contemporaries, Mohammad Azharuddin, said, I hope sympathetically, of Tendulkar's captaincy, 'He won't win. It's not in the small one's destiny.' After a short break, he went back to the job in 1999, taking over from Azharuddin himself, but fared no better. He resigned in 2000, when Sourav Ganguly took over. Seven years later, Rahul Dravid decided he had had enough and the job was again offered to Tendulkar, who refused it and suggested it should go to M.S. Dhoni. Tendulkar may not have been much of a captain himself, but he had spotted someone who was well qualified for the job.

One unhappy blemish on Tendulkar's career, for which the prosecution's case was perhaps never conclusively made, came on India's tour to South Africa in 2001. During the second Test in Port Elizabeth, the match referee, who was the former England captain Mike Denness, fined four Indians for excessive appealing and the captain, Ganguly, for not controlling his side. Tendulkar was also given a one-match suspended sentence for ball-tampering. Television pictures gave the impression he might at one point have been cleaning the seam. Denness fired from the hip and was accused of racism and was then refused admittance to the next Test match. Denness obviously had his reasons, but Tendulkar's character and general approach hardly suggest he would have stooped to this.

I have two innings of Tendulkar's still firmly in front of my eyes. On 14 August 1990, at Old Trafford, with the heavy weight of expectation on his shoulders, for he was only 17, he became the second youngest Test cricketer to make a hundred. In India's second innings against England, he counter-attacked with an extraordinary combination of nerve, skill and maturity, making 119 not out and saving India from defeat. I can still see him, only five foot five inches tall, standing on his toes and with incredible composure driving England's fast bowlers off the back foot to the square-cover boundary.

In 2003, the World Cup was played in South Africa and India played Pakistan at Centurion late in the qualifying round. India's target was 274 and I was lucky enough to be in the commentary box as Tendulkar made 98 in 75 balls, in the process taking apart Wasim Akram, Waqar Younis and Shoaib Akhtar, the most formidable pace attack in the competition. Pressure in cricket rises no higher than it does when India play Pakistan, which is the measure of this innings – one of the most thrilling I have ever seen. It was a phenomenal piece of batting as he smote these famous fast bowlers at their fiercest to all parts of the ground with a series of unbelievable strokes. India won the match by six wickets.

All types of cricket came alike to Tendulkar. He even became, in 1992, at the age of 19, the first overseas cricketer to play for Yorkshire, where a combination of charm and ability made sure the Tykes took him to their hearts. The IPL and Twenty20 came along towards the end of his career, when he captained the Mumbai Indians and was one of the leading run-scorers in the competition. At the end, he may have stayed on too long in order to take his tally of Test matches to a record 200, but after all he had done for India, so what? In India, the popular saying was 'Cricket is my religion and Tendulkar is my god.' Tendulkar was more modest: 'I am not a god of cricket. I make mistakes. God doesn't.'

As a final tribute after his retirement, he was made a member of the upper house in India's Parliament and, rather curiously, as he was not involved in any form of aviation, he was made a group captain by the Indian Air Force. For me, the memory of those effortless straight drives, played without almost any follow-through, and the punched strokes past cover off the back foot will always remain in my mind, along with that lovely innocent smile. I would happily settle for Sachin Tendulkar as my god.

T
THIRD UMPIRE

The third umpire is now the most important of the three. He is the Lord Chief Justice, as it were. The match referee may well dispute this, but the third umpire has greater control over the game. If the players are satisfied with the decisions which come from the umpires on the field, the third umpire does not come into it. But when any of the players dispute a decision that has gone against them out in the middle, it is 'sent upstairs' to the third umpire to adjudicate. He then has the benefit of all the many television replays and has to decide whether the original decision was right or not. If the on-field umpires should themselves be uncertain, they also have the right to ask the third umpire to advise them.

The third umpire has one crucial advantage over the umpires in the middle in that he sits behind the scenes and is effectively more anonymous and can take his time. When the Decision Review System (DRS) is activated, it introduces a moment of great excitement into the game which was not there before, when the decision of the umpires out in the middle was final. This is a bonus which has to be set against the fact that use of DRS can often take a long time, interfering with the rhythm of the game and slowing down the over rate. It is, of course, crucial that the third umpire interprets the visual evidence in front of him correctly. If he needs time to make sure he has got it right, so be it.

The original purpose of DRS was to eliminate the howlers that umpires are bound to make from time to time. If all the world can see on their television sets that a batsman is palpably not out, the game looks stupid if the decision is not changed. The third umpire does, therefore, have a greater responsibility than the two out on the field who have the 'prisoner' in front of them. The third umpire is a court of appeal.

I can see a point arriving when, after a period gaining experience as an umpire in the middle, certain umpires will then become specialist third umpires. I feel that interpretation of events on a screen requires slightly different qualities from those needed on the field. Instinct should not come into it, as it is bound to do when an umpire is in the middle of the action. Solid proof is the order of the day. The third umpire has the advantage of hindsight in that he does not have to make an immediate decision and can look at replays as many times as he likes. He knows what to look for and has time to do so. The danger is that I sometimes think third umpires feel it beholden upon them to make a definite decision, come what may. They may feel that, having all the advantages of second sight, 'I can't make up my mind' is not good enough. This is wrong. I believe there are plenty of occasions when the available replays do not give the definite answer and so 'don't know' and therefore 'not out' is the correct decision and anything else a bit of a guess. Third umpires must allow themselves to have doubts rather more than they do. 'Case dismissed' is the legal cry, and third umpires should not shy away from it.

T

THE TOSS

When the Laws of cricket were first written down, by a group of gentleman in the Star and Garter public house in Pall Mall in 1744, they stated that 'The pitching of the first wicket is to be determined by the toss of a piece of money.' Nothing could be clearer than that. But thirty years later the Law was changed, in the interest of supposed fairness I presume, to read, 'The party which goes from home [the visiting side – delightfully put] shall have the choice of the innings and the pitching of the wickets.' This was then abandoned in 1816, when they went back to the toss of a coin, and so it has remained.

It was also stated in these same Laws that if a piece of money was not available, a bat should be thrown in the air and the call would be 'round' or 'flat', indicating which side the caller thought the bat would come down. There is a lovely picture, intermittently seen in the Long Room at Lord's, of urchins, who would not have had a coin, throwing a bat up in this way to decide which of them would bat first.

The toss of a coin has remained until the present time, although in an age which considers it to be unfair if one captain should, for example, win all five tosses in a Test series, various alternatives are being suggested. Effectively, one would mean that after the first match, the choice of deciding who bats first should alternate. Luck would be eliminated. Another is that the visiting side should be allowed to make the initial choice, to guard against the home side preparing a pitch to suit themselves. Personally, I think this is nonsense and that if the visiting side is the better side, they will win the series regardless.

The toss has always been a small but delightful piece of theatre and is part of the essential character of cricket. It is a lottery that takes place before the game has started, but both captains can try to guard against losing the lottery by picking a side to cope with unfavourable conditions, maybe by taking a gamble. Do they play a third seam bowler, another batsman or a leg spinner? The toss is a moment of suspense and excitement at the start of each match, but before it is made, each captain hands the other the names of his players and there's no changing around after the toss. Moments like these are, I believe, sacrosanct and help make the game what it is, and they are all the better for being carried out in the middle of the ground so the spectators can enjoy the drama.

First the coin goes up, glinting in the sun. Then, as it falls, the heads go down to look at the coin and the winning captain makes his decision. When the captains turn to walk back to the pavilion, one may hit his leg with the flat of the hand, indicating to his players the need for the opening batsmen to pad up. The other may well bowl an imaginary ball so that his side will know it is their fate to be in the field. It is a great moment.

I remember going at the age of nine or ten with my father and mother to Lakenham to watch a Minor County match. My father took a somewhat cavalier view of my urgently expressed need to arrive in time to see the toss, albeit from behind the boundary, but for me it was still exciting.

There have been many jokes about successful captains using two-headed coins, but in recent times disturbing stories have circulated of real skulduggery occasionally creeping into the business of tossing. The persistence of the illegal betting industry on the Subcontinent has probably been one of the reasons and the arrival of spread-betting will not have helped. One story concerns two captains tossing before the start of an international one-day match. One of the captains, presumably by prior arrangement with the other, bends down and picks up the coin the moment it has come to rest, saying, 'We'll bat' or 'We'll have a bowl' – but neither of the captains has actually seen which way the coin has landed. I am sure there have been other variations of this same theme to enable the ungodly to profit. In order to stop this happening, the match referee now presides over the toss in limited-over and Test cricket.

There are so many dramas-within-dramas going on out in the middle at the time of the toss while we wait on our toes at the boundary's edge. As the coin goes up, there will be many captains who have not completely made up their minds what they are going to do if they win. There are others who will be devoutly praying that the opposing captain wins so that he does not have to make the decision himself.

Such is the charm, pressure and unpredictability of the toss. In no other sport is the toss so important and cricket would lose an important part of itself if we were no longer to see the captains walk out and go through the whole rigmarole of the toss. If we had to put up with an antiseptic announcement over the tannoy just telling us which side was going to bat, it would be a dreadful anticlimax and the start of a cricket match would be a much duller affair.

T

TRENT BRIDGE

Trent Bridge is my favourite cricket ground, although while making that massive statement I must admit that I have always regarded Lord's as something more than a cricket ground: it is surely the High Temple of cricket.

Trent Bridge is a magnificent cricket ground, pure and simple. It comes without airs and graces. It is a small but stately cockpit for cricket which has managed to maintain the homely feeling and lack of pretentiousness since cricket was first played there in 1838 under the auspices of William Clarke, the great lob bowler. The ground took shape during the nineteenth century. The old Trent Bridge Inn was pulled down and replaced with the current hostelry, stands were built on the west and north sides of the ground and in 1886 the present, defining pavilion was constructed. This pavilion has become the centre-piece of a ground which has been built up in its image. Today, it stands proudly at the southern end and the stands now stretching all round have the same style. Whether it is luck or coincidence, Trent Bridge has always been run and looked after by committees who have been sensitive to the aesthetic stand-ards of the ground. At the same time, they have looked after the character of the place and have been aware of the importance of making sure it has remained friendly and welcoming, for players and spectators alike.

I had the thrill of playing at Trent Bridge in 1956 when I was only 16. I first played for Norfolk that year in the Minor County Championship and we were up against Nottinghamshire Second XI. We drove up from Norwich and stayed at the old Black Boy Hotel in the market square. I cannot describe the excitement of going into the visitors' dressing room the next morning. This was where visiting Test sides had changed since Test cricket first came to Trent Bridge in 1899. The Notts Second XI was full of players who had been in the First XI for a number of years and their names were well known to me. I am sure we lost the match, but I can still remember the fizz of excitement as I first walked out onto the ground. Trent Bridge had just installed an Australian-type scoreboard which spelled out the names of the players on both sides. When I saw my own name in bold white block capitals, I felt I had reached the summit of life. While in the field, it was wonderful to look up after fielding the ball and see the light flash up alongside my name. The fact that twelve men, a boy and a dog is probably an overestimate of the crowd did not matter.

Being by then an avid reader about the game, I could hardly believe I was playing on the ground that had produced Harold Larwood and Bill Voce. It had also seen Stan McCabe make 232 for Australia in 1938 when Don Bradman called the others in the side onto the dressing-room balcony – which for two days in 1956 was *our* balcony – telling them, 'You'll never see the like of this again.' Of course, I was ever mindful of Denis Compton's progress wherever I went – in which corner of the room did he change? At Trent Bridge he made 102 in that first Test against Australia in 1938, 184 against them in 1948 and then in 1954 he made 278 against Pakistan. When once asked about that innings, he smiled and said, 'After I had got to a hundred, all I tried to do was get out.'

For many years the BBC radio commentary box was on the balcony on the first floor of the pavilion. There was a narrow and slightly rickety wooden staircase down to our box and once there, there was no room for manoeuvre. We squeezed in – just – and changing commentators after every twenty minutes called for an athleticism none of us any longer possessed. It was worth travelling a long way to see John Arlott leaving in a hurry so that his successor would be in position for the first ball of the next over. The window could sometimes be recalcitrant and refuse to open and Fred Trueman's pipe then became an additional hazard. The official scorers had their cubbyhole next door to ours and so it seemed that the umpires were making their signals to us. Brian Johnston would sometimes amuse us all by saying on air, 'Oh look, Dickie Bird's waving at us.' But what a wonderful position this old box was in. We were so close to the action that I almost felt I was fielding at fine leg.

Although our new box, in the Radcliffe Road Stand at the other end of the ground, is as good a commentary box as any in the world, I still miss our old friend. One reason for this is that the Nottinghamshire committee would always give the members of our commentary team the freedom of the committee room for the match. This meant that we had somewhere to watch in comfort when not on the air, with a constant supply of refreshments available, although I remember having to watch the committee's generosity with the white wine. It was wonderful for us too because the great and the good gathered in the committee room and we gleaned priceless snippets of information we could use on air. It also meant that if the weather intervened, we were able to find someone in the committee room to bring upstairs and interview. Our proximity to the committee room helped our product.

It is to the eternal credit of Trent Bridge that the friendly atmosphere which sweeps the ground extends to the chaps in white coats on the entrance gates. When you arrive at the start of the day they are really pleased to see you and do everything they can to welcome you into the ground. Sadly, on so many other grounds, those in the white coats appear to be looking only for one of eighteen different reasons to stop you coming in. This is the sort of little thing that is so important: people who have come to spend a day at the cricket remember it when they are treated like this, long after they have forgotten the score.

Trent Bridge is a ground which is known historically for its superb batting pitches. Neville Cardus once described Trent Bridge as 'a place where it was always afternoon and 360 for two wickets.' For long years it was made for batting, but then in the 1980s, when Nottinghamshire's new-ball bowlers were Richard Hadlee and Clive Rice, things changed. Ron Allsopp, the groundsman, began to produce pitches which made life rather more lively for batsmen. When questioned, Allsopp would smile and say that he was only trying to prepare pitches that would produce more interesting games of cricket. No one believed him, and Nottinghamshire won a County Championship or two. I dare say that one or two members of that benevolent committee had decided that it would do the club a bit of good to win a few trophies – and who can blame them if momentarily their feet turned to clay?

T

FRED TRUEMAN

It is difficult to know where to start with Fred Trueman. He was one of the great characters of the game and there cannot have been many better fast bowlers. A cussed Yorkshireman with a wonderful pithy sense of humour, blended memorably with an outspoken contempt for pomposity and a deep suspicion of the establishment, he had a cartwheeling bowling action and a late outswinger, both of which have never been bettered. He was known as Fiery Fred, certainly by opposing batsmen and probably by committee members too, for he was never one to mince his words when he spotted what he thought was an injustice.

Who will ever forget those strong legs, the curving, purposeful run and then that wonderful rhythmical action? The determined walk back would follow while he rolled up his right sleeve which had inevitably broken free as he bowled the previous ball and would do so again when he bowled the next. At the same time, he would toss that unruly mane of black hair back over his head. Then he would turn and smoothly accelerate before launching himself into that glorious high action, accompanied by the massive drag of his back foot as his arm came over. There was something wonderfully primeval about Fred's bowling which was underlined by the accompanying dark scowl.

He became the first bowler to take 300 Test wickets and it took him only 65 matches. In his early years Fred was very much a free spirit. His enthusiasm and his commitment as a fast bowler were never in doubt, but his impetuous character was badly handled early in his career. He erupted into Test cricket against a weak Indian side in 1952. Their batsmen showed a marked apprehension when facing genuine fast bowling. In the first Test of the series, at Headingley, India trailed by 41 after the first innings and then, in the first 14 balls of their second innings, they lost four wickets before they had scored a run. Trueman, bowling at a blistering pace, took three of them and Alec Bedser the other. At that time, Trueman was doing his national service in the RAF and was lucky to have a commanding officer who was happy to give him leave so that he could play for his country.

One of India's batsmen in that series who was especially uneasy against Fred's pace was H.R. Adhikari, who later rose to the rank of colonel in the Indian army. When India toured England in the early 1970s, Colonel Adhikari was their manager. During a break for rain in a Test at Old Trafford, Brian Johnston brought the colonel into the small commentary box. Fred was sitting there and Johnners said to him, 'Fred, you remember Colonel Adhikari, don't you?' Fred came back as quick as a flash, 'Aye, Colonel, glad to see yer got some o' yer colour back.'

In the 1952 series, Fred's captain was Len Hutton, the first professional to captain England in the twentieth century. Hutton and Trueman, who probably rubbed each other up the wrong way, both played for Yorkshire under Norman Yardley, England's captain for a time after the war. In 1953–54, Len Hutton took the England side to the West Indies and neither he nor Charlie Palmer, a weak player-manager, looked after Trueman, whose youthful enthusiasm and prejudices ran away with him. Hutton, whether by choice or on instruction from the authorities, did not like his players to mix with their opponents off the field of play. This did not suit Trueman, who was friendly with some of the West Indian players, and Hutton was upset when his instructions were disobeyed and so too were those running English cricket. Trueman's vigorous approach to the game also upset the West Indian crowds, who nicknamed him 'Mr Bumper Man' and sang uncomplimentary calypsos about him. When Trueman returned home, his good-conduct money was withheld without any reasons being given, which rankled with him for the rest of his life.

The following summer he was not picked for any of the Tests against Pakistan, nor was he chosen to go to Australia in 1954–55. He played in one Test in 1955 against South Africa, two the following year against Australia and was not asked to go to South Africa in 1956–57. Those in charge of England's cricket were most reluctant to forgive him his perceived sins from that West Indies tour, and for that Len Hutton and Charlie Palmer's failure to pay attention to him in the West Indies was to blame. The remarkable fact is that England played 118 Test matches from Trueman's first Test in 1952 against India to his last in 1965 against New Zealand, and he, with claims to being England's greatest ever fast bowler, was selected for only 67 of them. The main reason was that the establishment did not care for him and this was why he finished with 307 Test wickets and not somewhere in the neighbourhood of 500.

Readers may deduce a slight anger in my tone and I must now admit my prejudice. Fred Trueman joined *Test Match Special* a year or two after me and I hugely enjoyed having Fred in the summariser's chair while I was commentating. He was not the gruff, beer-swilling character he was often depicted as. He was always fun to work with, called me 'H', which no one else did, was never lost for a word and he had a prodigious and most entertaining memory of all those matches he played for Yorkshire and England. There was no better companion for listeners when rain stopped play. As a summariser, he would not tolerate sloppy cricket. I shall never forget saying to him at the end of an over, 'What do you think of this, Fred?' And back he came with a scowl almost before the words were out of my mouth, 'Can't watch this rubbish.' And then, even more mystifyingly, 'I dunno what's going off out there.' It was a growl, but the chuckle was never far away.

Above all, Fred was a kind man and I have one extraordinary story as evidence which was told to me by Pat Marshall, who wrote about cricket and rugby for the *Daily Express*. He was a good friend of Fred's and once, when he was covering a Yorkshire match at Headingley, he stayed with Fred near Skipton. On the second day, he was being driven by Fred to Headingley and they were going along quite a small country road when another car went past. Suddenly Fred slammed on the brakes and, without saying a word, got out of the car and walked back thirty or forty yards before disappearing into the ditch at the side of the road. He soon came back and they started off again without him saying anything to Pat. After a couple of minutes, Fred said, 'That other car ran over that rabbit and I wanted to make sure it were dead.'

Fred was a great family man and was especially happy when his daughter married Raquel Welch's son. She came to the wedding, at Bolton Abbey, and this was probably one occasion when, in describing the event, Fred allowed his imagination to run away with him.

T

TWELFTH MAN

The position of the twelfth man was once clearly defined, but in recent years this player's precise duties have become blurred. Even the name itself is scarcely used except when the final XI is announced and the unlucky one is then officially designated as twelfth man. Dressing rooms were once populated by the team and the twelfth man, one physiotherapist at most, perhaps a selector and the occasional visitor. That was all. Now, apart from the two main coaches, there are 'emergency fielders' galore; you can hardly see yourself for batting, bowling, fielding coaches, psychoanalysts and statistical wizards and a whole army of physiotherapists. In any event, 'twelfth man' is old-fashioned terminology. These days, once he has been left out of the side, he rushes back to play for his county. If he stayed, he would get lost in the dressing-room crush!

When his side were in the field, the twelfth man used to wait, booted and spurred, ready to take the place of any of the fielders who, for whatever reason, had to come off. It was important to have a twelfth man who was a good fielder, but it was an unwritten law that if he was a specialist in any particular position, he would not be asked to field there. It was the sort of gentlemanly principle that in the old days was very much a part of cricket.

I worked in the commentary box with one highly unusual twelfth man. John Arlott was not a hugely talented player himself, but being a Hampshire man, he was a passionate supporter of the county side. There was an occasion before the war when he was watching his county in an away match and one of their fielders was injured. They had travelled without a twelfth man. As a result, Arlott, as the only other able-bodied Hampshire man on the ground, took off his coat, borrowed some kit and made up numbers in the field. For those who only knew him in later life, when he was distinctly portly, it would have required quite a leap in imagination to visualise a sprightly Arlott diving this way and that. The accolade of being twelfth man for Hampshire followed him all his life and he enjoyed it.

Another famous twelfth-man incident occurred at Lord's in 1984. England had set the West Indies 342 to win and had high hopes of winning themselves. As it was, Gordon Greenidge made an amazing 214 not out and the West Indies won by nine wickets. During the West Indies' first innings, one of the England players had to leave the field. A member of the MCC ground staff, Don Topley, was acting as England's emergency fielder, having begun the day selling scorecards. Before long Topley, who later played for Essex, was fielding at deep backward square leg in front of the Mound Stand when Bob Willis was bowling to Malcolm Marshall. Marshall hooked and Topley ran round the boundary and, at full tilt, held a remarkable one-handed catch. While he was taking the catch his foot just trod on the boundary rope and, after much discussion, the umpire, to Willis's dismay, raised both arms to signal six.

When I was young, I was told by my father that in the pre-war days one of the twelfth man's duties was to make sure that, when a tray of drinks was taken out for the fielding side, there was a whisky and soda, a gin and tonic or whatever other tipple the captain may have wanted. I am sure that while captaining England, Douglas Jardine, Freddie Brown, maybe J.W.H.T. (Johnny) Douglas and one or two others needed sustenance of this nature to keep them going. For modern twelfth men or emergency fielders, bar training is no longer an essential requirement.

U

UMPIRES

Umpires come in all shapes and sizes. In my experience almost all of them at the top level of the game have been charming and delightful men and often memorable characters. They are so important too, for it is they who control the game, interpret the Laws and give the crucial decisions which will determine the course of a match. Just as important, they are, or should be, the on-pitch disciplinarians who make sure the standards of the game are upheld.

The lower down the ladder you go, the more some umpires have a tendency to bristle with officiousness as they presume to know all the answers, more than justifying the age-old taunt 'Give a man a white coat . . .' White coats give people the feeling that they are now in authority and, come what may, should make their presence felt. Which can have unfortunate repercussions.

They are, all of them, by the very nature of their job, the game's permanent Aunt Sallies. That is something they have to live with, but often these men in white coats are most unjustly mocked. If a fielder falls over trying to stop a ball, it is business as usual; if an umpire is struck by a fierce stroke, falls over in trying to get out of the way or has his hat blown off, it produces roars of laughter, from players and spectators alike.

The wonderful David Shepherd, who was vigorously and humorously rotund, was magnificently superstitious. When the score of the side or an individual batsman reaches 111, or 'Nelson' as it is known in the trade, superstitious cricketers sitting in the pavilion like to keep their feet off the ground until another run has been scored. When he was umpiring, Shep wisely did not try and keep both feet off the ground simultaneously, otherwise he and Humpty-Dumpty would have had a lot in common. He contented himself with skipping around out in the middle, raising first one leg and then the other, which caused considerable merriment on the pitch and in the stands. We made the most of these moments in the commentary box and, being a large man, he cut a priceless figure as, with a twinkle forever in his eye, he indulged in these deliberate callisthenic displays which added to everyone's enjoyment.

Shep was a great umpire, not only because of his ability to make the right decisions, but because of his unflappable and calm manner. It was this which caused him to be sent to umpire any series where tempers might become frayed and unhelpful crowd interruptions were likely to happen. His calming influence and his diplomacy were remarkable and he always had the respect of the players.

Umpires come under a lot of pressure. It is an impossible job for someone who has never played the game, for in a way cricket is much more than just the Law book – which is complicated enough. It is important an umpire should have the feel for cricket that perhaps comes only to those who have played and therefore understand the subtleties of the game. Of course, there have been terrific umpires who have not been players at any significant level, but they are the exceptions that prove my rule.

Great responsibility goes with the job and not only as far as the game in progress is concerned. The decisions of umpires can also play a part in the progress of young players at the start of their career, at all levels of the game. Confidence can so easily be ruined by careless or casual umpiring. This can cause players either to be dropped or to be kept in the side, which at the professional level can have a serious effect on their financial future. Umpire's reports on incidents during a game can have far-reaching consequences for a player's career. In my time watching, I have sometimes wondered whether the importance of the umpires is as fully understood and respected as it should be by those who employ them: the game's administrators. There have been times when I have doubted they have the support and the back-up they have every right to expect when it comes to upholding the game's standards.

Some of the controversies that have happened in Test cricket illustrate problems that umpires face at all levels. There was the famous drama at Lord's during the Centenary Test against Australia in 1980. On the third day, the Saturday, play was interrupted by rain and there was a long delay because two used pitches were extremely wet. The umpires, Dickie Bird and David Constant, made repeated inspections and, with the sun shining, the packed crowd became exasperated, none more so than some of the members in the Pavilion. When the umpires returned to the Pavilion after their fifth inspection, a few members of MCC, yes, members of MCC, assaulted Constant as he walked up the steps towards the door into the Long Room. Were Bird and Constant being too cautious? Had the members had too much to drink? Probably a bit of both. Players are understandably reluctant to continue a game if they feel they may slip and injure themselves on wet grass, and umpires will sympathise with this. On the other hand, spectators have paid good money and obviously want to see as much play as possible.

The most dramatic umpiring decision I have seen was made by the Australian Darrell Hair, the polar opposite of David Shepherd. He was an intimidatingly large man who did not get many out of ten for smiling and he fell over backwards to do what he considered to be right and in accordance with the Laws of cricket. He was fearless and when, as the senior umpire at The Oval in 2006, and with his partner West Indian Billy Doctrove's full agreement, he found the Pakistan team guilty of ball-tampering, he awarded England five bonus runs. After the tea interval which followed the lengthy on-field discussions prompted by his decision, the Pakistan side did not take the field. In strict accordance with the Laws, Hair waited a few minutes before removing the bails and awarding the game to England. This immediately became an international incident. The Pakistanis accused Hair of racism and he was subsequently struck off the international panel of umpires by the ICC. He, in turn, accused the ICC of racism, but dropped the case when he was reinstated on the panel. He only stood in two more Test matches before deciding to retire, almost certainly because the legacy of this incident made life in the middle extremely difficult for him.

Hair is not a man who has ever been plagued with self-doubt and he had been rated as an extremely good umpire. He was not one to be trifled with. His abrasive manner will not have helped him, for he was in every sense the unsmiling man in the white coat. He stuck to his ground throughout this whole furore, for he was certain the Pakistanis had been tampering with the ball. His decision immediately changed his life in no uncertain terms. For nearly a week he and his wife had to leave their house in Lincolnshire and move into an hotel, and his life has not been easy ever since. This incident shows that in the modern world the umpires' decisions are no longer final and with lawyers hovering in the background, it makes a difficult job a great deal harder. This, of course, happened long before the days of the Decision Review System. In similar circumstances now, the third umpire and the match referee would also have their say, which would spread the responsibility. When three of the Australians were accused of ball-tampering in their series in South Africa in 2018, the resulting fuss was much less pointed and bitter as far as the umpires were concerned.

At the moment, many of the leading umpires are from England, which may reflect the training they have had in the huge amount of county cricket that is played. One of my favourite umpires is Ian Gould, who has just retired from the international panel. He is the jolliest of men, an outstanding umpire and not in the least self-important, as umpires can become. He came on a Derrick Robins tour to Australia and New Zealand in 1980–81 when I was the assistant manager and social secretary and we had an awful lot of fun. These adventures turn you into friends for life. Richard Illingworth is another who is not only charming but extremely able too. I always enjoy watching Marais Erasmus, a big man from South Africa who, unlike some of his countrymen, is not short on humour. Steve Bucknor, the tall Jamaican, was also the friendliest of men, and of course Dickie Bird was unstoppable. Well into his eighties now, he still turns up at most Test matches, never stops talking and always comes up with good stories from his days as an umpire.

One of my greatest umpiring friends was Lou Rowan, a detective in the Queensland drug squad. He stood for a while in the 1960s and 1970s, often in partnership with Colin Egar from Adelaide. He stood through the series against Ray Illingworth's side which won the Ashes in 1970–71. In the final Test in Sydney, the crowd on the Paddington Hill started to have a go at John Snow, who was down on the fine-leg boundary. Objects were thrown and it became unpleasant. In protest, Illingworth led his side off the field, but the umpires stayed and it was Rowan who told Illingworth that if he did not bring his side back on the field, England would forfeit the match. They came back, in ill humour, and I don't think Illingworth and Rowan ever sent each other another Christmas card.

V

MICHAEL VAUGHAN

As captain of England, I wonder if Michael Vaughan ever received the praise he deserved. England had not held the Ashes for eighteen years when Vaughan's side took on Ricky Ponting's Australians in 2005. At the end of one of the best series ever played, with four of the tightest finishes, England held on at The Oval to a 2–1 lead with the greatest difficulty. Vaughan, who had taken over the captaincy from Nasser Hussain two years earlier, had a good series with the bat, but it was his tactical know-how and cool captaincy that took England to victory.

The way in which Vaughan had held his nerve was remarkable after his side had been comfortably beaten in the first Test at Lord's, where Glenn McGrath was the chief executioner. The story of the remaining four Tests only needs to be told briefly, but they all went down to the wire. Having looked comfortable winners in the second at Edgbaston, England were, in the end, extremely lucky to win by two runs. Australia's unlikely last pair of Brett Lee and Mike Kasprowicz had put on 59 for the last wicket before Kasprowicz was wrongly given out caught behind off his glove when his hand was not in contact with the bat. In the third, at Old Trafford, Australia, needing 423 to win in the fourth innings, were saved by Ponting, who made 156, but even so their last pair of Lee and McGrath had to survive the last four overs to make sure of the draw.

In the fourth, at Trent Bridge, England, who had made the running throughout the match, had to score 129 to win. They made a steady start and then Shane Warne removed both openers and proceeded to mesmerise the rest of the batsmen. He finished with 4–31, but if luck had been with him, he could have won that match for Australia. As it was, England had three wickets left when Ashley Giles shovelled Warne to midwicket for four. England were now 2–1 up in the series and, to win the Ashes, had at least to hang on for a draw in the last match at The Oval. What a game it was. England led by six on the first innings and began their second on the fourth evening. When, in the early afternoon the next day, they were 199–7, it looked as if Australia would have plenty of time to get the runs. England's innings had been kept going by Kevin Pietersen, whose eventual 158 was one of the great Test match innings. He now found a stalwart partner in Ashley Giles and their eighth-wicket stand of 109 saw England to safety and their first Ashes victory since 1986–87 in Australia. I cannot remember a more exciting day's cricket.

For all four of these Test matches, Michael Vaughan had held his nerve. He not only kept the side together, never allowing panic or disbelief to creep in, but at the crucial moments he was also able to give his players the inspiration to produce their best. He strode purposefully with those long legs of his from mid off to mid off and never suggested for one single moment that he was not fully in control. His tactical decisions were as good as his ability to bring out the best in those under him. He has, as I have discovered more recently in the *TMS* box, a naturally cheerful demeanour. Above all, Vaughan knows his own mind and has always had the confidence to back his judgement, which he still does today as a broadcaster without trying to ram his opinions down the listeners' throats. However forthright he may sound, he also makes you feel that a smile is never far away and he has a really good sense of humour.

In some ways Michael Vaughan had a curious and in the end a somewhat unlucky England career. He captained England in 51 Test matches and won 26, which is more than any other captain. Mike Brearley, who won 18 of his 31 matches, has a higher percentage of victories to his name, 58 per cent as against 50 per cent. One big difference between the two was that Vaughan, until near the end when injuries were taking their toll, was very much worth his place in the side as a batsman, while Brearley's position was always questionable.

Vaughan was born in the town of Eccles, in Lancashire. His talents were first spotted by the Yorkshire coach Doug Padgett, who had seen him play in his school side. He ran into the young Vaughan in Sheffield, where he was watching a county match, and suggested he should think about joining Yorkshire. But in those days Yorkshire were still sticking to their own self-imposed rule, which was that only those born within the county boundaries were allowed to play for Yorkshire. Some years later, with Vaughan in his teens, this restriction was lifted and Padgett then offered him a place in the Yorkshire Academy. It is surprising that no other county had shown an interest in him in the meantime.

Vaughan soon made his mark and in 1993–94 he was asked to captain the England Under-19 side on a tour to Sri Lanka and, later in 1994, at home against India. In the old days, England captains were usually in charge of their county sides and their ability as a captain was a known quantity. Central contracts began for England players in 2000, when Nasser Hussain was captain and Duncan Fletcher the coach. From that moment onwards, future England captains were not going to be given the job of captaining their counties, for whom they would now almost never be available. Vaughan, who had little experience of captaincy, did a wonderful job with the Under-19 side in Sri Lanka. John Barclay, the former captain of Sussex, was the manager of that tour and he told me that Vaughan was much the best player in the side, which gave him the respect of the others, and that he already had the ability to listen and to take advice. He was extremely popular not only with the other players, but also with their Sri Lankan hosts. In short, he was a natural.

Vaughan was selected to tour South Africa in 1999–2000 with the full England side and played in the first Test in Johannesburg. I was in the commentary box and I shall never forget the first half an hour of that game. When Vaughan came in, England were 2–2 and one over later they were 2–4. Vaughan played a most composed innings of 33, putting on 56 with Freddie Flintoff. It may not sound much, but with Allan Donald on the rampage it was impressive. Eighteen months later, in 2001, he made his first hundred for England, against Pakistan, and toured India the following winter, where he became the seventh batsman in the history of Test cricket, and the second Englishman after Graham Gooch, to be given out 'handled the ball'. In Bangalore, he tried to sweep Sarandeep Singh and brushed the ball away with his hand. He said at first he was trying to give the ball to short leg, but came clean later: 'I should just have held up my hands and said, "I got it all wrong. I'm an idiot."'

Maybe his most remarkable achievement in 2002 came during the Test at Trent Bridge against India. He bowled

Sachin Tendulkar, who was 92, with one of his part-time off-breaks. It was a beauty, pitching in the rough outside the off stump and turning about two feet as it found its way between Tendulkar's bat and pad and hit the off stump. Vaughan also made 197 in England's first innings and scored 900 runs in the seven Tests that summer. This was the prelude to Vaughan's best tour ever, when he scored three hundreds in an Ashes series which England lost 4–1. Vaughan's three centuries were all big hundreds too, 177 in Adelaide,145 in Melbourne and 183 in the last Test in Sydney, which England won. The way he kept pulling McGrath from only just short of a length was remarkable. Vaughan was tall, elegant and classical at the crease. He made 633 runs and became the first batsman to score more than 600 runs in a series in Australia for twenty-two years. In 2002, his *annus mirabilis*, Vaughan scored 1,481 Test runs in the calendar year and for a time was second only to Viv Richards, who had made 1,710 in 1976.

He took over the England captaincy from Nasser Hussain in 2003, and like Hussain he formed an excellent and important relationship with the coach, Duncan Fletcher. Sadly, he never found his devastating batting form again and, as with many England captains, the cares of the job did not help him. His supply of runs began to dry up, although the barren patches were interspersed with the occasional big score. He also had the bad luck to suffer increasingly from injury, which in the end precipitated his retirement. You can never take Michael Vaughan's outstanding record as England captain away from him, any more than you can deny those three hundreds in Australia – or his shrewd and charming common sense on the airwaves.

W

SHANE WARNE

Shane Warne must surely have been the best bowler cricket has ever known. His figures are staggering. He took 708 wickets in 145 Test matches between 1992 and 2007 at an average of 25.42, figures which bear testimony to his phenomenal accuracy. A wrist-spinner's art is perhaps the most complex of all. It is an extremely difficult discipline to control and traditionally leg-spinners have been spendthrifts. When they get it right, they can be unplayable; when it goes wrong, batsmen roll their eyes and feast for all they are worth. Warne's control was remarkable for any wrist-spinner, but for one who spun the ball so much, it was nothing short of mind-boggling.

Wrist-spinners have to be extroverts if they are to live with the downside of their trade. Warne was certainly that, although as far as his bowling was concerned, he never had much downside to worry about. On the field and off it, Warne, has taken on any challenge that has come his way with a zest for life that not many have been able to rival, including a much-publicised dalliance with Liz Hurley (she was by no means the only lady who failed to pick his googly) and a year's suspension after testing positive for a banned diuretic just before the 2003 World Cup.

Warne's character was revealed for all to see with his famous first ball in a Test match in England, which became known as the Ball of the Century. At Old Trafford in the first Test in June

1993, he ran in to bowl to Mike Gatting, no longer England's captain but still a considerable batsman. It was Warne's instincts that made him go for broke. Realising the moment was upon him, he imparted as much spin to that first ball as he could find in his wrists and fingers. It pitched at least a foot and a half wide of Gatting's leg stump. Gatting pushed out a speculative front pad in the direction of the ball, knowing he could not be lbw as the ball had pitched outside the leg stump. But he could only look on in horror as the ball bit and turned in a way a cobra would have envied, whipped across his pads and hit the top of his off stump. Gatting could only stare, mesmerised by what had happened. Warne had well and truly arrived, as a man and as a bowler.

As a leg-spinner, Warne had the complete armoury. There were two leg-breaks, one rolled, the other highly spun. He bowled two different googlies, the one much harder to read than the other. There was the top-spinner, and the flipper, his most dangerous ball. It was bowled like a leg-break but came from the back of the hand and was pushed through faster and lower. The danger for a batsman was that, seeing the ball was shorter, he would aim to pull, but it would come through much quicker than he expected and was likely to hit the stumps or have him lbw. Then there was the 'zooter'. I never heard Warne meaningfully explain the zooter. He was a master of the public relations industry, and the zooter was perhaps an invention of Warne's to make the batsman believe he had one more weapon up his sleeve. The secret of his success was the phenomenal control he had over all these deliveries. Leg-spinners are not generally known for bowling maiden overs. Warne was the exception.

Warne's knowledge of cricket was considerable and he would probably have made an excellent Test captain. He captained Australia in one-day internationals with great success, but maybe the Australian authorities feared that putting him in charge of the Test side would be a step too far. He had the knack of hitting the headlines for the wrong reasons and they probably thought he would have been too risky an appointment. Shane Warne, like Ian Botham, had a reckless, devil-may-care side to his nature, but if he had not had this, I do not believe he would have been the bowler he was. Warne's instinct told him to take everything on, no matter what. There was an infectious charisma about him and also a naughty innocence which spurred him on to believe he could get away with anything. He once turned down a dinner invitation because he was taking his children out. 'I may be a **** husband,' he said, 'but I'm a good father.' In a sense, he was an eager victim of his own success, which will have given him this sense of impregnability. Warne's name became universal coinage; he was known and talked about far beyond the boundaries of the cricket. Few players have had that universal appeal; W.G. Grace, Don Bradman, Garry Sobers, Imran Khan were others.

It is always good to bump into Shane Warne. I first met him early in his career when he came to Sharjah in the United Arab Emirates to play in a tournament arranged and televised by Mark Mascarenhas and his company WorldTel. Warne was as much outrageous fun then as he is now. He was cheerful, optimistic, refreshing and engaging and in those days that wide-eyed innocence was even more noticeable. More recently, it was Warne, with that same look, who introduced me to Jägerbombs with devastating effect. In 2016, England were playing the third Test against Pakistan at Edgbaston. On one evening I went back to our hotel in a taxi with Michael Vaughan and Phil Tufnell. We agreed to meet later for a drink and dinner. Red wine began to flow most agreeably and it was soon apparent that solids were unlikely to be on our menu that evening. After a while, and almost simultaneously, Warne and another bottle of red arrived and the evening gathered pace. Suddenly Warne said, 'Blowers, you'd better try this,' and pushed a biggish glass across the table towards me. There was a light brown liquid swilling around in the bottom and I did as I was told. It was rather good, but as I drank it, another smaller glass which was inside the bigger one hit me on the nose. There was more to drink in that glass but it was a much darker colour. Anyway, I had that too, amid much laughter, and I liked it. I eagerly accepted another and I fear there may have been at least one more after that. I have to say that the stamina of Messrs Vaughan, Tufnell and Warne was decidedly suspect, for when the next morning I suggested we should have a repeat performance that evening, they ran for cover.

We all have our own special memories of Warne on the cricket field. Mine principally belong to the 2005 series in England when Michael Vaughan's side regained the Ashes for the first time since 1986–87 in Australia. In the five Test matches, Warne took 40 wickets and came so close to saving the day for Australia. It was ironic that it was Warne who allowed England to escape with a draw and so regain the Ashes in the last Test at The Oval. On the last day, Kevin Pietersen played his extraordinary innings of 158 which saved England. When he had made 15 he drove hard at Brett Lee outside the off stump and the ball flew at shoulder height straight to Warne, a fine catcher at first slip, and he dropped the most straightforward of catches. Pietersen and Warne were both playing for Hampshire in the County Championship and when Pietersen was eventually bowled by Glenn McGrath, Warne ran down the ground from first slip towards the pavilion to pat Pietersen on the back and congratulate him on his innings. It was a wonderfully human moment.

The other piece of cricket I shall not forget from that series in 2005 came on the last day of the fourth Test at Trent Bridge when England had been left to score 129 to win. They were given a reasonable start by Marcus Trescothick and Andrew Strauss. After Mike Kasprowicz had bowled only two overs, the ball was thrown to Warne. In quick succession he removed Trescothick, Vaughan and Strauss, and after Brett Lee had sent back Ian Bell, England were 57–4. If ever a man bowled his heart out that afternoon it was Shane Warne. He was most unlucky to take only one more wicket and in the end England won by three wickets. Warne had made us all feel it was a much more slender margin than that. Again, Warne was quick to congratulate Ashley Giles after he had scored the winning runs. What a man: cricket would have been infinitely the poorer without him, and, being the man he is, he has raised eyebrows and temperatures off the field almost as much as he has done on it. He is a most engaging character and, in my view, the greatest bowler the game has ever known – and he could bat a bit too.

W

THE WAUGH TWINS

Not difficult to tell apart, off the field or on it, the Waugh twins were, in so many ways, contradictory characters. Steve, older by four minutes, was a hard man, a leader, a shrewd, clinical, calculating thinker, someone who always knew exactly where he was going and what he wanted. He was not a man who suffered fools gladly and as a cricketer he took no prisoners. Not for nothing was he known by his colleagues as the 'Iceman'. When he retired, he wrote an autobiography, *Out of My Comfort Zone*, which filled more than 800 pages. He wrote every word of a book of precise detail himself and maybe this argues that he felt there was a need to make a point or two, which, in turn, may illustrate a certain need to justify – in spite of the 'Iceman' exterior. It showed how aware he must have been of everything going on around him. Steve Waugh was not someone you messed with.

Mark Waugh's character was very different. Even their walks told the story: Steve strode purposefully from one point to the next, while Mark's genial amble had within it more than a hint of carefree humour and a lack of overwhelming concern. With him, you did not feel you had to earn his smile; it came readily. His strokes came just as fluently and easily, and he had them all. I was lucky enough to watch his first Test innings, when he made 138 against England at the Adelaide Oval in 1990–91. It was one of those occasions when, in the commentary box, as stroke followed stroke, we just looked at each other and shook our heads. It was beautiful, it was simple, it was orthodox, and we all knew we were in the presence of something pretty special. But genius needs to be accompanied by discipline, otherwise corruption can creep in. Although Mark had all the ability in the world, he was unable to control an irresponsible urge to have fun. From time to time, it amused him to attempt an outrageous stroke which would get him out – or at least he could not restrain himself from playing it. He found it difficult to maintain the intense concentration his brother had consciously built up, and he had a habit of ruining things with lazy strokes you would never have caught Steve playing at any time in his career. Having said that, Mark was one of the outstanding strokemakers of his generation, but, like David Gower, he could be intensely irritating as he appeared on occasion simply to give his wicket away. But these dangerous strokes would come off frequently enough that, risky though they appeared to normal mortals, to batsmen like Mark Waugh and David Gower they seemed legitimate. When they did not come off and cost them their wickets, it looked like blatant shrug-of-the-shoulders carelessness and irresponsibility. The perpetrators were ridiculed, not to say vilified. This did not appear to worry Waugh any more than it worried Gower. It was simply the way they were.

While Mark was all about the joy of playing, Steve was only about the business of winning. In *Out of My Comfort Zone*, he describes at some length the battle he had not only with the bowler but with himself while playing Curtly Ambrose in Trinidad in 1995. Waugh avoided a bouncer, Ambrose stared,

Waugh instinctively tore into him, Ambrose came back and on it went, and with Waugh writing that he regretted he had started it, Richie Richardson, the West Indies captain, had to drag Ambrose away. It makes a similar scenario between Allan Donald and Mike Atherton at Trent Bridge in 1998 seem positively civilised. Atherton was as tough as Waugh, but less outwardly bristly. Donald, although distinctly guttural, was not as big as Ambrose and did not have to be pulled away. The West Indies won the match, with Ambrose taking nine wickets, and Waugh reckoned his 63 not out was one of his finest knocks. Atherton's, which took England to victory, was certainly one of his best innings.

Mark Waugh would have been a charming dinner companion, but being of an easy-going nature, he allowed himself, along with Shane Warne, to become involved in a betting scandal in Pakistan in 1994–95. Apparently, Salim Malik had said to Mark and Shane that there would be $200,000 for off-spinner Tim May, Warne and the two Waughs if Australia did not bowl well on the fifth day of the first Test in Karachi, when the match was thrillingly poised. Steve heard about this later when the Australians were in Rawalpindi, and his answer was predictably splendid: 'Tell him to **** off.' For the record, Pakistan won by one wicket after their last-wicket pair had put on 57 runs, a result which still raises a question or two.

For all Mark's batting brilliance, it would be Steve I would have chosen to bat for my life. He had a determination perhaps only rivalled by another fine Australian captain, Ian Chappell, although he and Steve Waugh were sworn enemies. Chappell had accused Waugh in print of being a 'selfish cricketer', which Waugh described as being 'tantamount to being accused of treason', and they had locked horns. On a lovely afternoon at Lord's, I would have loved to watch Greg Chappell unfolding all those handsome strokes of his. If my life had depended upon it, I would rather have seen brother Ian coming out to bat. In their similar ways, Steve Waugh and Ian Chappell are perfect illustrations of the reason why Australia have won more Test matches than England.

Steve Waugh was a brilliant batsman who had worked out in detail how best to succeed. He taught himself the supreme importance of an impregnable defence. There were times when he forced himself to ignore the opportunities presented by half-volleys and long hops. Steve Waugh was as shrewd and unforgiving a captain as Chappell was himself. He demonstrated this in the early stages of the World Cup in England in 1999 when Australia played the West Indies in what was a very one-sided contest. The West Indies were bowled out for 110 and Australia were cantering home when Waugh realised it was to Australia's advantage to try and help the West Indies through to the last six in the competition. He and Mike Bevan were batting and they now took 20 overs to score the last 20 runs, for their slow overall run rate would give the West Indies a better chance of qualifying at the expense of New Zealand, who had already beaten Australia. Waugh was much pilloried for what happened. Waugh justified his actions later by saying, 'We're here not to win friends, just the World Cup.'

No captain has ever fought harder for Australia than Steve Waugh. He was made of granite and wrought miracles when it seemed that nothing could save them. He had a single-minded determination and an unshakeable faith in himself. Although Steve was able to play his strokes as well as the next man, it was his dedication to survival that is his chief memorial. He loved a fight and if he felt the world was against him, it suited him to perfection. He said, 'I never minded being the villain because it set me up against the rest – a scenario that turned me on.' The difference between Waugh and Chappell was that Waugh needed a fight, while Chappell was a magnificent fighter if he had to be. As he grew older, Waugh's style of batting became more risk-free, more resolutely determined, and he was perhaps more ready to feel he was leading the fight in a rearguard action sooner than he should. In his book, he makes another revealing statement about his character through his batting: 'Getting runs ugly is an art that all but the geniuses of the game need to master, so that they can attain consistency.' This shows both dedication and obsessiveness in unusual quantities.

Both Mark and Steve were more-than-useful bowlers. Mark varied between off-spin and medium-paced seamers, while Steve also used the seam at medium pace and took 92 wickets in addition to scoring 10,927 runs, with an average of 51.1 in a record 168 Test matches. Mark scored 8,029 for an average of 41.8 in 128 Test matches and was a brilliant fielder and catcher in just about any position. They were also wonderfully successful in the one-day game. Mark and Steve inherited starkly contrasting genes which produced astonishing results. Who is to say which was the better cricketer?

W

W.G.

Few sets of initials are so meaningful and so easily identified as 'W.G.'. William Gilbert Grace remains as the colossus who bestrode cricket in its relatively early stages in a way no one else has done since. He is still spoken about as part myth, part prehistoric superman and always with both awe and affection – and perhaps, as time goes by, with disbelief, for we live in an age in which the importance of historical figures such as W.G. is not appreciated as it should be.

Although more Errol Flynn than Winston Churchill, W.G. remains almost as easily identifiable as Churchill, and both bestrode their different stages in comparable fashion. I am sure Churchill would have admired W.G.'s approach to a game of cricket. He was as formidable a player as he was a character in that larger-than-life, mischievous way of his. It is this imposing John Bull-like image, together with his astonishing record, that identifies him even now as the commanding figure he was all that time ago. 'For Queen and Country' seemed to be stamped large on W.G.

Let us deal with his extraordinary ability as a batsman. It is important to remember that when W.G. began to play important cricket – at the age of 15 – the condition of most of the pitches he played on was appalling. They made batting an extremely hazardous, not to say impossible, pastime. Some of the bowlers he faced on those dreadful surfaces were also genuinely fast. His career figures reveal a man who dominated the game and his contemporaries too. W.G. played 1,493 first-class innings, scoring 54,896 runs with 126 hundreds and an average of 39.55, together with a small matter of 2,876 wickets.

He came from a Gloucestershire family steeped in cricket and learned the game in the family garden, where he had no fiercer supporter or critic than his mother. He made a remarkable start. He was almost 17 when he took 13 wickets for the Gentlemen of the South against the Players of the South in 1865 and he was 18 when he made 224 not out for England against Surrey at The Oval. In the course of that game, the young W.G. was allowed by his captain to go to Crystal Palace and win a quarter-mile hurdles race. Over the next forty-one years, he made no fewer than 6,008 runs for the Gentlemen against the Players, in addition to taking 271 wickets. In both 1871 and 1876, he scored over 2,500 runs. In 1876, in three consecutive innings, he made 344 against Kent, 177 against Nottinghamshire and 318 not out against Yorkshire. A few weeks earlier, he had made 400 not out against Grimsby, who had twenty-two players in the field. And on it went.

In 1880, at the age of 32, he made 152 in the first Test match England played at home against Australia. Six years later, also at The Oval, he scored 170 against Australia. Far from his powers declining in cricketing old age, W.G. had perhaps his most extraordinary season of all in 1895 when, at the age of 47, he scored 2,346 runs. He began with 103 against Sussex at Lord's. A week later he completed his hundredth hundred, making 288 against Somerset. Then came 257 and 73 not out against Kent. He needed to score 153 on 30 May to become the first batsmen ever to make a thousand runs in May. He made 169.

While W.G.'s batting feats were prodigious, his bowling was also impressive, as his tally of nearly 3,000 first-class wickets suggests. Even in his time, he was an old-fashioned bowler. He was a slow bowler with a round-arm action who cleverly varied his flight, bringing the ball in from the leg. He was, too, an amazing fielder to his own bowling, stopping or catching anything that was hit back to him, however hard.

He was effectively modern cricket's founding father. When W.G. first came on the scene, the game was still a pleasant, domestic country pursuit a long way from anything approaching an international stage. The wealthy aristocratic patrons were in control of a game used for much of the time as a vehicle for gambling. W.G.'s arrival caused quite a stir. Here was a Gloucestershire boy with a prodigious talent who did not speak in clipped aristocratic tones. His vowels were squeaky and easily recognisable as Gloucestershire-based. His talent was formidable and his zest and enthusiasm for the game was inexhaustible, as was his concentration at the crease.

First, it was his talent which took the game by surprise. It was not long before this combined with his domineering character and his pantomime appearance to produce a figure who was able first to dominate the game and then to change it. Over the next twenty years, W.G. not only held sway over the game as it then was, but he steered it almost single-handedly to the point where Test cricket began. By then, it was recognisable as the game which is played today, and W.G. was the bridge that made this rapid transformation possible.

No one was more aware than he was of his ability and of his importance to the game. He had no qualms either about making as much money from cricket as he could. The stories about him have become a matter of legend. He was tall and robust and his beard made him probably the best-known figure in England at the end of the nineteenth century. It is more than surprising that Lytton Strachey did not include W.G. among his Eminent Victorians.

There are a countless stories about W.G.'s reluctance to leave the crease when dismissed. Once, when a ball just flicked his off stump, he picked up the bail and, as he replaced it, said to the umpire, 'Windy day, umpire.' To which the umpire is said to have replied, 'Ay it is, and mind it don't blow yer hat off on way back to pavilion.' W.G. was fiercely competitive; he had a phenomenal ability, an enduring and unshakeable concentration and what was then a unique ability to adapt his game to suit the prevailing conditions. His attitude was splendid. 'The faster they bowl, the better I like them' was how he put it. On another occasion, when replacing the bails when he had been bowled, he turned to the bowler and said, 'They've come to see me bat, not you bowl.' These stories have turned into W.G. clichés over the years, but they still tell us a lot about the man, his presence, his humour and his effect on the world around him. When he was young, he qualified as a doctor and although cricket took up a huge amount of his time, he was extremely conscientious on the medical front, without ever losing his twinkle. After one difficult birth, he told friends, 'I lost the mother and I lost the child, but with great skill I managed to save the father.'

It was the character of the man that was so important. Don Bradman was perhaps the only other batsman to transcend the game in the way that W.G. did, and Garry Sobers was another who stood far ahead of his contemporaries. But these two did not change the game as W.G. had done, principally because they played at a time when the game was more set and assured in its ways. Bradman's bat may have been larger than life and Sobers the greatest all-rounder the game has known, but neither Bradman nor Sobers were as mesmerising and immortal characters as W.G.

One can only wonder what W.G.'s legacy would have been if he had been offered a lucrative contract by a company who made razor blades. A beardless W.G. does not bear thinking about.

W

THE WICKET

Traditionally, the wicket is the three stumps and two bails twenty-two yards apart at each end of a cricket pitch, rather than the surface on which the game is played. Why 'wicket'? Maybe because in the dim and distant past, when shepherds threw turnips at their mates, they tried to ward them off with their crooks while attempting to protect a small wicket gate behind them.

Over the centuries, as cricket has grown into the game it has become, the wicket itself has moved on from two stumps with a long bail across the top to its present dimensions of three stumps and two bails. Is there anything as exciting as arriving at a ground before the start of play and spotting the two sets of gleaming stumps sticking out of the ground at each end? They are waiting for the umpires to appear, extract the bails from their pockets and carefully place them on top of the stumps. It is the defining moment which says that a game of cricket is upon us.

Then, later, there is nothing much more exhilarating than seeing a fast bowler tear in, beat the batsman and shatter the stumps so that the bails fly into the air with that wonderful and sickening finality. A middle stump knocked out of the ground is one of the most satisfying sights in all of cricket. My favourite middle-stump moment came at Headingley in

1981 when I was on the air at the very end of one of the more remarkable Test matches of all time. After it looked as if England would be beaten by an innings and plenty, Ian Botham had made his uniquely heroic 149 not out with important help from two bowlers, Graham Dilley and Chris Old. Australia had to make 130 to win. After chugging uneventfully uphill from the Football Stand End with the new ball, Bob Willis changed ends and was suddenly inspired to find pace, rhythm, accuracy and movement all at the same time. He took 8–43 and England won by 18 runs. At the very end, I was on the air in the old commentary box in the Football Stand. Australia needed 19 runs to win with one wicket left as Willis ran in to bowl to Ray Bright, a left-arm spinner who could bat more than just a bit. He had already made 19 and England and Australia held their breath. Willis bowled, Bright pushed half forward, the ball was through him and the middle stump cartwheeled three yards towards wicketkeeper Bob Taylor. England had won and pandemonium broke loose. Yes, that was my best wicket ever.

The wicket moment which is perhaps the most famous of all came at The Oval in 1948 – and I can remember hearing it described live by John Arlott on the radio. Don Bradman, who I had watched when he batted in the second Test at Lord's, came out to bat for the last time in a Test match, needing to score four runs to average 100 in Test cricket. It was a highly charged moment. The crowd stood, Norman Yardley, the England captain, called for three cheers for the Don from his players. Bradman then took guard to face leg-spinner Eric Hollies. He played the first ball defensively. The second was a googly which Bradman did not appear to read out of the hand.

It turned through Bradman's defence and bowled him. Bradman walked back to the pavilion, briskly as always, cheered every inch of the way, taking a Test match batting average of 99.94 up the Oval steps with him.

Think what those shepherds have to answer for.

W

WORLD CUP 2019

The World Cup final at Lord's on 14 July 2019 must have been the most remarkable game of cricket ever played. The drama was incredible as England beat New Zealand, in the end because they had hit more boundaries during a match which finished first as a tie after 50 overs each and then as yet another tie after two extraordinary Super Overs, cricket's equivalent of extra time. Thanks to television replays, we all know the final dramatic details of this last match in exact, inch-by-inch detail. At the time, these details were more a frenzied kaleidoscope of furious and passionate sporting conflict as you saw what you saw, but it is never easy for spectators at the ground to see the whole picture. The last few overs transcended everything that had gone before on the day itself, in the semi-finals and in the interminable sequence of preliminary matches. To many, they became the competition.

This final kaleidoscope begins when Jos Buttler joins Ben Stokes, with England, who need 242 to win, heading for defeat at 86–4. With a potent mixture of the explosively orthodox, daredevil improvisation and a useful dollop of luck, they put on 110 at what would have been a fast enough rate if they had stayed together. Buttler then holes out and with the lower middle order scampering about like rabbits caught in the headlights, it looks as if there is too much for Stokes, who was first to the nets at eight clock that morning, to do on his own. Somehow he keeps going, but the required rate climbs to almost 13 an over.

Twenty-two are needed from the last nine balls. Stokes swings and the ball soars to Trent Boult at deep midwicket. He catches the ball a yard or so inside the boundary but loses his balance and steps onto the rope. Six runs. Fifteen are needed from the last over. Stokes is unable to score off Boult's first two balls and Lord's seems to have been hit over the head by a knuckleduster. Now a lunging swing at the third ball sends it over the leg-side boundary for six. Boult follows with a wonderful yorker, which Stokes works away to leg and sets off. He must get two to keep the strike. Martin Guptill fields on the boundary and the throw is on its way. Stokes makes a despairing dive for the crease and the ball cannons off his outstretched bat and flies on to the boundary at third man. The umpires quickly confer and six runs are signalled – two for the stroke and four overthrows. Stokes is on his knees, holding up his hands in an it-wasn't-my-fault gesture. It was not his fault.

Three are needed from the last two balls. They scramble a single to mid off from the first and come helter-skelter back for an impossible second. Adil Rashid sacrifices himself so that Stokes will keep the strike. I am certain Lord's has never been in such a frenzy as the injured Mark Wood shuffles out to join Stokes for the last ball, with two runs wanted. Stokes swings and off they go. They touch down for one, which brings the scores level, and set off frantically for the second and Wood is comfortably run out. It is 241-all and now comes the Super Over, something most people did not know about, which was in the law book for the remote possibility of a tie.

Those four overthrows were the cruellest of blows for the New Zealanders. It is said that Stokes even asked the umpires if they could be withdrawn, which they could not be, for all that had happened was in strict accordance with the Laws of the game. However, further examination showed that England should only have been awarded five runs. An overthrow starts at the moment the ball leaves the fielder's hand – I have to own up and admit that this is something I did not know. When Guptill let the ball go from the boundary, Stokes and Rashid had started for the second run but had not crossed and therefore only one run should have been added to the four overthrows. Of even greater significance was that this would have meant that Rashid and not Stokes would have been on strike for the fifth ball of the over, with four runs needed, not three. It is impossible not to feel extremely sorry for New Zealand, for luck does not often desert you as starkly as this.

In the Super Over, England bat first and Buttler and Stokes, who looks almost out on his feet, have the job of setting New Zealand a target, against the bowling of Trent Boult. Stokes picks up three off the first ball. With a single, Buttler gives him back the strike and with a tired flourish Stokes finds the midwicket boundary. This is followed by another single before Buttler carefully places for two, before despatching Boult's last ball off his toes to the midwicket boundary. New Zealand have to score 16 to win.

We see Jofra Archer loosening up in front of the Pavilion. Presumably because of his pace, Eoin Morgan has gone for the rookie. Many of us would, I think, have plumped for Chris Woakes's greater experience. England take the field, the two batsmen, Guptill and the left-handed Jimmy Neesham, follow them out and Lord's is making a noise which reminds me of a pressure-cooker with a loose top coming to the boil. Archer has never given away as many as 16 runs in an over in any of his 14 ODIs.

The scene is set and in he bounces to bowl to Neesham. He is looking for a yorker but slides the ball down the leg side and a marginal wide is called. It must be a truly sickening moment for the new boy and we all wonder again if Morgan has got it right. Neesham drives the next ball for two and then swings at the one after that and slogs it from the middle of the bat far over the midwicket boundary for six. It surely has to be New Zealand's match now. Seven runs are needed from four balls.

In comes Archer again, aiming for a yorker, and Neesham manages to dig it out on the leg side and a misfield on the boundary by Jason Roy gives him a second run. Now it is five from three balls. Two more to Neesham makes it three from two. Archer bowls again, this time to a good length, and Neesham can only find a frenetic single. And so to the last ball, with Guptill, who had been in no sort of recent form, on strike.

Archer turns at the end of his run, sees Guptill is ready. Countless millions hold their breath all round the world. A stupefied, punch-drunk Lord's can hardly bear to look. Archer bowls. Guptill stabs the ball away on the leg side. Roy, mindful of his error earlier in the over, swoops on the midwicket boundary and the flat throw comes storming back to Buttler. In a blur, the batsmen run one and turn desperately for the winning run, but Roy's return is pretty well on target. Buttler grabs the ball and lunges at the stumps and Guptill's despairing dive leaves him a yard short. The scores are again level, but England have struck the more boundaries and so have won their first ever World Cup.

Joy was unconfined, although no account of this incredible game of cricket would be complete without paying tribute to the way New Zealand and particularly their captain, Kane Williamson, took their defeat, for it was surely the most sickening moment any of them could ever have experienced.

These events at Lord's are the main reason that this final and therefore the 2019 World Cup will always be remembered, but it also produced two remarkable semi-finals in which the two most-favoured teams, Australia and India, were knocked out. India were beaten in the first semi-final by New Zealand who, on that occasion, found that luck was on their side. After nearly three weeks of blue skies, the weather changed and the day at Old Trafford was cloudy. New Zealand won the toss and batted first, making 211–5 before the weather brought the first day to a halt. The next day New Zealand got to 239–8. A target of 240 seemed well within India's reach, but it was a day when the ball swung and modern batsmen are not that well equipped to cope with the swinging ball and India were bowled out for 221. In the other semi-final, at Edgbaston, England thrashed Australia by eight wickets after bowling them out for 223. The scene was therefore set for a final between two sides who had never won the World Cup, which gave the last match an extra frisson of excitement.

The 45 build-up matches leading to the semi-finals were something of a mixed bag. I believe more than ten sides should have been allowed to compete, for this would not only have been a matter of great encouragement for some of the smaller cricketing nations, but it would also have increased the possibility of the shock results which are the life's blood of a tournament like this. As it was, the nearest we came to a real upset was when Afghanistan lost to India by only 11 runs. It was a World Cup which early on did not produce the close finishes which would have heightened awareness of the competition, and then there was some rain. There were too many empty seats in the early stages and the television figures were apparently not especially good. For the final, Sky, who held the television rights for the competition, allowed Channel 4 to share the broadcast once England had reached the final. Channel 4 had the bigger audience, raising again the importance of trying to ensure that some cricket is shown on free-to-air television. If this was the first significant step in that direction, it will be another reason why this competition will not be forgotten.

X

XI

The terminology of cricket can be deliciously old-fashioned. Not only does the luncheon interval linger on, as we have already seen, but those two beguiling Roman numerals 'XI' keep raising their heads. The noble concept of cricket had no truck with such ordinary words as 'team' or 'side' or even 'eleven'. It was a game which obviously had a classical education. When the early England XIs went to Australia, they played some matches away from the capital cities where the opposition was relatively weak. To try and make things a bit more even, they would not take on the Twenty-Two of, say, Bendigo, a mining town in Victoria. Instead it would be England v Bendigo XXII. Standards had to be upheld.

A 'century' is on the brink of becoming an old-fashioned word. It comes ultimately from the Latin *centum*, which means 'a hundred', while *centuria* describes a military unit of 100 men. Now, a word of caution: from the first century B.C., a *centuria* suddenly became a unit of only 80 men. How lucky this happened before cricket was invented, otherwise all those batting records in *Wisden* would have had to be devalued. In 2017, Geoffrey Boycott's reaction on *TMS* was one of instant horror when Jonathan Agnew, ably supported by our scorer and statistician Andrew Samson, told him that his hundred against a Rest of the World XI in 1970, in a series arranged after the South African tour had been cancelled, had been down-graded from first-class by the ICC. One dreads to think of his reaction if he were to find all his centuries were now worth only 80 runs each.

Z

ZIMBABWE

It is a miracle that cricket has survived at all in the country ruled for so many years by Robert Mugabe. Few things are as symbolic of England as cricket and I can only think that he regarded the game as so unimportant that he did not bother to turn his attention to it. This is even more surprising considering that the old Government House, where he lived while president of the country, is only just across the road from the Harare Sports Club, the headquarters of Zimbabwe cricket.

The irony is that before Mugabe, when Zimbabwe answered to the name of Rhodesia, Test cricket was never played there. During a tour of South Africa, the England players would come up to Rhodesia for a couple of games, and Rhodesians were qualified to play Test cricket for South Africa. Zimbabwe were first elevated to Test status in 1992, before they were quite ready for it, in an attempt to help them preserve the game by giving it added importance.

My own great affection for cricket in Zimbabwe began in England in 1983 when they were one of two sides from the Associate Members of the ICC who qualified for the World Cup finals. In one of the early games, they played Australia at Trent Bridge and I was one of the commentators.

I shall not forget that day, not least because of the curious start it had for me. I drove up the M1 that morning from London and left the motorway at the junction which took me past the Ratcliffe-on-Soar power station, which is close to the motorway exit. It was the time of the miners' strike, with all the problems about secondary picketing, and there was quite a queue on the slip road. I fell in at the back and eventually arrived at the round-about, where a policeman was sticking his head into every car. When my turn came a young constable leant through the window and asked me if I was coming to picket the power station. I was rather taken aback and gave a resounding 'My dear old thing!' and a beaming smile and he almost fell over in surprise. When he recovered, he waved me on, somewhat hesitantly at first. The third commentator that day at Trent Bridge was the Alderman, also known as Don Mosey. When I told him what had happened, he laughed so hard I thought he was going to choke.

The day got better still at Trent Bridge, for Zimbabwe proceeded to beat Australia by 13 runs. It was the first time I had shared a microphone with Bob Nixon, who was the Zimbabwe commentator. He was terrific fun and a really good commentator to work with. It was an amazing moment for him and this victory was a huge shot in the arm for Zimbabwe's cricket. It started the process which led to the country being elected to Test match status. Interestingly, the Man of the Match that day was Duncan Fletcher, who made 69 not out and took 4–42 in 11 overs at just above medium pace. Fletcher went on to become a successful coach of England and then moved on to look after India. On occasions he joined us in the commentary box as a summariser.

England made their first ever full tour of the country in 1996–97. I went for *Test Match Special* and it was a great experience. I had a brief and partial glimpse of the old Zimbabwe, for this was just before Mugabe began to flex his muscles as far as the European population and especially the farmers were concerned. One of the main reasons we were there was that the English cricket authorities wanted to show support to those who were running and playing the game against all the odds in that country. It was remarkable how the few people involved had managed to keep the game going as they had. Two Test matches were arranged and the first was in Bulawayo.

It was a wonderful game of cricket and the first time that a Test match had ended with the scores level with the side batting second, England, still having wickets in hand. It was therefore a draw and not a tie. This seemed the best possible start for what was in a sense a fraught goodwill visit by England. Zimbabwe had held their own in spite of England's coach, David Lloyd, proclaiming volubly afterwards that 'we murdered 'em'.

England needed to score 205 to win in a minimum of 37 overs. Soon after the innings began, I took over commentary from Simon Mann and simply kept going until it was all over, which must have been nearly an hour and a half later. Peter Baxter was the next man on, but I got so involved in it all I kept going, with Trevor Bailey and Chris Cowdrey as my summarisers. It was a shameful performance for which I have no adequate excuse, although I have to say I enjoyed every moment of it.

There was so much drama. The Zimbabweans were time-wasting for all they were worth and Ian Robinson, the home umpire – for at that time one was still allowed – was as ignorant of what constituted a leg-side wide as I was of the time. Thirteen runs were needed off the last over, three off the last ball and two were scampered. Phew. Why Peter and Simon have ever spoken to me since, I am not sure. Commentators on *TMS* who run over their twenty-minute limit are still said to be 'doing a Bulawayo'.

We moved on to Harare and Robert Mugabe announced that it was his intention to come to the ground early in the match and have lunch with the committee – not something he made a habit of doing. Before lunch he intended to hold a press conference in the big upper room in the pavilion. Peter Baxter decided this was a great chance to get back at me after my appalling performance in Bulawayo. He asked me if I would lead off the press conference by asking Mugabe half a dozen questions. I could hardly refuse. The leader arrived in a cavalcade of cars and the ground was heaving with security men. We had been told there were to be no political questions, and so it was obviously nothing more than a charm offensive.

Mugabe entered from the committee room and came across to me. Dodging his spitting and his halitosis, I asked him some rather wet questions about cricket and received one-word answers. Inspired by the courts at the back of the pavilion, I turned to tennis and had a better response. By agreement, the other journalists kept quiet, so that it would sound on air as if it had been an exclusive interview for the BBC, who had the radio rights for the series and therefore this interview. My job done, the others then piled in. With so many muscular secret-service men mingling around us, all armed to the teeth, I think we were all pretty nervous. It would be hard to imagine a worse interview, but at least I had done it.

That tour gave me many good reasons to remember with great fondness both Zimbabwe and its cricket. Not the least of them was that one of their players, Henry Olonga, a splendid commentator and a tenor whose 'Nessun Dorma' is as good as it gets, and who once publicly defied Mugabe, became a great friend.

PICTURE ACKNOWLEDGEMENTS

The author and publisher would like to thank the following
for permission to reproduce photographs:

Section One
Hulton Archive/Getty Images, Popperfoto via Getty Images/
Getty Images, Central Press/Getty Images, Patrick Eagar/
Popperfoto via Getty Images/Getty Images, Gareth Copley/
Getty Images, Central Press/Getty Images, Topical Press/
Getty Images, Barratts/S&G and Barratts/EMPICS Sport,
Bob Thomas Sports Photography via Getty Images, Sport and
General/S&G and Barratts/EMPICS Sport, Ken Kelly/
Popperfoto via Getty Images/Getty Images, Popperfoto via
Getty Images/Getty Images, Central Press/Getty Images,
Patrick Eagar/Popperfoto via Getty Images/Getty Images,
Adrian Murrell/Getty Images, Fairfax Media/Fairfax Media
via Getty Images, Bob Thomas Sports Photography via Getty
Images, News UK Ltd/Shutterstock.

Section Two
AFP/Getty Images, Tom Shaw/Getty Images, Hamish Blair/
Getty Images, Professional Sport/Popperfoto via Getty
Images/Getty Images, Paul Gilham/Getty Images, Katja
Ogrin/Getty Images, Mike Hewitt/Getty Images, Mark

Dadswell/Getty Images, Popperfoto via Getty Images/Getty Images, Michael Steele/Getty Images, Ryan Pierse/Getty Images, Ryan Pierse/Getty Images, Gareth Copley/Getty Images, Popperfoto via Getty Images/Getty Images, Glyn Kirk/AFP/Getty Images, Gareth Copley/Getty Images, Gareth Copley/Getty Images, Andrew Fosker/BPI/Shutterstock,

All other photographs are from private collections.

Every reasonable effort has been made to trace the copyright holders, but if there are any errors or omissions, Hodder & Stoughton will be pleased to insert the appropriate acknowledgements in any subsequent printings or editions.

INDEX